URBAN RUINS
MEMORIAL VALUE AND CONTEMPORARY ROLE

LA CALCINA
HOTEL E RISTORANTE
MEGEZIA SRL
Dorsoduro, 780 - 30123 VENEZIA
C.F. e P.IVA 04178250272
PEC: megezia@legalmail.it

"WHY ARE WE FASCINATED BY RUINS? THEY RECALL THE GLORY OF DEAD CIVILIZATIONS AND THE CERTAIN END OF OUR OWN.
THEY STAND AS MONUMENTS TO HISTORIC DISASTERS, BUT ALSO PROVOKE DREAMS ABOUT FUTURES BORN FROM DESTRUCTION AND DECAY.
RUINS ARE BLEAK BUT ALLURING REMINDERS OF OUR VULNERABLE PLACE IN TIME AND SPACE."

(Dillon 2014)

URBAN RUINS
MEMORIAL VALUE AND CONTEMPORARY ROLE

ELISA PILIA

6	**LITERARY AWARD**
	"LA CALCINA – JOHN RUSKIN – WRITING ON ARCHITECTURE"
8	**PREFACE**
	CLEMENS F. KUSCH, IN THE NAME OF THE COMMITTEE
13	**ABSTRACT**
15	**INTRODUCTION**
23	**PART I**
	HISTORIC DEVELOPMENT OF THE CONCEPT
24	**1. TERMINOLOGY, DEFINITION,S AND CONCEPTS OF RUINS**
	1.1. Ruin – rudere vs rovina
28	1.2. Wreckage - relitto
	1.3. Other terms: remains and fragments – resti, frammenti, macerie, vestigia
31	**2. RUINS IN HISTORY**
	2.1. A growing aesthetic value
33	2.2. The romantic outlook
35	2.3. The modern cult of ruins
45	2.4. The post war debate
58	2.5. Present-day ruins: conflicts and natural disasters
59	**3. TYPOLOGY AND CLASSIFICATION**
	3.1. Origins
62	3.2. Function
65	3.3. Location
66	3.4. Degree of ruination
69	3.5. Other classifications
71	**PART II**
	CONTEMPORARY APPROACHES
72	**1. LITERATURE REVIEW OF THE CURRENT DEBATE**
79	**2. TENDENCIES AND MAIN SCHOOLS OF THOUGHT:**
	A GEOGRAPHICAL OVERVIEW
	2.1. Global overview
81	2.1.1. Conservation Approaches
85	2.1.2. Integrative Approaches
91	2.2. UK vs Italy – English and Italian approaches to ruins
	2.2.1. The United Kingdom
107	2.2.2. Italy

119 **3. URBAN RUINS: ISSUES AND VALUES**
    3.1. Urban policy
127   3.2. Sustainability
        3.2.1. Cultural aspects - values
130   3.2.2. Social factors - values
        3.2.3. Environmental aspects - values
132   3.2.4. Economic aspects - values
141   3.3. Aesthetic issues. Dealing with the 'lacuna'

145 **PART III**
A METHODOLOGY FOR RUINS

146   1. Research design: an overview
148   2. From current methodologies to a new protocol for intervention
      2.1. Technical approaches
150   2.2. Value-based approaches
153   2.3. Critical notes
155   3. Proposal for a holistic and transdisciplinary approach
158   3.1. Macro Level. The ruin as 'urban tile'
160   3.2. Micro Level. The ruin as 'stone document'
161   3.2.1. Geomatic survey
166   3.2.2. Archaeometric and archaeological analyses
172   3.3. Assessment. Ruin as 'treasured urban element'
177   3.4. Threats and opportunities: SWOT analysis
179   4. Application of the methodology in Cagliari
      4.1. Macro level analyses | The historical urban landscape
185   4.2. Micro Level | The Convent of Santa Chiara
189   4.3. Assessment of values
193   4.4. Instuitutional current approaches
197   4.5. Compatible interventions and new uses
203   5. Definition of new contemporary values

207 **CONCLUSION**
213 **BIBLIOGRAPHY**

222 ACKNOWLEDGEMENTS

LITERARY AWARD
"LA CALCINA – JOHN RUSKIN – WRITING ON ARCHITECTURE"

This monograph was submitted to the *"John Ruskin – Writing on Architecture"* Award inaugurated in 2018 in Venice. The award was established by the RO.SA.M association and the La Calcina Hotel in Venice, where Ruskin stayed often during his Venetian visits. The idea was to support a cultural initiative concerning the work and writings on architecture edited by John Ruskin and to select texts on architecture that were unpublished or published in collective works or journals at the date of the award, offering the possibility to give them visibility also in concomitance with the Venice Biennale of architecture.

A committee was formed composed by prof. Giancarlo Carnevale as president, prof. Guido Zucconi, prof. Luigi Prestinenza Puglisi, prof. Vincenzo Melluso, and architect Dr. Clemens Kusch. Furthermore, a scientific board was nominated including prof. Marina Montuori, the architect Esther Giani and the founding members of the cultural association RO.SA.M, Roberta Semeraro and Marco Agostinelli.

The different sponsors and the support of University of Venice, RO.SA.M and the editor DOM-Publishers who offered to publish the first prize also made the award possible. Since this is the first edition, the initial task of the committee and the scientific board was to define the call for proposals as well as the participation conditions. First of all, previously published written works were excluded to narrow down the wide range of participants, encouraging the visibility of unknown academics and authors and the call was so opened to historical and critical texts, essays, papers and PhD theses, which had not yet been published at the date of the call. No indication regarding the length of the texts had been defined with the idea of dividing them into possible categories, once the texts where submitted. Languages were limited to Italian, English and French, easily understood by the committee and scientific board.

The definition of topics was particular difficult due to the wide range of possible arguments and the risk of finding highly different texts for comparison and judgment. The Award was finally *"addressed to all academics who wrote on the city, in particular Venice, not only in its historic-artistic complexity and density, but also in light of the contemporary matters: the co-existence between new and old, the possibility to 'conserve', allowing the needs and necessities of the modern society and the further future developments and challenges"*.

At deadline of the call on April 15, 2018, 57 texts had been submitted, a number exceeding all expectations. The writings included short essays on different topics with very personal approaches, papers and conference contributions as well as Master's and PhD dissertations on specific historic topics and urban and architectural analysis and theory.

While first reading of the writings, the committee considered it necessary to divide the first award into two categories: monographs and short essays. Then, all submissions were analysed in terms of their coherence with the call. After a first selection to exclude texts that were not scientifically relevant or far from the call, the committee selected ten works and finally, with full consensus, chose the work by Elisa Pilia *"Urban ruins. Memorial Value and contemporary role"* for the first category. This was chosen *"for the original approach to a complex theme, combining historical analysis and critical investigation between the Mediterranean and Anglo-Saxon contexts, enriched by a series of apparatus."*

Pilia's PhD thesis was considered perfectly coherent with the call of the award, especially for its aspects on *"the coexistence between new and old, the possibility to 'conserve' allowing the needs and necessities of the modern society and the further future developments and challenges"*. The thesis is articulated in different parts, expertly documented and written in good English.

For the second category of short essays, the committee chose a text by Elisabetta Concina *"La Ca' d'oro, da icona monumentale a modello di architettura veneziana tra Ottocento e Novecento"* (The Ca' d'oro, from monumental icon to Venetian architecture model between the 18th and 19th century) for *"the detailed historic and critic investigation, open to significant future perspectives of research."* Finally, the committee also assigned the Special Venice Award to an essay by Rossella Barozzi entitled *"La Corinthia Macchina. Jacopo Sansovino e la Scuola Grande della Misericordia"* (La Corinthia Macchina. Jacopo Sansovino an the Scuola Grande della Misericordia) for *"its extensive and articulated study supported by innovative tools"*. For the *"Old and New"* Special Award the committee recognised the paper by Davide Del Curto *"Il restauro é morto? Viva il restauro!"* (Restoration is dead? Viva restoration!) *"for the attention to the ongoing dynamics on the restoration field"*.

After this first highly successful edition, the aim is to hold the Award every two years, in concomitance with the Venice Biennale of Architecture, and during the same year, support the Award with other cultural events on architectural writings. For further information see www.premioletteraio-lacalcina-johnruskin.com.

PREFACE
CLEMENS F. KUSCH, IN THE NAME OF THE COMMITTEE

Ruins have always been part of European cities in more or less significant ways. The origins and causes like their eras of construction or of ruined conditions are numerous. In fact, ruins are not only vestiges of ancient Empires, but they can have more recent origins: wars, fires or simple disuse with no new functions, for example the many derelict industrial structures in European cities and countryside.

Therefore, the topic is broader than immediately expected. In the future, the design of contexts characterised by ruins of different kinds will always be more common, in the attempt to preserve, recover or reuse ruins for new purposes.

In the recent past, the topic of the development of European cities is not more related to areas to convert from agricultural to urban uses but rather focused on already developed contexts, this avoiding the devastating consumption of land that has significantly marked urban development over the past 60 years.

While working in urban contexts, it is frequent to face ruins that are both 'monumental', testimonials to particular historical and artistic values, and 'minor' ones, whose cultural values are not recognised or absent but at the same time they represent opportunities for maintaining or reusing structures and highlighting urban stratifications.

This stems from the widespread belief that the "*new*" – deleting traces of the past – should not be considered an absolute and essential value. Many destructive interventions were pursued in name of a "*new*" that does not establish dialogue with the past because it is believed to bear ideas and "*better*" conceptions than the past, causing herewith inevitable loss.

Moreover, considering recent projects, it is more and more in doubt that new architectures with their technological hypertrophy and formal and structural audacity can survive longer than ancient architecture, even if they went through important transformations and restorations, but have come down to us with better quality than many more recent buildings. Thus, the study of ruins encourages dialogue with 'the past' and stimulates the search for new solutions that do not pursue simple demolition and new construction indifferent to the traces of the past.

Ruins as traces of the past do not only represent the "*physical*" inheritance in cities but also have always recalled the history of places, wars, invasions, devastations, or simple abandonment. Ruins are therefore exceptional testimonies to place-history. Investigations into their origins have given rise to thinking by writers and philosophers that explore the relationship between ruination and memory. In the philosophical meaning, ruination becomes a "*narration*" as well as an educational tool not only for those working in historical contexts but, in a more general way, for people who face time and frailty.

Over time, different European countries have developed different kinds of "*coexistence*" with ruins and of design for their recovery. In the present book, with no pretence of systematic and definitive cataloguing, the principal modalities and approaches to design are analysed placing particular attention on the Mediterranean and Italian worlds as compared to Anglo-Saxon formulations. Overall and simplifying, there are two main positions: the "*romantic*" Anglo-Saxon one which is somehow 'braver' in terms of the design and transformation of ruins. A "*brave*" position from the Italian point of view might favour a more "*scientific*" approach. Generally the necessity to maintain entire signs of the past is held in high consideration along with clearly differentiating new interventions from older ones, guaranteeing the legibility of the different historic layers. But on the other hand, this position has often led to excessive caution with the consequent abdication of any intervention.

A third meaningful way to deal with ruins has been developed in Germany where war destroyed entire cities and reconstruction was divided between the need for historic restoration versus the affirmation of new construction as the identity of the modernity and the acquisition of democracy.

More recently, with many polemics and confrontations, the reunification of two Germanies proposed the theme of reconstruction and the intervention on ruins a second time after world war destructions. This came about especially in East Germany where many monumental buildings like the Frauenkirche in Dresden or the Castle in Berlin were left in ruins after the war. Subsequently, in reunified Germany, they were reconstructed according to the principles of rebuilding "*where it was and as it was*" (in Italian: *com'era dov'era*) as the assertion of history and identity of reunified Germany. In the case of the Frauenkirche in Dresden, reconstruction was integral while the case of the Castle in Berlin, it was limited to the principal façades. The possible approaches, widely analysed and illustrated in the text, regard others along with the geographical areas mentioned. These can also be classified according to typology of approach: on the one hand, integral restoration and rebuilding "*where it was and as it was*" criticised because of the creation of "*historical fakes*"; and on the other, the – sometimes – excessive stress on not always meaningful traces. Between these two positions are several other degrees of intervention objectively illustrated in this monograph without expressing any absolute value. Such typologies were contextualised by considering historic, geographic and also ideological backgrounds. With this clarification of the different approaches, it can be asserted that it is not possible to attribute absolute value or academic applicability to a specific operative method. In contrast, each typology of intervention can be applied to specific cases with diversified approaches and to different degrees.

Therefore, an approach might be different if a building was recently destroyed by a traumatic event, absolving a high symbolic value. In this case reconstruction "*where it was and as it was*" appears to be legitimate, while such an approach could not be taken into consideration for – as an example – a Roman antiquity. Furthermore, an intervention can be determined according to the necessity of reusing a ruin to give it a new and specific function as well as a modern structural performance and environmental comfort. In this case as well, the possible scenarios can anticipate different degrees of intervention. This awareness implies the necessity to trust the sensibility and preparation of professionals who, even as a team and in a range of possible methodologies, intervene on ruins with subjective approaches. Whatever approach is pursued, its definition stems from deep knowledge of an artefact. Just how this knowledge process preempts and supports the design is efficaciously presented in this book in the case of the Santa Chiara Convent in Cagliari.

Based on this specific case study, an ad-hoc methodology for the analysis of ruins is presented through the illustration of techniques for understanding and representing a ruins' conformation. This is carried out through historical documentation and currently-available photogrammetric tools. Such accurate and detailed analysis implies precise content: any "*ideology*", depending on the conditions of different nations, should be supported by deep knowledge of the ruins' context and the specific characteristics of the different countries. This requires first and foremost deep knowledge of an object's spatial context before projecting any further hypothesis for intervention.

Without such in-depth analysis any projects risks being superficial causing the elimination of important as well as generating misunderstanding of the origins of the ruin. Only after this phase of knowledge gathering is completed can design be initiated and decisions made as to which parts to maintain, enhance or eliminate.

In this way, analysis is not only a documentary phase but strictly interacts with design, allowing context to inform design choices.

This process of accurate knowledge gathering is important if a project is to preserve a ruin as a pure testimonial or if a ruin is to be restored with a new use. In all cases the choice cannot be based exclusively on the mere temporal consideration of the different parts, associating each of these to a value: in other words the older a part, the greater its value and thus renders opportune its preservation. In other cases, an intervention is carried out in name of the recovery of an "*original*" condition, which most probably never existed. If this can be legitimate, as in a case of archaeological sites like "*frozen*" Pompeii, it does not appear to be valid for structures that were continuously modified over history. If the criterion of "*age*" is the only one for justifying preservation, this would signify deleting all temporal signs and negating changes over time, removing important parts of the ruins' "*narration*". Thus, if age cannot be considered a criterion for deciding which approach to deploy for preservation, then the question becomes how to decide what is worth preserving and what not? In my opinion, there are two determining factors: the first is based on deep knowledge involving different disciplines, such as archaeology, art history or engineering; the second is more subjective, leaving professionals free to define their approaches, the parts to preserve and those to transform. In fact, an exclusive scientific approach is a utopia, since the designer is influenced by context conditions, especially in the case of functional reuse. The rigorous analysis of the general debate on theories and the specific case of Cagliari, which was the underlying motivation of the research project, is influenced in the research of Elisa Pilia by a particular sensibility and "*attachment*" to specific place and city as if the sorrow for its decline, transformed into ruin, recognises the need for new kind of "*care*" and, at the same time, for the realisation of the potential for a new and more aware life that must maintain the signs of history and through those the memory of people that have lived and spent their lives in this places.

ABSTRACT

This research project focuses on the role that ruins play in urban centres in terms of meaning, testimony, values and opportunity; it was developed on the international level. After an historical and contemporary outline of theoretical and practical approaches to ruins internationally, with an in-depth analysis and comparison of the British and Italian approaches, the aim is to delineate a transdisciplinary and integrated methodology that allows the investigation of the strategic values of such artefacts and their potential contribution to a sustainable requalification of the historic urban cores.

This protocol was tested on the urban ruins of the historical centre of Cagliari, a mid-sized port city on the southern coast of the island of Sardinia. Here, the ruins left by the aftermath of aerial bombardment by the Allies during the World War II represent something of a blight on the landscape beyond the mere presence of fallen masonry and overgrown vegetation. They also represent an absence, a series of voids at nodal points in the historic centre that have neither a current function nor any plans for future use. This is largely caused by the complicated management of the built urban context and ineffective planning procedures that drive non-intervention approaches. Approaching the problem initially through the lens of architectural conservation, this research considers the urban issues along with aesthetic, economic and social questions relating to the reuse of ruins. A comparative evaluation of the international cultural and legal frameworks creates a basis for identifying possible strategies and guidelines to safeguard and re-use the historic urban ruins such as those placed in Cagliari.

INTRODUCTION

The decision to carry out a comparative study on urban ruins on the international level stems from the awareness that these architectures, while widely investigated on the theoretical and practical levels, still raise complex issues and debate that deserve further scientific investigation in the field of urban and architectural conservation.

The survey of the state-of-the-art of these studies shows how ruined structures are considered to be some of the most complex and permanent symbols in Western culture (DeSilvey and Edensor 2012, 465). This interest is clarified by the fact that they have been widely investigated over centuries during which they transformed and developed different nuances and meanings. Nevertheless, from World War II on, and especially in the last decade, approaches to ruins have changed, bringing new emphasis and interest to the academic field: the vast literature confirms this tendency regarding both rural and urban contexts. Thus, it seems important to recall the significant contributions of Tim Edensor (2005) who conducted important research on ruins, defining a first state of the studies on the topic. In these ten years, he also recognised an intensification of interest, both in academia and among the broader public, in what he called 'contemporary Ruinenlust' (DeSilvey and Edensor 2012, 465), a sort of obsession with ruination and decay.

In general, scholars throughout the world have studied the role of ruins in different fields of the human sciences (Augé 2004; Dawdy 2010; Stoler 2008), archaeology (Gordon 2010; Ruggieri Tricoli and Germanà 2013; Ruggieri Tricoli 2011), human geography (DeSilvey and Edensor 2012; Edensor 2005, 2007; Hatherley 2010), literary studies (Hell and Schonle 2010), arts and history (Aston 1973; Dillon 2006; Ferri 2015; Makarius 2004; Woodward 2002) about the values of ruins (Stead 2003; Featherstone 2005); architecture and composition (Desrochers 2000, Oteri 2009, Ugolini 2010),

1. Cagliari, Italy.
Wartime ruins of Portico Vivaldi-Pasqua.
© *Elisa Pilia*.

urban studies (Göbel 2015), landscape studies (Matteini 2009; Capuano 2014), tourism studies (Pálsson 2013), symbolism, relationship between ruins, nature and culture (Simmel 1911, Roth et al. 1997, Woodward 2002; Pálsson 2013), aesthetic studies (Zucker 1961; Ginsberg 2004); architectural conservation and preservation (Ashurst 2007; Billeci, Gizzi et al. 2006; De Martino 2004, 2017; Fiorani 2009; Gazzola 1967; Gizzi 2006; Marino 1989, 2002; Picone 2012; Thompson 1981, 2006).

In general, if the extensive literature focuses on ruins in the architectural field, offering broad attention to theoretical (aesthetic, philosophical) and design issues, this scenario has provided stimulus to rethink these misunderstood architectural objects that have been often restored with controversial interventions. This has created the need to codify a transdisciplinary approach that, starting from in-depth exploration, understanding and knowledge of ruins, might offer a solid basis for the assessment and enhancement of their values as well as subsequent sensitive intervention respectful of their history, form, stratifications, materials, and context. Furthermore, such an approach should focus on all the issues: urban, architectural, economic, aesthetic and social, and the possible and compatible reuse of ruins geared toward processes of rehabilitation and enhancement of urban contexts.

Based on these premises, this research, developed through a circular structure, considered the historic centre of Cagliari, the regional capital of Sardinia characterised by a high presence of medieval ruins (fig. 1), as an opportunity to re-consider these problems on a local scale. In fact, Cagliari (fig. 2) now is at the centre of a vigorous debate on how best to make use of such abandoned and neglected heritage causing so much urban decay. The city still manifests the visible scars of war, which have contributed (and continue to contribute) to the gradual, ongoing decay of its historic neighbourhoods and which today are experienced and considered the mere wreckage of history. In recent years, the question of how to face this urban decline has taken on added importance since the municipal authorities, after more than a decade of a series of ineffective plans, has recently designed a strategic plan for the historic centre. Although it recognises the strategic role of these urban ruins, it does envision a new role and a new set of functions or strategies for them. In fact, the proposals, according to an urban approach strictly within the Italian tradition, are still a far cry from a comprehensive knowledge-building process which can allow the deep understanding necessary for new intervention scenarios. It seems essential to define and conduct a transdisciplinary and holistic study of these ruins to provide a new set of guidelines deriving from international comparison and inspiration, while bearing in mind that their memory values must be re-thought in the contemporary world.

In this sense, the detailed international comparative research, carried out at the Scottish Centre for Conservation Studies (ESALA – Edinburgh School of Architecture and Landscape Architecture – College of Art – University of Edinburgh) was an essential starting point both in cultural and methodological terms. In particular, this investigation is not only a mere state-of-the-art on global theories and practices, but an important critical work that highlights strong and weak points as well as best practices and criticisms in each context, providing possible fundamental suggestions for resolving local issues.

Thus, after a global overview without neglecting other European methodologies and practices, the study focuses on two approaches: the British and the Italian ones, chosen for their long traditions in conservation and the sensitivity to ruined heritage which developed into two different approaches. On the one hand, the Anglo-Saxon conservation field has several interesting contemporary interventions for the enhancement and promotion of its ruined cultural heritage. These are designed on a value-based approach that bases its process of conservation or transformation on the assessment of the tangible and intangible values of the building or urban fabric. On the other hand, the Italian approach, focused on more detailed analysis, has become characterised by obsessive research into the preservation of history, memory and identity which has led to practices of non-intervention or extremely slow processes of rehabilitation.

These reflections led me to think that cross-pollination between the Anglo-Saxon value-based approach and the Italian conservation tradition might lead to the definition of a new experimental methodology to be tested in Cagliari's historic centre. Therefore, Cagliari and its ruins can be considered the experimental case of research for developing a broader study of the problem, defining and testing a new methodology based on the comparison of international experiences and issues in order to delineate practical guidelines for intervention.

The main general research questions are then:
- How can we enhance the meanings of those aspects of the built environment that are often misunderstood due to their fragmentation and incompleteness and consequently perceived as place of abandonment and negligence?
- What methodologies can we pursue in order to reach an appropriate degree of intervention that will relate intelligently to their surroundings?
- How can we transmit the historical values embodied in these ruins to the future through contemporary conservation and preservation projects?
- Eventually, what new functions can be attributed to these ruins in case of intervention and reuse?

2. Cagliari, Italy.
Aerial view of the historic centre.
© *Elisa Pilia*.

Theoretically speaking, the dilemma may have arisen from the misunderstanding of the concept and application of the conservation discipline. In fact, the sources showed the necessity to think about conservation not only as an operation connected to the past, but also as an action in the present that should resolve contemporary necessities and issues within old structures, bringing them into the future. It is, indeed, a complex act. As Frank Matero (2011, xvi) asserts, *"conservation is both creative and modern and the real goal of conservation is not simply to preserve the past but to find new sustainable approaches in which past and present are both well-balanced, considering the knowledge and skills coming from such different disciplines as architecture, history, anthropology, economy etc. Not least, conservation is a 'dynamic process'"* (Matero 2011, xvii) involving the society that inhabits and uses the spaces.

Architectural, urban, social, cultural and economic issues, and the needs of the contemporary city are in constant flux and for that reason, they should be considered in their continual transformation. Conservation is an act that modifies heritage, maintaining continuity with the past and the evolution of meaning and uses of places. Only by keeping in mind this dynamic process can we provide an appropriate response to these main questions. Considering the concept of conservation in these terms, in order to answer these main questions, research was carried out along three specific lines of enquiry. The first considers ruins within the broader context of the historic urban landscape defined by UNESCO (2011) as *"the urban area understood as result of a historic layering of cultural and natural values and attributes, extending beyond the notion of 'historic centre' or 'ensemble' to include the broader urban context and its geographical setting"*.

The second concerns the problem's architectural dimension. It looks at ruins as benchmarks of the historical built environment that document themselves and embody a wide set of values. It involves all aspects relating to the building such as its history, structure and development, material composition, and state of conservation. They are essential for understanding the case study and for proposing intervention. The third, instead, deals with the identification and assessment of tangible and intangible values embodied in these artefacts, their significance and needs, by seeking to determine the operative principles for their conservation, safeguarding, re-enhancement and sustainable adaptive re-use

The study opens with a clarification of the concepts of ruin in both English and Italian languages. This was important for establishing some important key terms and meanings commonly used with confusion in the literature and by designers, especially in Italy where 'ruin' can be expressed with the terms *'rudere'* and *'rovina'*. This linguistic explanation (part I), useful for conceiving worldwide ruined architectures, is followed by a selective analysis of the historical development of the concept of ruins along with the study of the contemporary theoretical and practical approaches to ruins in Europe and internationally (part II). Approaching the problem through the lens of architectural and urban conservation, this research conducts an in-depth exploration of the 'historical city' considered as a dynamic environment and palimpsest of stratifications that must be deeply investigated in terms of its history, development, modifications and the issues concerning policy, economy, the needs of the local community, and the current state of conservation of the built environment and its potential re-use. Furthermore, it faces issues tied to processes of urban transformation that involves the economic, social and aesthetic dimensions. Then, a comparative study of the international cultural and legal frameworks, and the in-depth analysis of the UK and Italy create the basis for codifying a transdisciplinary methodology aimed at identifying specific guidelines for safeguarding and finding the proper level of intervention for historic urban ruins in Cagliari, which are deeply investigated according to the protocol defining possible strategies to transfer to similar contexts (part III).

In conclusion, the goal of the research project was to codify a general methodology that could allow a holistic comprehension of ruins for the definition of sustainable interventions or, at least, some specific guidelines for enhancing its ruined urban heritage as an important testimony to local memory and identity.

"WHEN WE CONTEMPLATE RUINS, WE CONTEMPLATE OUR OWN FUTURE.
TO STATESMEN, RUINS PREDICT THE FALL OF EMPIRES, AND TO PHILOSOPHERS THE FUTILITY OF MORTAL MAN'S ASPIRATIONS. TO A POET, THE DECAY OF A MONUMENT REPRESENTS THE DISSOLUTION OF THE INDIVIDUAL EGO IN THE FLOW OF TIME; TO A PAINTER OR ARCHITECT, THE FRAGMENTS OF A STUPENDOUS ANTIQUITY CALL INTO QUESTION THE PURPOSE OF THEIR ART."

(Woodward 2002, 2-3)

PART I
HISTORIC DEVELOPMENT OF THE CONCEPT

3. Athens, Greece.
Ruins of the Temple of Hephaestus.
© Elisa Pilia.

The first part of the dissertation provides an overview of the modern concept of 'ruin' as the result of the prolonged historical development of both theories and practices.

First, an in-depth analysis of the terminology currently used to define these structures examines the differences in meaning between the English terms, 'ruins, remains, wreckage, and fragments' and the Italian '*rudere, rovina, relitto, resto, vestigia,* and *frammento*'. This analysis is necessary not only to explain the origins, etymology, and linguistic evolution of these terms, but also to understand the differences between the two languages. Furthermore, it is important to underline that problems of interpretation occur within each language, as in the Italian where the words *rudere* and *rovina* are frequently misunderstood and improperly used, creating problems of interpretation that can have consequences for the preservation project. This is a basic and very essential point for identifying the topic of this research and for subsequent investigations.

Next, an international survey of the variations in the historical meanings of ruins is presented. Since antiquity, various bodies of knowledge such as the arts, philosophy, literature, and architecture have contributed 'to defining and developing' different approaches and theories regarding such assets.

Finally, the chapter explores the different ways of classifying ruins depending on approaches to materials and typologies – origins, buildings types, location, degree of deterioration - or according to precise interpretations by scholars within specific architectural topics. Among the wide range of ruins included in this preliminary survey, special emphasis is placed on the cultural debate regarding the World War II period and its contemporary legacy. In general, Part I establishes the study's theoretical and lexical premises, reframing the evolution of the perception of the ruin and reviewing the various attempts at classification. It also introduces and brings into focus the research topic: ruins of traditional architecture from the post-war era within historical urban contexts.

1. TERMINOLOGY, DEFINITIONS, AND CONCEPTS OF RUINS

Different terms have been used in the English and Latin languages to describe buildings in a state of ruin; their meanings and subsequent interpretations have changed over time in relation to different cultural contexts.

The terminology is extremely broad in the English language but it is especially so in the Italian scientific literature. Three terms are most frequently used in English, usually in the plural: ruin/s, remain/s, wreckage/s, and fragment/s while in Italian *rudere/rudero* and *rovina* are the foremost terms, together with *relitto/i, frammento/i*, and *resto/i*, which, while less used, are, in any case, synonyms for expressing these incomplete architectures. Having considered the different nuances of these terms in different countries and authors' interpretations over time, the analysis first turns to the etymology of each lexical expression and to the definitions provided by the most widely utilised dictionaries (Oxford, Cambridge, Merriam-Webster, and Treccani). These definitions are then compared to the way in which the words have been used in the scientific literature, highlighting several conflicting interpretations and cases of inappropriate usage demonstrating that a general misunderstanding of the concept of ruin was one of the causes for invasive and unbalanced interventions on this particular type of structure (Di Blasi and Robbiati 1996, 22). Thus, clarification of the terms appeared urgent and crucial as a first step. The analysis also recognises important and nuanced distinctions in both languages, a crucial point for understanding the differences between the Anglo-Saxon and Italian approaches to intervening upon such structures. In detail, this clarification is useful for considering ruins in Italian cities such as Cagliari, whose wartime ruins are termed *rovine* or *ruderi* without any distinction in the scientific research or in technical documents.

In addition to the aforementioned reasons, lexical analysis is a fundamental tool for the philosophical investigation of possible connections between terminology and related values, whether tangible or intangible.

1.1. RUIN – RUDERE VS ROVINA

The Oxford English dictionary (2016) reports that the origins of the English word 'ruin' are partially borrowed from French words *ruwine* and *ruine*, and partially from the Latin word *ruīna* The evolution of its use is considered here. In the 12th century, the word was specifically related to devastated and destroyed objects or for representing the downfall or decay of individuals or society. Only in the early 13th century did it begin to refer to the collapsed remains of buildings. Considering the classical Latin roots, it is important to remember that *ruīna* meant "*headlong rush, headlong fall, downward plunge, collapse (of a building), fallen mass of debris, collapsed remains of a particular building or town, destruction of hopes or position, collapse, downfall, source of destruction*".

In a similar way, the Latin noun was also borrowed by other Germanic languages, in some cases via the French, in which the word was the feminine *ruine* used in the 16th century to refer to a ruined building. The modern meaning of an architectural ruin referring appeared in the dictionary as: "*the state or condition of a fabric or structure, esp. a building, which has given way and collapsed*", or in the plural, "*material which remains after the decay and collapse of a structure*" synonymous with debris, wreckage, remains.

This meaning is quite different from the one used in the Oxford Dictionary of Architecture (Curl & Wilson 2015) in which ruins are presented with the strong emphasis of eighteenth-century English. The definition appears to be a thematic interpretation of one among the several ways of conceiving ruins: "*carefully contrived specially constructed 'ruins' (sometimes called folly) or real ruins (e.g. of a castle or abbey) were often incorporated within the 18th English Picturesque landscape, a fashion that spread in Europe. Some architects (e.g. Chambers and Soane) established their architectural works as worthy of the best Classical Antique models by arranging for them to be depicted ad imaginary ruins, inspired by the Grand Tour and the influential engravings of Piranesi*".

The American Merriam-Webster dictionary agrees with the Oxford dictionary on the date of its first use in the 12th century and considers the origins and the etymology of the word from the middle English *ruine* deriving from the Anglo-French and Latin etymons. Furthermore, the Webster Dictionary defines ruin more generally as "*the remains of a decayed or demolished city, house, fortress, or any work of art or other thing; as the ruins of Balbec, Palmyra or Persepolis*".

The similarities of Anglo-American definitions are also evident in the Cambridge Dictionary (2016) that, again, defines a ruin as "*the broken parts that are left from an old building or town*".

Other authors have provided a definition of ruins with different interpretations and from different points of view.

In the fifteenth chapter of his book 'The Aesthetic of Ruins', Robert Ginsberg analysed the terminology of ruins from an aesthetic point of view (2004, 285 – 314). He defined a ruin as "*the irreparable remains of a human construction that, by a destructive act or process, no longer dwells in the unity of the original, but may have new unities that we can enjoy*" (Ginsberg 2004, 285). According to his thinking, if we consider the 'absent original' of a work that had value, we project negative meaning onto the word 'ruin', underlining loss and regret. In contrast, in the aesthetic discourse ruins are considered 'artworks'.

Ginsberg said:

"assigned to that entity whose unity has been destroyed, 'ruin' apparently could not be valuable in aesthetics. When we reflect that the ruin is all that remains of something valued, we do accord it some aesthetic weight. It is valuable as the remnant of the original. It keeps the absent present. The original may become so mingled in mind with the remnant that we are willing to treat the ruin and the presence of the original, not only a reminder or part of it. In such cases, we regard the ruin as a cultural treasure" (286). The same author considered that not only in an aesthetic sense does ruin have a positive meaning, considered what it is and not what it was, but also poetry and arts in general assumed the positive meaning deriving from the picturesque and symbolic expressions (288). His argumentation goes beyond the mere explanation of the word ruin to analyse the terminology surrounding this concept. His classification is interesting:

D words – damage, decay, dilapidation, decline, destruction, deformity, devastation, desolation as negative words that declare the end of the structures; R verbs – repair, restore, rebuilt, replicate, readapt, replace, reconstruct as verbs that permit the ruin to become something else, according to different degrees of intervention; P verbs – preserve, protest, protect, present, promote as proactive verbs that allow us to do something for ruins.

In Italian, the question is even more complicated since the English word 'ruin' corresponds to two words: the feminine *rovina* and the masculine *rudere*. If we look for their meanings in the Italian dictionary, Vocabulary Treccani, it seems that, while the roots of the words are different, the meanings seem to be the same. In fact, *rovina*, from the Latin word *ruīna*, means large destruction or total or partial collapse of a building. In its plural form, *rovine* also represents ruined material, produced for instance by the bombing of a city (Treccani Dictionary 2015).

Rudere, rarely *rudero*, on the other hand, finds its origins in the Latin *rudus – ruderis* and it is often used in the plural form, *ruderi*, to indicate rough remains of buildings or statues (Treccani Dictionary 2015).

Following this unity of meaning, despite the different roots, scholars have not provided precise definitions for the use of *rudere/rovina* using them without clarifying or distinguishing the two terms. At the same time, it can be asserted that the word *rovina* is more widely used (Augé 2004; Barbanera 2009, 2013; Ercolino 2006, 2014; Settis 2010; Tortora 2006; Treccani 2008; Ugolini 2010; Varagnoli 2008) than the word rudere (Carbonara 1997, 2011; Gizzi 2005; Marconi 2005, Picone 2012). Rudere and rovina both refer to artefacts in a state different from their original one and, as such, both can be transmitted to the future (Serafini 2005, 79). In contrast, according to other scholarly interpretations, the two Italian words should be considered differently. For Francesco Doglioni (2008), a leading figure in Italian conservation, *rudere* and *rovina* are different in how they fall into ruination in terms of their original building typologies and the quantity of material still in place. Only some types of architecture, such as military or monumental religious buildings, can become *rudere*. In fact, this 'noble state' is the destiny intended for "*big structures built to survive over ages and ages by magistri who knew the secrets of the lime*" (263). *Rudere* is a special state referring to buildings made of stone or brick bonded by mortar, raw materials well-cemented with the best technologies of the times. After deteriorating, these materials, in Latin '*rudus*', can be defined as *maceria* and still show the *firmitas* of the collapsed structures. If *rudere* is the mere remain of walls giving little information about the early building, *rovina* has recognisable features because it is still composed of intact elements and details. Doglioni added that a fragment of *rovina* could be a wonderful ruin, the decay of a work of architecture with recognisable elements, whereas a fragment of a *rudere* is merely a wall of stone (264). From this description, *rudere* cannot be recomposed from its remains while the *rovina* still has possibility and proper *venustas*. Moreover, it represents the action of ruination in its own meaning, including possible origins in traumatic or catastrophic events. Other authors, like Gianluigi De Martino (2004, 77), emphasised the absence of use or *utilitas* from ruined structures associating the word *rovina* to the action of ruination whereas the concept of *rudere* to specific objects (2017, 17). Nevertheless, this uselessness does not qualify ruins as 'dead monuments' (Giovannoni 1945), according to Giovannoni's definition, but rather the possibility to plan a project. Concerning the meanings of these words, Tatiana K. Kirova (2009) asserted that it can depend on the context in which ruins are placed. The archaeological ruin for instance (fig.3), can be considered a *rovina* that, in her opinion, has a positive connotation because of its antiquity. On the contrary, in an urban context, ruins, called *ruderi*, take on negative meaning because of their irreparable decay, and are thus linked more to material aspects than to aesthetic ones, also raising social questions for nearby residents (186).

1.2. WRECKAGE – RELITTO

As the Oxford dictionary suggests, wreckage finds its etymology in the word wreck. It had origins in the Anglo-Norman *wrec, wrech, wrek* that is also the source of medieval Latin *wreccum, warectum*. If a wreck is defined as *"that which remains of something that has suffered ruin, demolishment, waste, etc.; the dilapidated, disorganised, or disordered residue or remainder of anything"*, a wreckage is a *"material of or from a wrecked or shattered structure; a ruined fabric, building, etc..."*

According to Merriam-Webster, its first known use can be dated to the 19th century. It represents the broken remains of something wrecked or otherwise ruined, something disabled or in a state of ruin or dilapidation. In general, wreck and wreckage came to be used relatively late in the architectural field, having been used to represent fragments or remains of a shattered or wrecked vessels. The same word in Italian, *relitto*, from the Latin *relictus*, past participle of the verb *relinquĕre* 'to leave', and in its passive 'to remain' or 'to stay', identifies something that remains and survives even if in an isolated condition (Treccani 2016). In all languages, it does not refer directly to architecture but takes on metaphoric meaning, expressing a state of decay.

Again, Doglioni also analyses this concept. *Relitto* is something abandoned to its destiny (Doglioni 2008, 264). Comparing *rudere* and *rovina*, *relitto* does not derive from an event or building typology. Its nature is based on the loss of use and interest in its structures which can still be fully intact. Doglioni defined the *relitto* as a *"non-state"* (264), a condition of non-use that is more dangerous than *ruderi* and *rovine*. A new life for these structures can be made possible through renewed interest or their falling into ruination and becoming a *rudere*. The main difference from the previous words regards the quantity of materials; in fact a *relitto* could be intact and not be modified by time (Doglioni 2008, 256). Finally, *rudere*, *rovina*, and *relitto* are often interpreted as different typologies but it is also possible to find a combination of them in the same building. *Relitto*, on the other hand, is an intermediate state, between what is still present and the *rovina*.

1.3. OTHER TERMS:
REMAINS AND FRAGMENTS – RESTI, FRAMMENTI, MACERIE, VESTIGIA

Remains and fragments are two other common words used to refer to ruined structures. In Italian, they are *resti* and *frammenti* respectively. Both are used mostly in the plural and can be considered synonymous for defining *"that which remains or is left of a thing or things after other parts have been removed, used, or destroyed"* (Oxford 2016).

As Alessandra Quendolo reported (2014, 8) *frammento* comes from the Latin word '*frag-mentum*' and it has the same roots as two other words:

fragile and *frangere*. This could indicate a piece of something broken but also of something conserved (idem). In any case, these words have literally the same general meaning even if they have different roots. They define, with negative undertones, something that partially survives destruction or collapse. Also, these words are typically used to identify a singular and specific part of a more complex ruined structure.

The Italian *maceria/e*, translated in English as ruins, has been defined by Marc Augé as the ruins of modern history in contrast with *rovine*, born in the past in *"pure time"* (2004, 135).

Finally, *vestigia*, from the Latin *vestigium* is used to identify ruins from the World War II (Quendolo 2014, 8). It is a synonym of a footprint, sign, track, or marker in the landscape and it recalls the verb investigate - concerning the investigation of a monument that endures as a document and memory of an event.

In conclusion, this linguistic and semantic analysis shows that the Italian language is more complex than English due to the wide range of terms used to define ruins. Moreover, historical events and the linguistic evolution of the terms mentioned have complicated the linguistic panorama more than ever.

2. RUINS IN HISTORY

Having examined the terminology concerning ruins, its meanings and interpretations, this chapter presents the changes in viewpoints, interests and meaning that ruins have acquired over the ages. Ruins have been constant presences from antiquity to modernity with continual metamorphoses involving various historic and cultural fields including literature, painting, photography, landscape history, archaeology, restoration theory, architecture, urbanism, and sociology. As Barbanera (2009, 15) suggested, *"a ruin is a sentinel at the boundary of the time which is her enemy for his fluidity and fast flowing. On the one hand, ruins are behind the time because it has collapsed their structures; on the other hand, their physical presence and their resistance over the time confer to them the sense of time and the value of identity"*.

This idea of the ruin as a cultural memory to be preserved is a relatively modern concept that developed during the industrial revolution. People changed their habits and models to adapt their lives to the frenetic rhythm of new production, and they soon understood the value of ruins, important as a testimonial to the rapidly-changing times. Generally, the new approaches were determined by the historical, social, cultural, and especially economic events that involved our nations and characterised them in distinct ways. In Western countries, ruins generated two main responses. For some, ruins encompass a special material component that should be preserved due to its strong communicative and expressive nature; for others, they are lost places that should arguably be reconstructed. The debate/conflict unfolds among three positions: the aesthetic, the historic (Di Blasi and Robbiati 1996, 22) and the psychological.

2.1. A GROWING AESTHETIC VALUE

The ancient world did not confer value upon ruins or demonstrate any particular interest in them. Most probably, after the fall of the Roman Empire, the Latins began to consider ruins in a new way as they began to ponder the frailty of their actions and mortality (Barbanera 2013, 16–18). In the Middle Ages, the concept of ruin was linked to the Roman idea but also to the new Christian credo which supported a view of ruins as the death of the pagan world and the concept of luck as well as the fragility of human actions (19). Roman remains are ruins par excellence (fig. 4). In literature, Francesco Petrarca (1304–1374) overcame this view and began to emphasise the beauty of ruins, disapproving the state of abandonment of these pagan and Christian *vestigia, mura, columnae,* and *reliquae*. His speeches articulated a new desire for renewal, the need to remember a magnificent past through the study of ancient memories and symbols of identity like ruins. The interest in ruins changed the field of knowledge

4. Rome, Italy.
View of Roman ruins:
Imperial Forum and Colosseum.
© *Elisa Pilia.*

with Poggio Bracciolini (1380–1459) who introduced the archaeological dimension of these artefacts in his *De varietate fortunae Urbis Romae at ruinae eiusdem descriptio* (1431–1448). Through the accurate study of all features of the ancient structures such as their building techniques and materials, he demonstrated great sensibility for their protection. Ancient artefacts were for the first time conceived as integrated with modern ones. Leon Battista Alberti (1404–1472) focused on aspects of construction technology. He saw ruins, especially dating from the Roman era, as elements that revealed the building language, models with which to establish a new architectural morphology based on mathematics and proportions. His book *De re aedificatioria* (1404) is the result of this detailed research that compared buildings to the human body. Other artists like Giotto, Maso di Banco, Ambrogio Lorenzetti, Andrea Mantegna, Sandro Botticelli instead exalted the positive or negative symbolic role of ruins in their paintings.

During the age of humanism, literature and painting finally merged in Francesco Colonna's *Hypnerotomachia Poliphili* written in 1447. In 170 etchings, he represented ruins and wild nature in a romantic view of the past's lost beauty. From the 17th century on, Rome become that cultural hub where all artists travelled to see the vast ruins from the past and to learn more about their construction (29).

Therefore, following the Enlightenment – a long period of excess in the aesthetic of ruins – society was ready to appreciate the new aesthetics of the ruin whose maximum expression was developed by Piranesi.

2.2. THE ROMANTIC OUTLOOK

Contemporary fascination for ruins finds its main roots in the last two centuries (Rizzi 2007, xix). During the Enlightenment, the debate concerning ruins became increasingly important, due in particular to two significant events: the excavations and extraordinary discoveries of the archaeological remains of Pompeii and Herculaneum in 1748 and the French Revolution in 1789. At the time, archaeological remains stimulated such great interest in ruins that integral reconstructions and the creation of false ruins became a very common tendency (Di Blasi and Robbiati 1996, 22). Moreover, earthquakes in Lisbon (1755) and Messina (1783) gave impetus to rethinking the relationship between humans and nature. This power of nature on ruins was emphasised in Giovanni Battista Piranesi's (1720–1778) etchings.

During the 18th century, the poetic views of Piranesi highlighted the greatness of ruins (fig. 5). They became reference material for the reconstruction of the past and research into the building techniques of our ancestors. Piranesi emphasised their relationship with the forces of nature, pointing out the important role of nature in the origins and development of decayed structures. Roman and Greek ruins, considered by Piranesi to be superior

5. Etching of different views of Roman ruins in Pesto, the old city Possidonia in Lucania, by Giovanni Battista Piranesi (1778).
In Planche V url:
http://hdl.handle.net/10934/RM0001.collect.164949).

architecture, appeared for the first time covered with flourishing vegetation as *"an attempt at both recording the remains of classical antiquity and offering an archaeological reconstruction of the past"* (Ferri 2015, 83). Indeed, at the time, he promoted a totally new view of ruins, far from the modern way of conceiving an objective 'archaeological representation of the past'. In fact, he conferred a subjective sublime mood upon them, creating a new idea of landscape and the *"material evidence of the history"* (Ferri 2015, 87). During the same century, ruins and nature were also celebrated in the 'landscape garden', also called 'English garden' (Makarius 2004, 120). Nature acquired a new image as an aesthetic object where the components of the previous 'French garden', geometry and symmetry, were totally absent. Seemingly wild paths and landscapes were adorned with the presence of ruins placed in the landscape to stimulate the imagination and offer picturesque views. The picturesque was characterised by irregular shapes and additions with 'mysterious' features, including ruins, as described by the English artist William Gilpin (1724 – 1804) (Makarius 2004, 120). Ruins, seen from an aesthetic point of view as fragments produced by nature as well as witnesses of history, conferred identity upon places. It is for this reason that artificial ruins, 'follies', began to be widely deployed in landscape gardens as the 're-composition' of man's and nature's work (Roth et al. 1997, Woodward 2002). Thomas Whately (1771, 130) described why and how these ruins should be placed in gardens:

"they are a class by themselves, beautiful as objects, expressive as characters, and peculiarly calculated to connect with their appendages into elegant groups; they may be accommodated with ease to irregularity of ground, and their disorder is improved by it; they may be intimately blended with trees and with thicket, and the interruption is an advantage; for imperfection and obscurity are their properties; and to carry the imagination to something greater than is seen, their effect" (Whately 1771, 131).

Ruins given over to nature have a new appearance. They could also be divided into several pieces in order to recall a previous structure, placed with precise meaning and connections. These artificial ruins sought to imitate the work of nature and soon, from mere aesthetic practice, the tendency became a fashionable trend in which ruins were only objects used 'to furnish' and decorate gardens. With the same purpose, in 1762 Hubert Robert (1733 – 1808) built the *Temple de la Philosophie* in the park at Ermenonville, designed by René Louis de Girardin; it was left unfinished to symbolised the unknown future that was to come. Opposed to the idea of ruins in a garden, J. M. Morel instead asserted that ruins should only be placed in landscape and not in gardens. Generally, this period, characterised by love for artificial ruins as the *"re-composition between human and nature's work, become a 'ruin mania'"* (Roth et al. 1997, Woodward 2002).

Even if Greek and Roman ruins were considered important bases for scientific studies while medieval remains were seen as barbaric architectures having negative connotations, this was the period in which the 'gothic revival' began to become even more widespread, especially during the following century. Again, it involved all fields in which writers, painters, thinkers and artists expressed their arts. Maria Piera Sette (1996, 151) called this phenomenon the 'cult of ruins' and recognised two prevailing positions: first, the melancholic view of the ruin as a new artefact, a unique piece of art and nature, arising from the victory of time over man; second, the view of ruins as mutilated testimonials to the past.

Philosophical thought also developed in this period, carrying out the birth of the modern aesthetic of ruins. Central contributions were Edmund Burke's (1727–1797) 'theory of the sublime' and Denis Diderot's poetic of ruins (1713–1794) as fragments that reflect the past and the human condition. Ruins were thus considered to be a memento mori of civilisations, the *"visible effect of history in terms of decay, a symbol of eternity"* (Macaulay 1977, 23).

All of this was the basis for the formation of the modern conservative movement in the following period, considerably influencing the approach to ruins. Only in the 19th century with the development of this discipline as we understand it today did the consideration of ruins begin to evolve differently in relation to national traditions and ideological currents.

2.3. THE MODERN CULT OF RUINS

The late 19th and 20th centuries offered a series of cultural and philosophical experiences which conferred upon ruins further symbolic connotations and meanings (Matteini 2009, 47).

In particular, the semantic duality of ruins, already expressed in the Enlightenment when Roman ruins were considered an auspice for classical renewal, characterised the entire 19th century (Roth et al. 1997, 18). In terms of theoretical and practical approaches, the late 19th and 20th centuries were characterised by important occurrences in Italy, France, Germany and Great Britain with their scientific and nationalistic implications (Stubbs and Makaš 2001, 10-11). Italy and Germany faced restoration *"with a cultural pride and reinforced enthusiasm for political reunification"* (Stubbs and Makaš 2001, 10). Approaches in France and Britain instead, reflected their reaction to the social changes brought about by the Industrial Revolution, manifesting the revival of medieval architecture as *"a source for national origins"* (idem). In France, the emphasis on equality and emancipation stimulated by the Revolution influenced the propensity towards the development of the concept of 'national heritage' (Glendinning 2013, 67). If, on the one hand, it led to approaches to preservation supported by intellectuals like

Victor Hugo (1802–1885), Charles de Montalembert (1810–1870), Antoine Chrysostome Quatremère de Quincy (1755–1849), Ludovic Vitet (1802–1873), and Prosper Mérimée (1803–1870), as well as to the development of a system of centralised heritage management, on the other, it brought to the restoration discipline an ideology and a growing national competitiveness united by the idea of the superiority of Gothic architecture (78). Radical approaches were supported by Eugenè-Emmanuel Viollet-le-Duc (1814–1879) who, for the first time, provided a definition of restoration and introduced the concept of 'stylistic unit'. In his 'Dictionary of Architecture' (1866) he argued: "*to restore a building is not to preserve it, to repair, or to rebuild it; it is to reinstate it in a condition of completeness which may never have existed at any given time*". Thus, a monument "*might exist not as an object or as material substance but as an abstract ideal at one remove from historic 'reality', whose modern 'recreation' might, in its greater purity, answer the demands of a nation more effectively than 'authentic' old substance*" (Glendinning 2013, 77).

Ruins can be reconstructed after an accurate study of all the fragments and the context in which they were located (Picone 2012, 36). The case of the fortified city of Carcassonne (figg.6–7) was a clear example of this approach, having recomposed the ruins into an idealised medieval citadel with 'unity of style' and clear new additions. Towards the end of the century in the United Kingdom, an extraordinary passion for rebuilding and 'restoring' English cathedrals stemmed partially from the Victorian sense of religion and partially from aesthetic theory. With these ideas, the Camden society was founded in 1839, seeking 'to promote the study of the ecclesiastic architecture and Antiquities and the restoration of mutilated architectural remains'. The controversial results of the interventions carried out by its followers gave the origins to the Anti-Scrape movement between 1850–1890. In 1877, the conservation propagandist, William Morris (1834–1896), founded the SPAB, the Society for the Protection of Ancient Buildings that had "*immense importance in the development of the Conservation movement, as it was the ancestor of all modern campaigning society*" (Glendinning 2013, 122). SPAB was a 'private' group that revealed to the public issues relating to the threats to old buildings, in the past sponsored only by gentlemen protestors. Augustus Pugin's (1812–1852) religious conservatism and Ruskin's ideal of authenticity and defence of the 'living monument' continued the ideology of their predecessor, Morris. The theorist John Ruskin (1819–1900), particularly influential in the 'conservation of ruins', defines restoration as, "*the most total destruction which a building can suffer: a destruction out of which no remnants can be gathered; a destruction accompanied with false description of the thing destroyed. Do not let us deceive ourselves in this important matter; it is impossible, as impossible as to raise the dead, to restore anything that has ever been great or beautiful in architecture.*

6. Carcassonne, France.
View of the walled city restored according to the 'unity of style'.
© *Caterina Giannattasio.*

7. Carcassone, France.
The fortified walls of the city.
© *Caterina Giannattasio.*

That which I have above insisted upon as the life of the whole, that spirit which is given only by the hand and eye of the workman, never can be recalled. Another spirit may be given by another time, and it is then a new building; but the spirit of the dead workman cannot be summoned up, and commanded to direct other hands, and other thoughts" (Ruskin 1849, 185).

He argued that historical values were those that physically embodied the collective social and natural memory. No-one had the right to modify a building and no sort of restoration could be allowed except basic repairs. It is only with Ruskin that ruins enjoyed their highest theoretical acknowledgement: symbols of truth, they were the witnesses to themselves. In his book, The Seven Lamps of Architecture (1883), and specifically in the Lamp of Memory, he explained that "*[..] the greatest glory of a building is not in its stones, or in its gold. Its glory is in its Age, and in that deep sense of forcefulness, of stern watching, of mysterious sympathy, nay, even of approval or condemnation, which we feel in walls that have long been washed by the passing waves of humanity. It is in their lasting witness against men, in their quiet contrast with the transitional character of all things, in the strength which, through the lapse of seasons and times, and the decline and birth of dynasties, and the changing of the face of the earth [..]*" (1849, 172) (fig.8), introducing also the value of age. In the broader European context at the same time, the question of values had been already analysed by two other important figures: F. W. Nietzsche (1844–1900) and Alois Riegl (1858–1905). The first, a German philosopher (1844–1900), theorised about the identification of values. His statement, "*God id dead! We have killed Him!*" written in Gay Science - aphorism 125, meant the elimination of the highest values of this period which he called 'nihilism' and led to an important contribution in the reconsideration of universal values for all of Western Europe (Jokilenhto 2009, 213). These universal values, now based on specificity and relativity, were not imposed by religion but emerged as product of human culture. The second, an Austrian art historian, wrote Der Moderne Denkmalskultus (1903), in which, while developing the Ruskinian concepts of ruins, he explains his theory of values which distinguished 'intended' and 'unintended' monuments, estimable and appreciable according to the modern concept, 'Kunstwollen', a relative and not absolute evaluation depending on the beholder. 'Intended monuments' are only works that, due to will of their creators, show a particular historic period. They will remain ever alive and present in the consciousness of all generations. 'Unintentional monuments' instead, both historic and dating from antiquity, depend on modern human perception (fig. 8). The historical ones refer to a precise era decided by subjective human will; the second, more generally, are considered all human works, with no distinction of meaning or function but monuments because of having existed.

8. North Berwick, United Kingdom. Abandoned ruins of a dwelling in the Scottish wild landscape.
© Elisa Pilia.

In line with these typologies, Riegl classified two groups of values: 'memorial values' (age and historical values, and intentional values of memory) in counterpoint to 'present-day or contemporary values' (use, art, newness and relative art values). 'Age values' follow the law of aesthetics in which signs of decay impressed by nature are symbols to preserve without additions and removals. Inevitably, the continual and free action of nature will destroy a monument, so that the more ruins decay, their value of age and picturesque will increase. By contrast, historical values are based on scientific consideration noted only by scholars because they are embodied in monuments clearly built in a specific period and within a given field of human creativity. The only interest is in the initial state of construction of the monument; any signs of wear and weathering are disturbing. As a consequence, these signs should be removed in order to preserve the original work in the future. In that case, the monument is a document and its historical value decreases as the age value increases. Finally, the 'Intentional value of memory' embodies the function of preserving and conserving a present monument in eternity, avoiding its becoming and element of the past. Indeed, Riegl considered this value to be transitional towards contemporary ones and for that reason it envisages restoration regulated by legislation. Overall, if 'age value' is founded in the past while historical value tries to halt time, the intentional value of memory supports the immortality of the present in complete contrast to age value (Scarrocchia 1995, 55).

In contrast, 'present-day or contemporary values' are deeply rooted in natural and intellectual will. Use value for instance, cannot be eradicated for structures. Use is, in fact, the element that allowed our monuments to endure to the present and to satisfy our practical life. If it is in contrast with the 'age value', it can find accordance with the 'historical' one which can be adapted to new uses. At the same time, 'art value', in modern thinking, is possessed by all monuments according to Kunstwollan. It can be divided into 'newness value' for recently built works and 'relative art value' considered in relation to evolution over time and changing social need (fig.9). Newness value might be considered a value of the less educated mass and for that reason, it is the major enemy of 'age value' which require great training in aesthetics. As a consequence, the modern newness value has great influence in the community so that new architecture characterised by the completeness and unity of style are more appreciated than the old. 'Relative art value' instead, is based on the possibility of appreciating monuments from the past not only as monuments of human creativity but also in relationship to their conception, form and colour. In summary, a unique and valid standard of beauty cannot exist. At the beginning of the 20th century, Mark Dvorak (1874–1921), one of Riegl's followers, wrote the Katechismus der Denkmalpflege (1916) and expressed his opinion about

9. Edinburgh, United Kingdom. Old and new on High Street.
© *Elisa Pilia.*

how ruins should be restored. He asserted that *"a 'built' ruin is not a ruin, but a mediocre building"* as well as all other restored ruins that have been reshaped as ruins (Dvorak 1971, 55). He underlined the importance of ruins' authenticity and uniqueness and proposed some restoration interventions for preserving them by filling cracks, reinforcing damaged masonry and detached parts, keeping the natural irregularities of the structures without painting or modifying the finishes and leaving vegetation as an element of beauty. Furthermore, in a special section with suggestions, he advised keeping all interesting and unique elements by adapting the new intervention with compatible materials and forms (Dvorak 1971, 56). In Italy, the ideas of philological restoration promoted by Camillo Boito (1836–1914) and their evolution into the later scientific approach, theorised by Gustavo Giovannoni (1873–1947), contributed to considering ruins in their contexts, the city. Stratifications had absolute value that should not be eliminated, but preserved, valorising the documental character of ruins. Moreover, Giovannoni recognised the significance of a regular maintenance and appropriate reuse for architectures (Jokilehto 2009, 5). In 1931, the Athens Charter, the first Italian charter on restoration, specified how to intervene on ruins: *"in the case of ruins, scrupulous conservation is necessary, and steps should be taken to reinstate any original fragments that may be recovered (anastylosis), whenever this is possible; the new materials used for this purpose should in all cases be recognisable. When the preservation of ruins brought to light during excavations is found to be impossible, the Conference recommends that they be buried, accurate records being of course taken before filling-in operations are undertaken"* (Athens Charter 1931). Furthermore, the same attention on ruins is reported in the Italian Charter of restoration (1931). In the modern age, ruins also had a place in the fields of literature, philosophy and psychoanalysis. The 20th century opened with an important contribution to the French literature on the topics of time, memory and ruins: 'In Search of Lost Time' written by Michael Proust (1871–1922) between 1913 and 1927. There, the notion of physical decay stressed man's awareness of his vulnerability and the uselessness of his actions in front of his ruins as already seen in the Romantic period. But, from this perception Proust felt the necessity to speak about history; a history in which ruins were not only inspiration but also symbols of regeneration (Barbanera 2013, 14). George Simmel (1858–1918), philosopher and sociologist, added a significant contribution in 1911 in his writing Die Ruine. He wrote *"architecture is the only art in which the great struggle between the will of the spirit and the necessity of nature issues into a real place"*; when this balance between spirit and nature shift in favour of nature, architecture becomes a ruin where decay can be considered *"nature's revenge for the spirit's having violated it by making a form in its own image"* (Simmel 1965, 379).

As a consequence, the ruin of a building reveals in its state what other forces, the forces of nature, have grown in it, becoming a new entity. Although nature and spirit are in contrast, the fascination with ruins comes from the fact that they are works made by man but by nature. The difference between Proust and Simmel lies in the fact that Simmel did not consider ruins as a living element, but as elements of contemplation according to the 18th century. In Proust's thinking instead, ruins are contemporary elements. The slow action of nature in the creation of ruins was overcome by the rapid human ability to produce ruins (Barbanera 2009, 19). Thus, in this period nature is not a negative force as at the end of the 18th century, but a conjoined element, and architecture and ruins are composite elements of nature. In addition, the further development of botanic disciplines led to a naturalistic investigation of ruins. The English botanist pioneer Richard Deakin (1809 –1873), for instance, with some carried out a detailed analysis of all the species of plants grown spontaneously in the Colosseum, cataloguing and illustrating the flourishing flora that infested the ruins. He argued that flowers *"form a link with the memory, and teach us hopeful and shooting lessons, amid the sadness of bygone ages: and cold indeed must be the heart that does not respond to their silent appeal; for though without speech, they tell us of the regeneration of the power which animates the dust of murdering greatness"* (Woodward 2002, 23). His cataloguing, in 'Flora in Colosseum' (1855), contributed to defining a nature that fifteen years later was to be destroyed by the excavations of 'cold-headed' archaeologists (Woodward 2002, 24). As far as psychoanalysis is concerned, Sigmund Freud (1856–1939) compared urban ruins, specifically those in Rome, with his patients' memory thinking (*tracce mnestiche*): they cannot disappear and in some way, they can be brought back in the mind while real ruins will inevitably be lost. In 'Disagio della civiltà' (1930) the ruins of the Acropolis become a 'landscape of the soul', a slip of memory, something that overcomes easy sensorial perception (Matteini 2009, 47). Freud wrote *"the presence of the ruin activated a repressed memory that seemed both to project him backwards in time and to place reality itself – the status of the present – in crisis"* (Lavery and Gough 2015, 2). Finally, the creative side of ruins also found diffusion in other cultural endeavours such as Le Corbusier's travel journals (1984) or the 'wonderful ruins of Louis Kahn' (Barbanera 2009) and in literature with 'Ruins of Tipasa' written by Camus, that showed an innovative view of ruined landscapes, a moment of synthesis of architecture and nature, spirit and materiality (Matteini 2009, 48).

2.4. THE POST WAR DEBATE

The traumatic events of the First (1914–1918) and Second World Wars (1939–1945) significantly changed the debate regarding interventions on ruins in the 20th century. All the theoretical discussions and the progress made with the Athens Charter and the philological 'minimum intervention' had to be reviewed considering new ideas and psychological need. The urgency to save bombarded heritage resulted in a series of interventions designed on a case-by-case basis (Casiello 2011, 1).

At this time, ruins were not only destroyed monuments, but open wounds, the memories of traumatic events caused by human action. Even if Britain, Germany, France, Italy, Belgium, and the Netherlands were the European countries involved, the debate arose on an international level and it had to face the unprecedented devastation including not only monuments but entire industrial and heritage cities.

During the World War I, the destruction of cities such as Leuven and Ypres in Belgium and Reims in France and the coastal defence heritage raised the question regarding the 'memory landscape' (Glendinning 2014, 191). Ruined towns became symbols of *"commemorative built environment of community"* (idem) where the authenticity of materials was completely neglected and reconstruction *"was largely a phenomenon of fiction"* (idem). Then, destruction become even more severe during the World War II which was defined a 'total war' where everything, both human and architecture, was considered a war target (fig.10) (Lambourne 2001, 27).

The war's cultural destruction also raised questions regarding the responsibility of these devastating actions and the possibility of judging them as crimes. In fact, these were veritable 'war crimes', as reported in Article 25 of the 1907 The Hague Convention that, even if before World War II, specified that attacks and bombing, by whatever means, of undefended towns, villages, dwellings, or buildings were prohibited (33). Nevertheless, during the Nuremberg trials whose first inquisitor was the Reich Marshall Göring, the indiscriminate bombing of historic cities and the consequent destruction of monuments were not pursued as crimes dues to the absence of dogged legal determination that would have also accused Allied forces who committed such crimes (169). Overcoming these moral and legal issues regarding the causes of war damage, several other problems had to be solved on the practical side. As Valentina Russo (2011, 127) asked in her essay on wartime urban ruins: is there a difference in the collective sentiment between ruins generated by violent war bombings and ruins that come out of natural events such as earthquakes and floods? Post-war history and events teach us that this difference is huge. In fact, from the mid-20th century onward, each country reacted differently to these human destructions according to the degree of damage and national values.

10. Coventry, United Kingdom.
Signs of destruction and consolidation in the ruins of St. Michael Cathedral completely bombed during World War II.
© *Elisa Pilia.*

As a consequence, ruins took on contrasting meanings and interpretations and as result, were subjected to contrasting interventions. On the one hand, the scale of the ruins, and the urgency and necessity for new housing, often encouraged the demolition of bombed areas and their reconstruction in modern forms and materials. On the other hand, the preservation of ruins and the decision to keep them permanently in their ruinous state led to the creation of memorials to the dead and other destroyed buildings. Churches, with their spiritual implications, were the buildings that best carry out this function. They took on positive connotations as elements of survival and optimism to counter the negative forces of war. They become metaphors for the wounded populations in the bombed areas. In practice, this thinking was translated into the 'garden ruin' where monuments were surrounded with flowers and grasses like Christchurch Greyfriars gardens in London (figg. 11 – 12), recalling the 18th century romantic idea of ruin.

In contrast, this visual and aesthetic attitude was countered by the consideration that war ruins could not be romantic due to the deeply negative originating events. In this view, not all ruins could be considered aesthetically pleasing. They evoked negative feelings and recalled the conflict's tragedy. The phenomenon of *damnatio memoriae* was born from this other interpretation with restorations, replicas and mimetic reconstructions. Monuments that did not received attention between the first wave of intervention, between 1940s and 1950s, had less opportunity to be restored to their original appearance, indeed with some exceptions.

In the 1950s and 60s, interest in preservation, restoration and reconstruction as well as the introduction of new architecture within traditional buildings in historical centres saw its maximum diffusion. Generally, if in Europe the solutions adopted were the result of deep thought relating to social issues, they were not always respectful of the historical features and authenticity of places; sometimes they were mere creative experiments. Other times, the wave of reconstruction became a great 'opportunity': a special situation to resolve the previous unanswered questions regarding urban planning (Casiello 2011, 2).

Indeed, Germany, Britain, France and Italy had significant influence in the post-war debate regarding the treatment of and approaches to historical monuments.

In particular, Germany faced a unique period, having been divided into the Federal Republic of Germany in the west and the German Democratic Republic in the east while controlled by the three occupying powers: Britain, France and the Soviet Union, each carrying out their own policies for the nation's reconstruction (Lambourne 2001, 170). In the 1950s, strong differences between East and West came about due to different political conditions.

11. London, United Kingdom.
Christchurch Greyfriars gardens.
© Elisa Pilia.

12. London, United Kingdom.
Details of the garden surrounding the ruins of the former Christchurch Greyfriars. The wooden frameworks recall the lost pillars of the church.
© Elisa Pilia.

The East was characterised by a communist government that politicised reconstruction and preservation for ideological purposes (Stubbs and Makaš 2011, 211). This Soviet influence, focused on leaving destroyed monuments as ruins, is clearly manifested in the Dresden Frauenkirche (Church of Our Lady), destroyed during the nights of February 13th and 14th, 1945. The monument, left in ruins as an *"unofficial war memorial throughout the Cold War"* (Stubbs and Makaš 2011, 210) began to be rebuilt in 1994, only after German reunification. It became the most heroic late post-war case of architectural preservation of a reunified Germany that sought to establish a new identity. The archaeological conservation and cataloguing of all its 'fragments' gave way to an *anastylosis* reconstruction directed by architect Eberhard Burger, concluded in 2005 (fig. 13).

This was an also exemplary instance of reconstruction in terms of social participation and respect for social values (Pretelli 2011, 12). In fact, the community not only wrote a Manifesto for supporting reconstruction based on historic analysis and the restricted use of traditional materials avoiding glass and steel, but also raised economic resources to finance the rebuilding of the city exactly as it was before the war (Casiello 2011, 4).

The surrounding Dresden Neumarkt (fig. 14) is a case of 'stylistic' reconstruction of pre-existing forms but with the integration of building techniques to achieve modern standards of comfort. It will be completed only when the overall urban reconstruction is concluded (Pretelli, 2011, 29). Also in Nuremberg, the reconstruction introduced contemporary material and techniques among the traditional ones (fig. 15).

West Germany offered, instead, a golden opportunity to recreate cities based on modern styles and standards as in West Berlin, Cologne, and Frankfurt which maintained only small parts of their historic centres. At the same time, as in East Germany, contempt towards Nazi architecture led to the decision to demolish important symbols like the Paul Ludwig Troost Ehrentempel and the Feldhernhalle memorial in Munich.

The DDR, Central Institute of Denkmalpflege was instituted in 1961, the same year as the erection of the Berlin Wall. Although following the French cataloguing model, the Institute listed a restricted number of ruined monuments and, between 1950 and 1970, allowed the extensive demolition of urban areas due to poor consideration and understanding of historic architecture (Pretelli 2011, 17).

In this context, after the war and especially the demolition of the Wall in 1989, Berlin became complicated case in which theories were never applied in practice with a total lack of consideration of historic urban values. The city's widespread destruction raised the idea that it never could be functional again and that its future was as a ruined memorial city (Sachs 2011, 4).

13. Dresden, Germany.
The Frauenkirche.
© *Giulia Cuccu.*

14. Dresden, Germany.
The Neumarkt.
© *Giulia Cuccu.*

Berlin's destiny was different and everything that marked transformations during the post war years, the construction and the demolition of *die Mauer*, brought to light the numerous historical stratifications and wounds that the city suffered. Nevertheless, the city's transformation offers several examples of integration between old and new with a clear distinction of the different historical layers. A good case is the Kaiser-Wilhelm-Gedächtniskirche (Church of Remembrance) where the new bell tower was built in contemporary materials and forms near the memorial of the bombed out and ruined church. The Palast der Republik, built in 1976, was constructed on the ruins of the demolished castle.

The architectural 'theory of ruin value', codified by Albert Speer (1905–1981) during the war, was an *"expression of the wider Nazi ideology"* (Featherstone 2005, 301). In Architectural Megalomania, the architect explained the concept of ruin value as *"a method of construction that could transmit the heroic spirit of Hitler's Germany to future generations"* (302) that would lead to aesthetic immortality. Miming Greek and Roman building, Speer aligned the future ruins of Nazi Germany with these dead civilisations, symbols of cultural superiority 'and of imperishable symbols of power'. The use of marble, stone and brick was preferred for all new Nazi buildings, avoiding the use of steel and reinforced concrete (Woodward 2001, 29). Thus, Nazi Germany would have achieved immortality only through the pursuit of endless ruination (302). In Poland, ruined historic monuments were rebuilt in replicas 'in defiance' (Woodward 2001, 209) to the robust Nazi attempt to destroy their culture. Warsaw's façades were rebuilt in the same forms and materials based on photographic and documentary sources dating to before the bombings (fig. 16). The interiors and uses on the other hand were modified according to new needs (Casiello 2011, 4). Again, psychological need and social values drove reconstruction. In contrast, Russia exalted the ruins of its enemy.

Entire cities were completely destroyed throughout Europe. Oradour sur Glane, Le Havre, and Saint-Malo were only three examples in France, considered unique for the different theoretical and practical approaches to their reconstruction.

Oradour (fig. 17) was a small village of 650 inhabitants in the south-west of France which was bombed on June 10th, 1944. Its destruction was catastrophic. It was reduced to a place of ruined shells whose only inhabitant was silence. No artistic or creative projects were carried out in an abandoned town that today is a renowned tourist destination of remembrance (Woodward 2002, 211). With its strategic position, Le Havre was bombed on September 5th and 6th, 1944. It was rebuilt by August Perret between 1946 and 1958 in an attempt to unify classicism with innovation. A *tabula rasa* dominated the new city plan which, guided by the architect's personal

15. Nuremberg, Germany.
Old and new in the streetscapes.
© *Elisa Pilia.*

16. Warsaw, Poland.
Old town Market Place reconstructed according to the 'stylistic unity'.
© *Francesca Mulliri.*

vision, was re-founded and reconstructed. As Perrett said, *"the city does not need to be reconstructed but to be recreated"* (Perret 1946). His research for a new classicism and a new equilibrium between academic technology and formality stemmed from the distinctive character of modernism in France at the time. Destruction was, in fact, seen as a reason for the renewal for a past that could be recreated (De Martino 2011, 95). In 2005, the city was designated by UNESCO as a site of exemplary post-war architectural and urban reconstruction (fig. 18) (De Martino 2011, 77).

In contrast, Saint Malo, bombed in 1944, was reconstructed by Arretch in easier forms to recall the destruction of the war. The architect designed his project according to existing buildings with the use of traditional materials, avoiding mimetic additions.

In the over panorama of reconstructions, the United Kingdom showed a singular approach in total counterpoint to the other nations. Here, the separation between industrial and residential cities reduced the damage inflicted by the German raids which focused on industrial and strategic targets (Glendinning 2013, 238). The declaration by Kenneth Clark, chairman of the War Artist Advisory Committee (WAAC) and director of the National Gallery, who defined the 'bomb damage in itself picturesque' summarises post-war thinking in the UK and clearly explains how British culture considered its wartime ruins in a different way. Clark asked artists such as John Piper and Graham Sutherland to represent the *"glowing embers for the bomb sites in which more than 13.000 people died in the five months from September 1940 alone"* (Woodward 2002, 212).

As result, a series of books recorded the war damage. In 1942, the book The Bombed Buildings of Britain provided *"an obituary notice and a pictorial record"* (Richards 1942, 2) of the architectural casualties. The author, J. M. Richard, wrote the book stemming from the need *"to know what of real architectural value has in fact been lost, and to have the history and character of these buildings recorded so that they shall not have vanished without some kind of obituary tribute"* (Richards 1942, 2). This personal selection of 'pictorial records', considered to be as representative as possible, had the purpose to record the *"national architectural possessions that have become casualties, to illustrate the nature of the casualties and to accompany the illustrations with some notes about the character an history of the built concerned"* (Richards 1942, 2). As reported in several post-war documents, some 14,000 damaged religious buildings were catalogued according to the gravity of their destruction (Casiello 2011, 5). Then the SPAB had a fundamental role in proposing the preservation of all the ruins, supporting their consolidation and enhancement of their authenticity. An iconic war memorial from the World War II was Saint Michael's Cathedral in Coventry (fig. 19). Decimated by German bombing on the night of November 14th, 1940, immediately thereafter it

17. Oradour sur Glane, France.
View of the ruined village.
© Maria Annun-ziata Oteri in Oteri 2008, 42.

18. Le Havre, France.
The reconstructed city is an UNESCO site.
On-line access: http://gabisworld.com/data_images/top_cityes/le-havre/le-havre-02.jpg).

became an international symbol of the devastating war destruction in Britain. It rose again like a phoenix with a new form and materials near the ruined structures in a novel coexistence of old and new (fig.20). The project, designed by Basil Spence, became the expression not only of renewal but also *"of the Christian Faith in contemporary terms"* (Howard 1962, vii). The architect's approach was 'evolutionary' with the integration of modern ideas with past traditions (idem) (fig. 21). In Bombed Churches as War Memorials (1944), a number of devastated churches were proposed to be preserved as 'memorial ruins' for reminding future generations of the war's traumatic events.

In Italy, wartime bombing caused destruction in strategically placed cities where, for many years, reconstruction was driven by urgency (Bellini 2011, 11). *'Norme per i Piani di Ricostruzione degli abitati danneggiati dalla guerra'* (Code for the post reconstruction Plan of war damage cities) (DLL n. 154, 1 March 1945) played an important role in the post-war policies. Reconstruction was to be defined by each local city council in order to determine the areas allocated for demolition, reconstruction, repair, new construction, and areas of restriction as written in the second article of the Urban Planning Law dating from August 17th, 1945. Furthermore, a series of guidelines and instructions indicated the characteristics of the plans to be designed. These guidelines, *Istruzioni di massima per la progettazione dei Piani di Ricostruzione degli abitati danneggiati dalla guerra* were drafted by the Minister of Public Works on August 14th, 1945. These should seek to reduce the destructions and reconstructions that were already numerous. Then, after surveying the characteristics of the historical centres, the 'reconstruction plans' were to enhance their traditional features considering not only monuments but also the 'minor architecture' that was significant for the identity and value of places (Casiello 2011, 3). This period also meant renewal. In fact, the Italian restoration field made important progress and questioned the widely-accepted philological approach. The changeover from the monumental restoration approach to the urban scale approach was only one of the many transformations that came about. In fact, the restoration discipline, based on the study of single buildings, opened the field to the study of groups of buildings considered in relationship with their urban contexts. Moreover, the traumatic loss of places stimulated interest in the investigation of other deep relationships: between architecture and psychology and architecture and economy, which heretofore had not been considered. Bellini (2011, 12) also recognised a huge gap and contradiction between theory and practice as well as the absence of preliminary surveys of war damage and interdisciplinary approaches in the Italian post war debate (Bellini 2011, 14) also leading to controversial results. Modern architecture was completely ignored (Bellini 2011, 11).

19. Coventry, United Kingdom. Interior of the Cathedral ruins.
© *Elisa Pilia.*

20. Coventry, United Kingdom. External view and main entrance of the Saint Michael's Cathedral.
© *Elisa Pilia.*

At the same time, academic development regarding the concept of beauty, the picturesque, environmental and social values led to intervention typologies different from the rest of Europe.

Replicas and stylistic reconstructions of monuments can be seen in the San Marco bell tower in Venice (fig. 22) and the Santa Trinita bridge in Florence: two icons of Italian reconstruction.

The debate surrounding the reconstruction of historical centres broadened internationally with such important exponents as Roberto Pane (1897–1987) and Ernersto N. Rogers (1909–1969). Their discussions were published in the journal Casabella-Continuità (1957) where both recognised the need to find a harmonic relationship between old and new with the possibility to add contemporary structures. Pane distanced himself from English romantic conservation and supported reconstruction while considering the psychological and sentimental aspects more than the aesthetic ones. New additions had to be simple in form and geometry to enhance the value of the damaged and reconstructed architecture; this goal was achieved through the use of photographic and documentary materials. For Pane, destruction was a 'new event' but was not necessarily resolved with new tools. Furthermore, he stressed the importance of 'minor architecture' as a mirror of society.

The post-war period saw an increase in international collaboration and the development of new ideas, particularly in Italy with the contributions of Benedetto Croce, Giulio Carlo Argan and Cesare Brandi. If Argan contributed with the introduction of such modern concepts as 'conservative restoration' and 'artistic restoration', Brandi can be considered the *"foremost theoretician of conservation at an international as well as Italian level and laid the ground work for Italian pre-eminence in many conservation organisations and charters"* (Glendinning 2013, 264). He was the head of the Central Institute of Restoration in Rome and wrote a fundamental text, *La teoria del restauro* (1963) following and developing the previous values theories, defining a methodology based on the recognition of aesthetic and historic values called '*istanze*' (instances) by Brandi (see 3.3. in Part II).

In the following years, important issues such as the authenticity and integrity of monuments were debated, followed by important events, such as the publication of the international Venice Charter (1964), the foundation of UNESCO (1972), the Australian Burra Charter (1999) and the Nara Document of Authenticity (1995). their Operative trends and legislation in European countries have evolved in modern times by experimenting with different approaches. Yet still today the enormous problem relating to ruins is still open (see part II).

21. Coventry, United Kingdom.
The Saint Michael's Cathedral designed by Basil Spence.
© Elisa Pilia.

22. Venice, Italy.
View from the sea of San Marco bell.
© Elisa Pilia.

2.5. PRESENT-DAY RUINS: CONFLICTS AND NATURAL DISASTERS

The debate regarding war-time ruins cannot be considered closed since some architecture still lays in ruination from the events that are continuing to unfold in Eastern Europe. The same issues and questions that arose after World War II are still present as is the reconstructive tendency as was the case for The Mostar Bridge destroyed in the Bosnian war. In contrast, ruins such as the Yugoslav Ministry of Defence Building in Belgrade were intentionally left as memorials of war. This building, built between 1957 and 1965, was designed to resemble a canyon of the Stejskal river, where one of the most significant battles of World War II in Yugoslavia was fought, the street a river dividing the two sides. The building was severely damaged by bombing on April 30th, 1999. While the building could have been repaired, it was chosen not to; it was instead preserved as cultural heritage and monument to the Kosovo war. Today, it is Belgrade's most famous ruin and a popular tourist attraction.

Overall, if wartime ruins originated from violent bombings creating opportunities for reconstruction and the creation of War Memorials (fig. 23) symbols of memory and identity, in contrast they helped in 'the process of thinning out' (Giovannoni 1945) of slums and unhealthy urban areas. As Woodward wrote *"there are a hundred more examples in Europe alone but although each human tragedy is unique, the architectural expression is a variation upon familiar dialogue of fragmentation versus wholeness"* (2002, 210).

23. London, United Kingdom.
New Zealand War Memorial designed by architect John Hardwick-Smith and sculptor Paul Dibble in 2006.
© *Elisa Pilia.*

3. TYPOLOGY AND CLASSIFICATION

The chapter presents a classification of ruins useful for better understanding the different contemporary approaches to these structures that will be presented later. Four significant and qualifying words/concepts can be identified: origin, function, location and degree of ruin. These terms have been used to carry out typological analysis, and to understand the deep roots underlying their current state of ruin and the practices of non–intervention. Furthermore, they highlight other classifications provided by authors in the scholarly literature for comprehending the choices upon which current international and local practices are based. Again, these typologies can be applied to the case of Cagliari in order to clarify the context of this study, its theoretical and practical issues as well as the connotation of ruins in this historical setting. Overall, detailed and accurate examination is important for defining the key-typological concepts that allow to better understand interventions on ruins, especially focusing attention on those placed in urban contexts, mainly originated by war bombings and their consequent processes of disuse.

3.1. ORIGINS

Worldwide ruins find their origins in different historical and natural events that happened over time. Their different starting points confer different meanings, interpretations and connotations (positive or negative) upon them. Moreover, since ruins exist, many kinds of intervention have been shaped according to the causes of decay and consequently ruination. For convenience, this research divides ruins according to the speed of events that originated them: rapid and gradual. This first division helps underline the difference in approaches. 'Rapid ruins' are those caused by a sudden and unexpected event such as wartime devastation; they are also defined as man-made ruins due to their origins in human causes (Bevan, 2006; Lambourne 2001; Larkham and Pendlebury 2008; Casiello 2011; Treccani 2008). Natural disasters such as earthquakes are also considered rapid ruins (Giuffrè 1988; Wilford, 2008). Indeed, while both these processes of destruction are fast, these two classes have different practical results. As already mentioned, the cause is rooted in the difference in the collective sentiment (Russo 2011, 127) in relation to catastrophic events caused by nature or by humans.

As far as nature is concerned, different interpretations and considerations of nature led to different interventions or non-interventions. Regarding the first category for example, the mediaeval town city of Ghibellina, devastated by an earthquake in 1968, was monumentalised by Alberto Burri in 1984. He decided to suffocate ruins and nature under a concrete mound, destroying any possibility of rebuilding. In contrast, several other cities destroyed by natural events were completely abandoned to their deterioration such as Gairo Vecchia in Sardinia (fig. 24).

Wartime ruins, left without their aesthetic unity and function, have produced, on the other hand, different approaches to the violence and trauma of bombing. As seen in that case, the urgency of reconstruction as well as the fragmentary and temporary nature of the structures required immediate intervention in most instances. Two tendencies arose from these negative origins, which conferred different meaning to the structures.

On the one hand, ruins, interpreted as 'absences', were left as scars of war or demolished to emphasise the events' brutality. The loss and empty spaces in Weimar and Buchenwald are only two examples of this tendency. On the other hand, ruins, conceived as 'presences', led to conservative and interventionist approaches. In the first case, the preservation approach stemmed from the will to evoke the past and preserve the memory of history, leaving nature free to act and take over its space, creating a picturesque character. In the second case, instead, the interventions maintain the ruined structures as material remains for new experiments (Fiorani 2009, 351). The degree of interventions and additions can be different but in these approaches, the victory of human action over the forces of nature, completely cancelled through building new structures, is undeniable.

'Gradual ruins' can be divided into two categories. The first consists of the archaeological sites so widespread throughout Europe. They have been mostly excavated or rediscovered while building other structures and have always considered documentary monuments or texts due to their clear reading of past techniques and materials. The second includes those buildings that, due to economic, social and political transitions, were subjected to slow abandonment. In this category, we find ruins from antiquity linked with the historical events in each country. Examples can be seen in the ruined abbeys from the post-reformation period in the United Kingdom or the derelict villages resulting from the clearance of the Highlands in Scotland. Post-industrial ruins, mostly in Britain and in America, are also gradual ruins as their disuse and uselessness led to their progressive abandonment and consequent ruin due to processes of de-industrialisation in the 20th century (fig. 25).

Finally, a third category is comprised of the combination of rapid and gradual ruins, buildings that, after rapid and violent destruction, fell into disuse and abandonment until now. This is an intermediate category which can include the archaeological sites of Pompeii and Herculaneum which, destroyed by the violent eruption of Vesuvius and, after having been excavated, are again involved in a process of gradual ruination (fig. 26). It also includes wartime ruins, as will be shown in the case of Cagliari (fig. 27); after their destruction, some are continuing in their gradual ongoing process of degradation. Finally, it includes other ruins which, for socio-economic conditions, are still neglected and are awaiting reuse.

24. Gairo Vecchia, Italy.
The abandoned village in the Sardinian island.
© *Porcu Martina.*

25. Manchester, United Kingdom.
Industrial ruins in the area of New Islington.
© *Elisa Pilia.*

3.2. FUNCTION

Another category of ruins can be defined in relationship to their original uses, functions and structure typologies, from whatever era they date. They are divided into monumental, minor or residential and industrial ruins. As seen in the historical overview, this distinction appears useful due to the different roles that these typologies played over time and, therefore, their modifications. Monumental ruined buildings, linked to the loss or change in 'power' can be generally divided into religious and political ruins. The former comprise all those buildings characterised by spiritual and commemorative values insofar as they are places of religiousness and social identification. They include monasteries, abbeys, churches, and convents that fell into disuse. For instance, the role that churches played after World War II as architectural and spiritual memorials is notable.

'Political' ruined structures include all the built symbols of administrative power such as medieval defence and fortified heritage (castles, walls, towers etc.) but also modern military architecture, military installations and Cold War remnants (Davis 2008; Strange and Walley 2007) and post-Socialist state-built architecture (Andreassen et al. 2010; Lahusen 2006; Pusca 2010; van der Hoorn 2003). Furthermore, a third class is represented by all the buildings that, due to their impressive dimensions, styles, building technologies and social roles can be considered monuments such as theatres, schools and so on.

'Minor or residential' ruins are those that came from the destruction of dwellings located in historical urban or rural contexts. They are mirror of a community or their residents. Their disuse is strictly related to the socio-economic conditions of specific areas raising questions on the psychology of place, place attachment and identity, which were lost in some cases due to the different origins of the previously cited destruction. In this class can be included not only minor urban architectures, but also abandoned rural settlements (Armstrong 2010; DeSilvey 2007a; Gonza´lez-Ruibal 2005) and urban wastelands and edge lands (Farley and Roberts, 2011; Franck and Stevens 2007; Hudson 2010). Industrial ruins derive from the production of the capitalist development and the relentless search for profit (Edensor 2005, 20). However, they differ from the other categories because they are considered the results of modern industrialisation. In some cases, their perception has been hugely negative, represented as "*spaces of waste*" (Edensor 2005, 7) with no value. Also, they could be seen as "*spaces of danger, delinquency, ugliness and disorder*" (Edensor 2005, 7) especially with their suburban locations often close to railway lines and canals. They could also represent places of uncertainty in which formerly productive buildings are now rubbish (Thompson 1981). These have been also called 'new ruins' (Edensor 2012,

26. Pompeii, Italy.
The archaeological site.
© *Elisa Pilia*.

27. Cagliari, Italy.
A post war ruin in the historical centre.
© *Elisa Pilia*.

466), the results of decommissioned and useless workplaces born in the modern age (fig. 28). Factories, foundries and mills (Brandt 2010; Edensor 2005; High and Lewis 2007; Mah 2010) and derelict rail and transportation networks are also included in this category (Qviström 2012; Rosa 2011).

3.3. LOCATION

Ruins can be considered rural and urban in terms of their locations. This difference in context offers a range of issues and questions to face with a varied range of values to assess. They also concern different policies and legislation. If rural ruins (fig. 29) imply issues regarding the cultural landscape, urban ruins have to cope with a more complex system, the city, governed by a complex socio-economic and political logic.

The concept of 'cultural landscape' refers both to the way we view the environment that surrounds us as well as the environment itself and connects people to nature providing a setting for their interaction. Moreover, it points to culture because human interactions with the environment are settings for tangible and intangible values in the landscape. So, every rural ruin is a unique piece of art with values and feelings strictly related to the nature and environment of each country. Each landscape is also characterised by a different flora, fauna and materials that typify each ruin. Urban ruins (fig. 30) also involve the landscape but in terms of 'townscape', they are involved in different dynamics, that comprise different fields of investigation: economy, sociology, psychology of places and aesthetics. Thus, the two areas call for different approaches and rules. For instance, De Martino (2011, 33) underlined the difference in terms of policies for the protection of the wartime ruins located in either natural or urban landscapes. In the first case, ruins are considered to have an incomplete status; they play the role of testimonial, surviving fragment with a continuous and strong relationship with the natural landscape. In the case of urban ruins, the psychological aspects cannot be denied, evoking feelings of horror *vacui* due to the creation of lacunae. The need to fill these gaps and voids stems from factors that permit us to remember and recognise dramatic events and their signs. Thus, in urban contexts we might recognise two ruin typologies: the historical ruin and the real ruin still close to the dramatic events of their origin. The conservation approach to wartime ruins derives from their character of irreproducibility and the consequential desire to preserve the old city with its pre-existing artefacts. Notwithstanding, preservation has not been pursued, leaving space to stylistic reconstructions especially in countries strongly affected by the war. Overall, the difficulties in the approach to urban ruins stems from a series of motivations and issues that are found in the contemporary city, which, through planning, policies and spatial commodification, has often lost its sensorial character and place-identity.

28. Guspini, Italy.
'New ruins' of the former mining site of Montevecchio.
© *Andrea Pinna*.

3.4. DEGREE OF RUINATION

Ruins have manifold forms in relationship to the cause of their decay and depending on the strategies adopted during and after their abandonment and ruination. They can be classified by evaluating their state of decay, meant as the percentage of deteriorated or lost features expressed in degrees. This codification evaluates the structure's state of obsolescence which considers physical and structural deterioration, functional qualities, imagined perception, location, level of accessibility and natural factors involved in its decay as well as financial and economic influences (Tiesdel 1996). Obsolescence can also depend on the nature of the building materials and the technologies used during their construction.

The degree of decay has been defined in the following way:

- Structure without use: the structure is still entirely recognisable but has lost its functionality. Although it still manifests all the building elements, even if deteriorated, it is structurally unstable and cannot be used. This is the beginning of the process of ruination: the absence of use and consequent absence of maintenance. Its accessibility is not compromised.
- Low degree: structural parts of the building have collapsed. Typically, the roof and the ceilings are unstable. The building is accessible with protection but it is still legible. Its image perception is still understandable showing 25% of missing features and elements. The cost for its recovery increases as it needs to cover small additions and new roof elements.
- Medium degree: a progressive loss of structural parts is underway. Walls are collapsing and the physical decay of building materials compromises the legibility of the original building. The building is not accessible (50%–75% of loss).
- High degree: the building has completely lost its original image. All structural and functional elements are lost. In this case, ruins can be accessible as in the case when they become archaeological areas that, while they have lost their original aesthetics, can still be visited.

These degrees of ruin are distinguished by a percentage of loss that can be evaluated by calculating the hypothetical original volumes of the structures and the residual volumes after destruction. This calculus can be done through the use of historical surveys and maps and the modern geomatics techniques that will be illustrated later. Moreover, this parameter will be significant in the case study of Cagliari, where, by means of the map of war damage, the development of this degree of ruination can be clearly read and compared to the current state of the ruined structures. Finally, the consequent degree of intervention can be assessed.

29. Barumini, Italy.
The landscape ruins of Su Nuraxi in Sardinia.
© *Elisa Pilia.*

30. Cagliari, Italy.
The urban ruins of Aymerich Palace in the Castello quarter.
© *Elisa Pilia.*

3.5. OTHER CLASSIFICATIONS

Several scholars have carried out studies regarding the different interpretations and meanings of ruins, assigning different classes to them.

In particular, Di Blasi and Robbiati (1996) described ruins in three classes in their paper: 1) ruin as place of continuing change. Following Simmel's definition of architecture as a balance between spirit and nature, in their interpretation ruins are creators of a new form that describes the past at the same time. They are precious products of history and place of transformation; 2) ruin as place of memory, and an incentive to remember our past; 3) ruin as a thorny witness to history and contemporaneity, an irreversible object that has found difficult coexistence with new architecture because of its uselessness. Later, Paolo Torsello (2007, 185) attributed a positive meaning to abandoned structures as *'testo and pretesto'* (text and pretext) for new creative interventions. Furthermore, Donatella Fiorani (2009) made another interesting contribution linking the perception of ruins to the different interventions. She proposed seven categories: 1) ruin as statement of an empty space. It gives emphasis to 'absence' and includes mainly wartime ruins. As the author (2009, 342) said, not all absences will become ruins. Examples can be seen at the World Trade Centre in New York, in the ruinous conservation of the remains of Buchenwald based on the exaltation of the empty spaces or by contrast, the Cretto designed by Albert Burri, built between 1985 and 1989 on the ruins of the city of Gibellina destroyed by an earthquake in 1968; 2) ruin as evocative fragment. This conception considers the conservation of the ruin as a unique intervention for emphasising psychological and emotional components. The fragment is considered a *"photograph of the historical past"*(344). Examples are the palace of the National Bank in Warsaw or the tower of Cluny Abbey in France; 3) ruin as an anatomical body to explore in all its aspects; 4) ruin as a tool for understanding history and as an element of knowledge. This is the case of archaeological ruins that are investigated by means of actions of excavation and stratigraphic analysis often aimed at the production of new unburied ruins (fig. 31); 5) ruin as equal interlocutor, for researching a new balance and relationship between the old and the new as in Crypta Balbi in Rome; 6) ruin as remains and pretext, meant as material remains for new experiments and transformations, such as for instance the case of CaixaForum museum in Madrid designed by Herzog & de Meuron in 2008. Finally, 7) ruin as premise for reconstruction where the reconstruction itself is the death of the ruin as widely shown in the several cases of post-war mimetic intervention.

31. Athens, Greece.
Excavations below the entrance to the Acropolis Museum designed by Bernard Tschumi Architects in 2009, where a late antique, early Byzantine neighbourhood (7th – 9th centuries CE) has been revealed.
© Elisa Pilia.

"RUINS POTENTIALLY EPITOMISE THE PERENNIAL TENSION BETWEEN WHAT IS PRESERVED AND WHAT IS LOST, WHAT SEEMS IMMEDIATELY UNDERSTANDABLE (OR USABLE) AND WHAT NEEDS INTERPRETATION (OR RECONSTRUCTION) [...] TRAUMA AND DISCONTINUITY ARE FUNDAMENTAL FOR MEMORY AND HISTORY. RUINS HAVE COME TO BE NECESSARY FOR LINKING CREATIVITY TO THE EXPERIENCE OF LOSS AT THE INDIVIDUAL AND COLLECTIVE LEVEL.
RUINS OPERATE AS POWERFUL METAPHORS FOR ABSENCE OR REJECTION AND HENCE, AS INCENTIVES FOR REFLECTION OR RESTORATION."

(Settis 1997: vii)

PART II
CONTEMPORARY APPROACHES

32. Pisa, Italy. The conserved stratifications in the project of reconstruction of S. Michele in Borgo. Designed by Massimo Carmassi (1979–2002).
© M. Ciampi in De Vita 2015, 75.

This chapter provides an overview of the current international debate regarding the ways in which ruins have been interpreted both in theory and in practice. This debate has stimulated discussion regarding key concepts such as the binomial perception of presence – absence, reflexivity, memory and time, identity and place-attachment as well as politics.

These theoretical considerations are followed by a global overview regarding today's broadly-accepted design approaches to buildings in a state of ruin. Europe, the Americas, Eastern countries and Australia all deploy different approaches in solving the complex issues associated with ruins, adopting different terminologies. The two main tendencies that can be identified are conservation and integration. In this panorama, the United Kingdom and Italy are compared insofar as they are the two European countries in which, for over two centuries, theoretical and practical approaches have contributed significantly to the international debate, establishing consolidated methodologies and tendencies. Scotland and Sardinia are also the subjects of a more in-depth analysis.

In addition, the research examines the main questions regarding processes of regeneration of the urban contexts in which ruined buildings are located. These problems are analysed, underscoring positive and negative experiences, models and tools and values that can be used for the definition of a transdisciplinary approach.

Overall, the overview of general urban issues is useful not only for identifying and delineating methods of investigation, policies, classes of values and case studies that can be considered best practices for the creation of a shared transdisciplinary methodology, but also for defining the basis for understanding the same issues in the Cagliari case-study context. Thus, this section is also important for delineating local operative guidelines.

1. LITERATURE REVIEW OF THE CURRENT DEBATE

The unresolved debate on how best to preserve ruins, especially after World War II, continues among academics the world over, raising questions that merit further investigation. This is clearly evidenced by the numerous conferences, published articles and monographs addressing the issue. In contrast, this complex theoretical discussion does not find its application in the practical field where numerous projects regarding ruins have shown how these incomplete architectures are still increasingly rejected due to their complex underlying issues (Fiorani 2009, 342). These involve a wide range of disciplines, ranging from architectural conservation to the urban field and include economic, political and social questions. However, as Carbonara asserted (2011, 18), in different ways, their main intention was to grant more meaningful future roles to these fragmented, incomplete and useless artefacts.

Architecturally speaking, ruins are complex structures that necessitate re-consideration and/or design for their conservation or reuse. They are dynamic objects (Gizzi 2006, 25) that are not part of one precise period but change continuously; they are the result of stratifications (Serafini 2005, Carmassi 2007) that should be preserved (Carmassi 2007, 63) (fig. 32). Mario Manieri Elia (2006) identified them as 'transitional objects', testimonials that transmit something different from what they are. They are *heteroutopias*, difficult to replace due to their enormous significance; their re-integration into social and urban life should indeed preserve these characteristics.

In contrast, ruins take on different meanings when approaching the question from the philosophical or anthropological points of view. They cannot accept human intervention but only distance as a sign of respect. George Simmel (Simmel 1958, 379) argued that they carry connotations of spirituality and their destiny is to return to their natural state (fig. 33). Following the same line of thought, Marc Augè (2004) considered them to be testimonials to 'pure time' for which any further human action is an end. Again, these two opposing observations have shown how, from different perspectives, the concept of ruins can be controversial and complex in today's debate.

According to these two approaches, the international literature can be divided into practical and theoretical explorations.

Several important talks and papers have been published in the theoretical field regarding the arts, politics, sociology, philosophy, anthropology and economic matters. Two international conferences were organised in the Americas between 2005 and 2006: *Ruins of Modernity* (2005) organised by the University of Michigan in Ann Arbor, and '*L'Imaginaire des ruines*' (2006) organised by the Université du Québec in Montréal. In particular, the first focused on analysing the entanglement of political, philosophical, and aesthetic discourses generated by modern ruins

(Hell and Shonle 2010). On the European level, *La ruine et le geste architectural* (2007) should be mentioned; it was organised by the Société française des Architectes in Paris and published in the same year (Hyppolite 2015). It was divided into three main topics: sonographies, poetry, and beauty. The goal was to provide an in-depth analysis of the interdisciplinary dialogue regarding ruins as a *'geste architectural dans sa decomposition'*.

In Italy, two important contributions were considered: *Relitti Riletti. Reread Wreckage. Transformation of ruins and cultural Identity* (2007) organised by Marcello Barbanera at the University La Sapienza, Rome (Barbanera 2009) and *Rovine e macerie. Obliare, rimembrare, riedificare* (2005) edited by Giuseppe Tortora at the *Centro per la Filosofia italiana* in Pompeii (Tortora 2006). Both events, published in subsequent years, dealt with the theoretical and historical aspects underlying the difficulties in the practical approaches.

Articles regarding theoretical questions and specific case studies were published in other proceedings of international conferences and journals. Several issues of the Journal of Architectural Conservation examined the question. In detail, they address the preservation of urban ruins in Britain (Stanford 2014), structural conservation, stabilisation, and related issues (Avent 2011) as well as key studies such as *Urban regeneration and the management of change for the city of Liverpool* (Rodwell 2014). In the on-line journal, *Performance Research. A Journal of the Performing Arts,* an entire volume entitled *On ruins and Ruination* (2015), was dedicated to the multidisciplinary concepts of memory and *utopia*. Additionally, in the *Journal of Architecture,* Desrochers presented ruins under a modernist conception of heritage considering both the concepts of conservation and sustainability (Desrochers 2000).

In Sardinia, the conferences *Il rudere tra conservazione e reintegrazione* (2003) organised by Bruno Billeci, Stefano Gizzi and Daniela Scudino in Sassari (Billeci et al. 2006) and *Antiche ferite e nuovi significati. Cagliari e la città storica* (2007), organised by Caterina Giannattasio at the University of Cagliari demonstrated that the issues relating to abandoned and neglected architectures are still controversial even on the local scale. Monographs on the topic are numerous principally in the Anglo-Saxon context. In 1981, Michael Thompson, inspector of ancient monuments for the Ministry of Works in London, was the first to carry out an in-depth study of the preservation of authenticity (Thompson 1981). His subject was historic ruins in Britain; his detailed work was *"an attempt to give an account of the treatment of ruins without straying into the architect's sphere on one side nor into the official aspect in the other"* (Thompson 1981, 7).

He faced such topics as 'preservation and display', as the title highlights, but also retrieval, restoration, representation, access to and interpretation of ruins, defining British approaches as compared to the Italian and the French. His mature research found space in another publication that, after less than thirty years of investigation, dealt with changing attitudes toward ruins since the 18th century (Thompson 2006). Instead, *English Ruins* by Jeremy Musson (2011), and *American Ruins* by Vergara Camillo José(1999) provided overviews of the origins and typologies of ruins in the two countries. *Conservation of ruins* (Ashurst 2007) fills a huge scientific gap on the theme, describing and analysing the genesis and causes of this phenomenon, providing detailed practical instructions for the conservation and stabilisation of ruins and describing procedures for their protection.

Other theoretical monographs discuss the influence of ruins in art, history, philosophy, and literature (Macauley 1953, Woodward 2001, Augè 2004) and their aesthetic analysis in terms of material, form, function, incongruity, site, and symbol (Ginsberg 2004). In Italy, monographs and contributions in edited books deal with theoretical and methodological aspects (Gizzi 2006, De Martino 2004). They underline the complicated gap between theory and practice highlighting open questions and key studies (Doglioni 2008; Oteri 2009; Ugolini 2010; Confronti 2012). Regarding wartime ruins, several authors provided contributions in Italy and Europe (Casiello 2011; De Martino 2011, 2017; Fiorino 2015; Lambourne 200; Picone 2011; Pretelli 2011; Russo 2011; Richards 1942) deeply analysing the European issues and reporting on the most important post World War II approaches. In particular, Treccani (2008) and De Stefani and Coccoli (2011) reconstructed the post-war Italian debate and trends seeking to fill a knowledge gap regarding this problematic period. The publication clarifies the complex economic and administrative policies that sought to solve architectural and urban issues as well as the ideologies underlying the practical approaches. Around the same concept, Brian Dillon (2011) examined the development of ruin aesthetics from the early modern era to the present.

Lastly, numerous PhD theses have investigated the topic. Important to this research is Hanna Katharina Göbel's (2015) contribution to the sociological realm with her thesis *The Re-Use of Urban Ruins: Atmospheric Inquiries of the City*. Together, these scholarly works provided a rich array of cues for further elaboration of theoretical perspectives, but they ignored questions specifically concerning ruins in historic urban environments. Several research projects considered the theme by illustrating cases and projects, identifying critical and theoretical issues in different disciplines, in a sectorial rather than a transdisciplinary way. Therefore, the immense question of how to investigate these artefacts in their multifaceted complexity is still open.

33. Stirling, United Kingdom.
Detail of Castle Mar's Wark ruins.
© *Elisa Pilia.*

In addition, considering all the references investigated, other studies explored intangible and contemporary interpretative constructs regarding the 'materiality' which confers qualities upon ruins that can stimulate sensorial experiences and memories; they also explored the coexistence of the concepts of absence-presence, relationship with nature, temporality and political and economic power (Edensor 2005, 2011). In fact, *"the space in which ruins are placed is characterised by multiple relations between things, space, non-human life and humans"* (124). These are in continual transformation that give their mute materiality the ability to speak of history (Hell and Shönle 2006, 652).

THE ABSENCE-PRESENCE DUALITY *"Ruins are simultaneously an absence and a presence [...] They are an intersection of the visible and the invisible"* (Roth et al. 1997, vii). They can be considered an absence because their original function has been lost, along with their 'invisible whole' but, at the same time, their fragmented presence is testimony to durability and immortality. Thus, in their presence, ruins narrate what Nature cannot: about their previous structures, the people who made and used them. In their absence they recall the people or the events that destroyed them. Tatiana Kirova (2008) discussed the topic, considering presence as materiality and 'potential absence' as lack of use (185). Finally, in their current state, they represent those who left them in that state of dereliction or memorialisation (Roth et al. 1997, vii). The presence–absence duality speaks of the tensions between that which has been preserved and that which has been lost, between that which can be immediately used and that which should be interpreted. Ruins are metaphors of absence and, at the same time, of reflection.

REFLEXIVITY On the concept of reflexivity of ruins, Hell and Shönle (2010) argued that the semantics of ruins is not stable because of the potential vacuity of meaning insofar as it works as a uniquely flexible and productive metaphor of modernity's self-awareness and reflexivity. This is because it represents vacuity and loss as constituents of modern identity (6). The same authors defined the relationship between beholder and ruin. In their view, beholders define ruins that could not exist without their creativity and interpretation. At the same time, as Diderot maintained, they claimed that ruins are part of society's subjectivity; they emancipate our senses and desires, and enable introspection. *"The ruin enables individual freedom, imagination and subjectivity"* (Hell and Shönle 2010, 8).

MEMORY, IDENTITY AND PLACE-ATTACHMENT These anthropological aspects also evoke the psychological implications of memory, identity, and place attachment. Edensor (2005) argued that, through our observation of ruins, we might learn to adopt a more open approach to reading and narrating urban space as well as the signs and layers hidden in the histories and materiality of places (2005, 161). To intervene on ruins, we should also consider how they are perceived and the way in which their memory is narrated. Often this memory will not be available in materials or stories but it *"might be part of broader, less identifiable forms of apprehension, borne out of experiencing structures of feeling grounded in the habitual and the sensual"* (Edensor 2005, 161). Ruins are characterised by the 'value of inarticulacy' with their impossibility of recounting their history from beginning to end due to their fragmentary nature and multifaceted meanings. Therefore, time and memory are two factors that contribute to defining the uniqueness and peculiarity of these structures. As Guggenheim (2009, 40) asserted, *"memory is a specific way in which a person relates to time"* and it is the ability to remember. The process is subjective and objects are the elements that help remember. In urban space, buildings can be considered the objects that stabilise time and memory. Consequently, ruins are 'buildings' that best embody the two sensorial elements of time and memory. In other views, ruins that originated from the destruction of war designate the location of memory in which trauma has taken place (Trigg 2009, 88). They are physical remains that have an aesthetic existence that must be faced. They are fragmented presences that can be filled by the imagination. Indeed, ruins are testimonials of history and temporality (89). Thus, memory is considered a social component that depends on historical thought and, like history, it is socially conditioned and altered over different generations (Kalman 2014, 21). Ruins mark the fluidity of space and our times (Bauman 2007). They offer different ways of remembering the past. Therefore, the city should be seen as an archive of layers, traces and memories to protect instead of a mere place where only some preferences find space.

POLITICS Ruined structures are also political and economic issues (Hell and Shönle 2010; DeSilvey Edensor, 2012). As Edensor asserted, ruins can offer spaces where interpretations and practices are free to be experimented; they are opportunities *"for challenging and deconstructing the imprint of power on the city"* (2015, 4). Ruins can also offer strategic points for a multi-level reading of a city by means of effective urban policy. In addition, they can be considered both symbols of failure and of growth as in the case of the devastated city of Detroit where ruined factories and abandoned infrastructure represent the passive acceptance of failure and at the same time they become forces for increasing collective resistance and evolution. In light of these considerations, ruins can become opportunities with great creative potential, key ingredients in the regeneration of places and in the consolidation of place identity (2011, 474).

2. TENDENCIES AND MAIN SCHOOLS OF THOUGHT: A GEOGRAPHICAL OVERVIEW

Today, a widely shared framework for theoretical and practical approaches to urban ruins cannot be found in the international context. This is due to the fact that such approaches are expressions of theoretical orientations deeply related to the historical events and the current value systems in each country. Difficulties in practical approaches stem from the considerable gap that endures between project and restoration since the 18th century (Varagnoli 2008, 835).

This global overview looks at two contradictory approaches, conservation and integration, illustrating different applications. The analysis focuses principally on the Anglo-Saxon and European experiences which have become the background for the most principal and commonly-accepted approaches. The widespread heritage of ruins in Great Britain is carefully enhanced and managed by the two main national institutions, Historical England and Scotland. Here, the long tradition of the protection of ruins and urban conservation areas has brought special attention to well-codified conservation planning policies. Scotland as a whole and in particular Edinburgh have offered virtuous examples in terms of interventions on ruined structures (fig. 34) which are mainly absent in conservation areas. This is also a result of the existence of the 'Buildings at Risk' registry regarding listed buildings and vacant buildings in conservation areas that have fallen into a state of disrepair. The same virtuous examples cannot be found in Sardinia where there has been a notable lack of policy and funding for improvement, with ruins completely neglected. Only few interventions, regarding singular monuments in the past, have been undertaken, leading to widespread decay awaiting proper attention.

2.1. GLOBAL OVERVIEW

In the international context, a commonly accepted framework for theoretical and practical approaches to urban ruins cannot be found; this is due to the fact that such approaches are deeply related to the historical events and current values system in each country. Difficulties in practical approaches stem from the considerable gap between project and restoration that began in the 18th century (Varagnoli 2008, 835).

Varagnoli (2008) maintains that we should consider several aspects of contemporary projects for urban ruins. First, the relationship between the knowledge-gathering and design phases. With some exceptions, the author recognised a general lack of interdisciplinary approaches in the planning process. Historical and specialised surveys that are often acclaimed as essential bases for correct design are totally excluded from the creative process. This absence makes the contemporary project self-referential, creating problems in historical areas (Varagnoli 2008, 837).

34. Edinburgh, United Kingdom.
Detail of new additions in Advocate's Close.
© *Martina Loi.*

Second, the failure of design derives from the absence of a specific planning culture that is able to correctly interpret historic space and materials in order to adapt them to new necessities (Carmassi 1999, 17). Often, the architectural quality of restoration interventions is not satisfactory. Modern conservation principles, recognised as minimal intervention, compatibility, reversibility, distinguishability, respect for authenticity are rendered banal or, in contrast, are used opportunistically. For example, distinguishability sometimes becomes an element for justifying new and devastating additions. Further unresolved issues can be recognised: lack of a shared methodology between the conservation project and the design of new parts; the opportunism of the 'abuse' of the distinguishability principle to investigate new composite designs; the need to identify the overall values of an old building (Varagnoli 2008, 838).

Finally, it cannot be denied that urban ruins play a different role today from the one in the past especially during the 18th century. They are unique in light of the different kinds of natural and human events that characterise them. Overall, contemporary tendencies linked to ruins are strongly related to the concept of ruins as-evidence (Stanford 2000, 28) and to their aesthetics.

This international overview is mainly focused on the Anglo-Saxon and European experiences that have established the background for the main widespread approaches.

Even with its different cultures, languages, politics and histories, Europe is a vast continent whose architectural conservation practices had such an advanced start and swift development as to influence the rest of the world. Europe is a leader in the field (Stubbs and Makaš 2001, 2) playing a significant role in the formation of the two global cultural heritage institutions: UNESCO and ICOMOS, founded to share values and protect cultural diversities. The European administrative and legal frameworks have been considered unique and proactive in the promotion of such cultural initiatives as: the European Capital of Cultures and the safeguarding of cultural heritage with several Conventions (European Cultural Convention 1954; European archaeological heritage Convention 1969; Granada of the Convention for the Protection of the Architectural Heritage of Europe 1985; Framework Convention on the Value of Cultural Heritage for Society 2005) and Charters (European Charter of the Architectural Heritage 1975). Other organisations, including Europa Nostra, established in 2002, "*have played a crucial role in promoting and protecting the architectural heritage of Europe*" (Stubbs and Makaš 2001, 5).

Although collaboration between nations has been fundamental, especially in the 20th century, each bears witness to different experiences especially in Western and Eastern Europe. Indeed, Western Europe, cradle of the earliest interest in ruins, has defined the principal global approaches.

As far as the Americas are concerned, they reflect the trends of their own distinct historical, social and economic development. While the United States and Canada have advanced systems and institutions of protection due to the influence of the Western Europe countries and especially Britain, significant threats and difficulties persist in the western and southern hemispheres, in Mexico, the Caribbean region, and Central and South America. With their affinity to the common source of theoretical approaches and techniques, this research takes into account the two most evolved states: the USA and Canada.

Considering the ample international debate regarding contemporary interventions on ruined buildings (Bloszies 2012; Carbonara 2011; Di Martino 2017; Ferlenga et al. 2008; Klanten & Feireiss 2009; Fiorani 2009; Giannattasio 2009; Oteri 2009; Thièbaut 2007; Ugolini 2010), as previously noted, it can be asserted that the different degrees of intervention can be summarised by two main approaches: conservation and integration. On the one hand, conservation considers ruins as documents to transmit to the future by preserving their historical identity. On the other, the integrative approach sees an opportunity for a new aesthetic reconfiguration of the ruin in the combination of old and new.

2.1.1. CONSERVATION APPROACHES

The conservation of ruins focuses mainly on a clear reading of the building fabric, and the enhancement of its historic character through different kinds of intervention such as stabilisation, consolidation, and archaeological conservation.

The Burra Charter (2013) defines this approach as *"all the processes of looking after a place so as to retain its cultural significance"* and it is *"based on a respect for the existing fabric, use, associations and meanings"* (art. 3). Born in the United Kingdom from the formation of the modern conservation movement, it is based on a 'critical methodology' (Jokilenhto 2009, 4) that refers to the Ruskinian concept of ruins as evocative fragments and witnesses of history. The UK can be considered the global leader in a field in which conservation became an established component for architectural and planning practices in the 20th century (Stubbs and Makaš 2001, 59). The appreciation of authenticity and respect for historic patina are manifested in the innumerable cases of ruins especially castles and monasteries, models for all European nations.

Many examples are present in England and Scotland as will be shown later, but also in other countries such as Portugal where the Convent do Carmo (fig. 35), a Gothic monument devastated by an earthquake in 1755, was left as an evocative reminder of destruction, or the famous Cistercian church of San Galgano, designed by Gino Chirici in Italy.

Here, this conservation tendency, focusing on the "*maintenance of the architectural object in its current physical condition, without adding or subtracting anything from the aesthetic corpus of the artefact*" (Fitch 1990, 46), has taken the name of '*conservazione a rudere*' (conservation as ruin) or pure conservation. Its foremost contemporary exponent is the architect Marco Dezzi Bardeschi, who recognises absolute conservation as the only intervention for emphasising the ruin's stratification (see par. 2.2.2).

Stabilisation, consolidation and protection, which focus on maintaining structures 'as they are', regard safeguarding and reinforcement, often with physical application of adhesives or supports within materials. In light of the aforementioned historical background, the conservation approach also finds its bases in Brandi's historic *istanza* and in the 'age value' concept codified by Riegl (see part I, par. 2.3).

Preservation, instead, refers to the process of "*maintaining a place in its existing state retarding deterioration*" (Australia ICOMOS 2013, art 1.4). It is focused on the maintenance of structures in their existing forms and conditions, respecting their history and eras of construction; it derives from the 'anti-restoration' approach promoted by SPAB. This concept is used in American English for identifying conservation while in British English it means "*routine management and maintenance*" (English Heritage 2008a).

The preservation approach can be considered a lesser degree of intervention than conservation, based only on maintenance.

Another prevalent tendency, defined by Stanford (2000, 32) as the 'freeze-the-masonry' approach', believes that ruins should be frozen in time as 'bionic ruins' that can survive into the future. This concept stems from the idea that historical values and traces should be preserved untouched, in the same state in which the structures were transferred to us. Finally, the author recognised a further level of intensive conservation, the 'verdant approach', which permits ruins to exist in symbiosis with nature (35). Ruined structures are symbols of a past in which vegetation, which requires active management, guarantees a site's aesthetic experience. Ruins are not objects to display but organisms, as in the cases of Wigmore Castle in Hertfordshire, Tickhill Castle in South Yorkshire, where English Heritage decided to consolidate the structures as romantic ruins fully integrated with their landscapes.

35. Lisbon, Portugal.
Ruins of the Convent do Carmo.
© José Morais Arnaud.

2.1.2. INTEGRATIVE APPROACHES

The integrative approach is characterised by different degrees of intervention, transformation or additions. The codified practices are restoration, adaptive reuse/rehabilitation, also called parasite architecture, reconstruction, replicas. 'Restoration' means to *"return the artefact to the physical condition in which it would have been at some previous stage of its morphological development"* (Tiesdell et al. 1996, 172). This approach finds its roots in the stylistic unit claimed by Viollet-le-Duc (see part I, par. 2.3) and is still adhered to today, although to a lesser extent. In fact, in this case a ruin *"is restored to its form at a specific date in the past, which may or may not be the original date of construction"* (Kalman 2015, 12). Different kinds of interventions can be found in the concept of restoration. From 'stylistic restoration' or 'façadism', strictly focused on the recreation of the built fabric as in Viollet-le-Duc's iconic case, for instance of the fortified city of Carcassonne, it is also possible to find restoration based on the ruin's critical interpretation and typological restoration. One such example is the theatre in Sagunto (Spain) designed by the architects Grassi and Portaceli at the end of the 20th century. Here, the architects designed a new idea of classical theatre using contemporary materials and techniques.

Other tendencies favour the integration of ruins into an existing urban fabric, seeking a balance between the aesthetic qualities of the modern built environment and pre-existing ones. It can be asserted that, today, much attention has been focused on the consideration of the building as a 'text' (Marconi 1993). According to Alois Riegl, it is necessary to guide interventions according to the values present in the ruins – whether historical or contemporary. In this search for a new relationship between new and old, two emerging tendencies developed: adaptive reuse and constructive conservation.

Another integrative and interesting and singular approach defined by the name, 'archaeological restoration', has its basis in the archaeological concept of intervention and authenticity as Boito claimed in the 18th century. This purist and extreme trend can be seen in the Acropolis in Athens (fig. 36) where all successive stratigraphies have been eradicated in order to enhance on the ruins' classical period. In this case, the desire to emphasise the ruins' classical layer led to an aberrant restoration practice and new additions are made with the same Pentelic marble of the original fabric (fig. 37).

In fact, 'rehabilitation - adaptive reuse' is also very common today, especially in Spain but also in the United Kingdom, Germany and the US. It is defined as a kind of recycling that converts ruins into something better-suited to contemporary needs in a sustainable way and with minimum impact. New contemporary uses are identified by maintaining the components that contribute to a building's cultural significance and altering or adding others that do not (Australia ICOMOS 2013, 1.9). So, different terms

36. Athens, Greece.
View of the Acropolis from Filopappou Hill.
© Elisa Pilia.

37. Athens, Greece.
Detail of the additions in the Parthenon.
After an archaeological approach, the intervention has involved the reconstruction of the structures with a massive use of the local stone:
the Pentelic marble.
© Elisa Pilia.

identify the same approach in different countries. In the US, this is called rehabilitation while in Australia it is adaptation. Adaptive reuse can also involve extensive integration and modification. In this case, additions can complete the structures in different ways and with the use of different materials.

The Franciscan Convent in Santpedor (Spain) designed by David Closes in 2011 is a case in which a building's rehabilitation was carried out by differentiating new elements from the original ones in the historic church. The project preserved all aspects of the building's past, without still-visible or hidden traces, wounds or scars. The aesthetics and appearance take on the highest significance although it is possible to design the permanent loss of layers and materials in order to emphasise some historical phases rather than others. Another example in Lisbon is the Thalia Theatre by Gonçalo Byrne and Barbas Lopes. In 2008, the ruined structure of the 19th century theatre, destroyed by fire twenty years after its inauguration, were rehabilitated and reused through the combination of conservation and the addition of new parts.

As far as the intervention approach is concerned, Sara Marini (2008) compared this trend to the field of biology and called its results 'parasitic architectures'. A technologically and aesthetically diverse integration is a parasite on the existing structure allowing the coexistence of old and new. According to this concept, new additions can be three different types of parasite:

- 'endoparasite', when the parasite is placed inside a 'shell', having forms perfectly adapted to the old structures. It is partially visible from the outside but it completely changes the ruin's identity. Examples can be seen in the S(ch)austall designed by FNP architects in Germany or in the Decovete Studio designed by Haworth Tompkins in Suffolk (England) where small ruined structures hosted respectively new wooden or Corten cores (fig. 38). A most significant example is the Moritzburg museum extension in Hall (Germany), designed by the architects Nieto e Sobejano in 2008. The interior of this ruined fifteenth-century castle has been redesigned creating a wise coexistence of old and new, a clear case of the ruin used as 'container'.

- 'ectoparasite', in which the 'exophage' is fixed to the ruin. In this case, the new structure can take on different forms while the ruin serves a static function. The intervention can be also considered autonomous in terms of technologies, design and materials. The rehabilitation and extension of the Music School in Louviers (France) designed by OPUS 5 architects in 2012 offers a clear example of this kind of parasitism (fig. 39). Here, the walls of old convent of Penitents built in the 17th century, an extraordinary example of a 'cloister on water' (Area 148 2016), were enlarged with contemporary structures without losing their historical stratigraphies and signs. The old/new contrast can be seen as a poetic image of sound, a new key element in this structure.

38. Suffolk, United Kingdom. Decovete Studio designed by Haworth Tompkins (2009).
© Philip Vile.

39. Louviers, France. Music School Louviers designed by OPUS 5 architects (2012).
© Opus 5.

'parasitism' occurs when the new structures establish a relationship of extreme dependency with the ruin. It completely changes form and identity with respect to the previous structure which becomes a secondary element and can disappear completely. This is the case with Caixa Forum, a museum housed in an 1899 abandoned power station in Madrid (Spain), converted and designed by Herzog & de Meuron in 2008 (fig. 40). The structure's metamorphosis and transformation undeniable. The extensive demolitions and new additions completely changed the building's original nature.

The Netherlands is the nation with the greatest degree of experimentation even if this contemporary approach is rapidly increasing throughout the rest of the world. Finally, but no less undertaken in international contexts, are 'reconstructions' intended as the return of a destroyed place to a known previous state and consisting of rebuilding what has been lost and destroyed with the addition of new materials. Thus, reconstruction differs from integration insofar as it re-establishes the image of the ruin that had been completely lost.

This approach has many examples, especially in the recovery of ruins of war or natural calamities. After these sudden and destructive events, as already mentioned, the state of urgency as well as social demand and the psychological need for place-identity compels the reconstruction of national or historical symbols. This approach can also include 'replicas' or 'anastylosis', philologically realised in modern times, like the Frauenkirche, the Noto Cathedral, and the Mostar bridge.

40. Madrid, Spain.
Caixa Forum, designed by Herzog & de Meuron (2008). Front and main entrance.
© *Martina Porcu.*

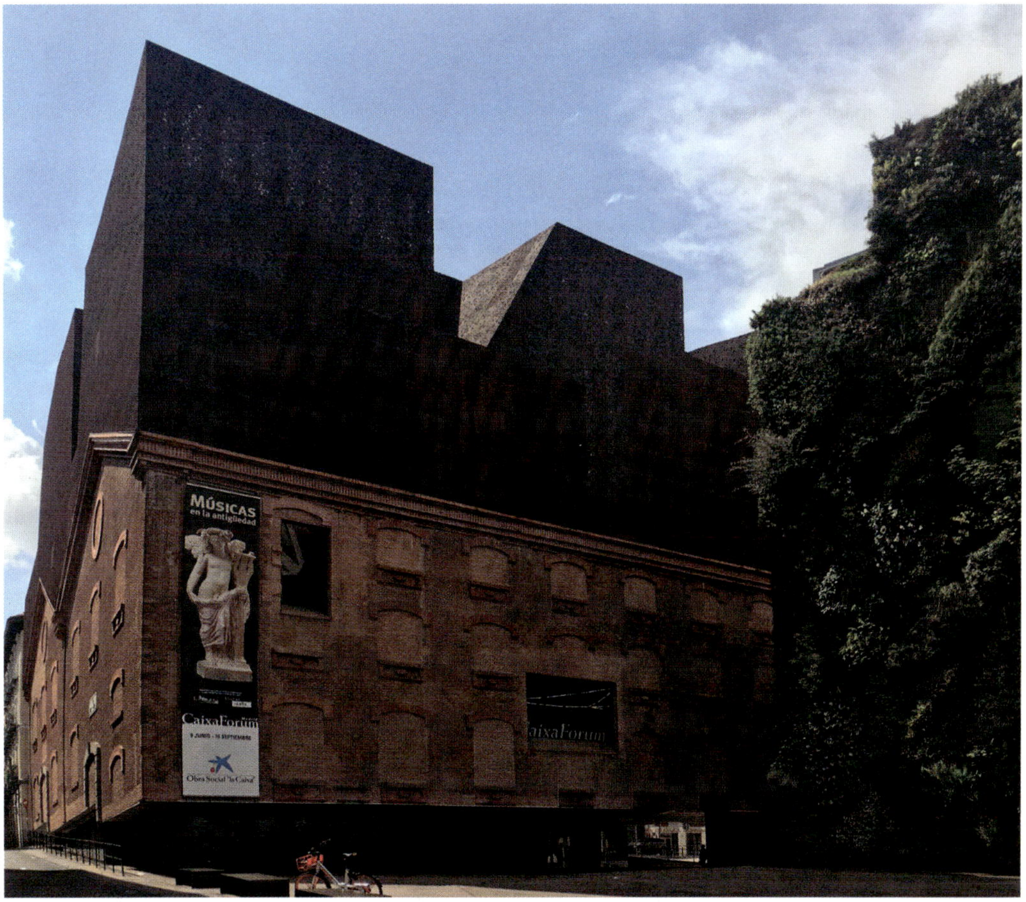
MÚSICAS
en la antigüedad
CaixaForum
Obra Social "la Caixa"
CaixaForum

CaixaForum

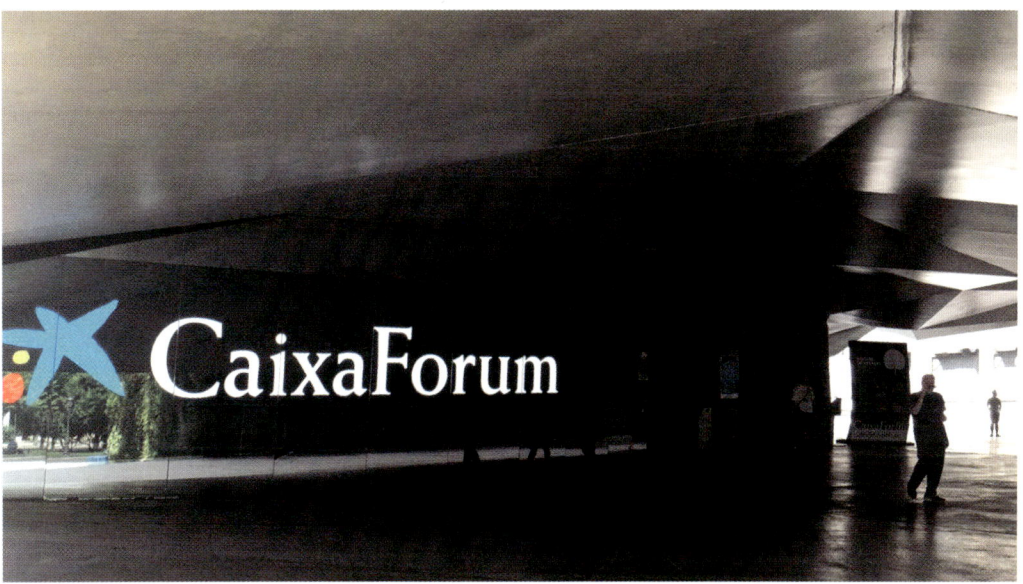

2.2. UK VS ITALY – ENGLISH AND ITALIAN APPROACHES TO RUINS

This paragraph investigates two countries that have significantly contributed to the discourse concerning ruins, the United Kingdom and Italy. Both have been, and are still characterised by strong conservation approaches, albeit in different ways.

While the value-based British approach has seen several contemporary interventions for the enhancement and protection of its cultural heritage, in Italy the obsessive pursuit of the preservation of history and memory has lead to non-intervention or exceedingly slow rehabilitation processes. Both contexts were studied in terms of their practical trends and polices with a focus on the regions of England, Scotland and Sardinia. In this case, Scotland and in particular Edinburgh, capital of Scotland and World heritage site, were studied in order to determine both best practices and criticalities, useful also for the Cagliari case.

Overall, the differences, in terms of practical interventions, in protection policy as well as methods and techniques of investigation led to the design of a common 'Anglo Italian methodology' to test on the local context. Furthermore, through their analyses, positive practical case studies suggested different themes for further reflection in order to understand and resolve some difficult issues in Cagliari.

2.2.1. THE UNITED KINGDOM

There is no doubt that in Britain ruins are much more highly considered and preserved than in the rest of the world. This is related to the high presence of structures in state of ruins. Roman ruins (fig. 30), castles, churches, monasteries, and abbeys along with other building types such as palaces, residential buildings, and military installations are located throughout the islands. Moreover, even if reduced in number, there are also cases of abandoned villages, dockyard structures, pitheads, mills, and, generally speaking, industrial ruins (Kent, 2003). The origins of these ruins can be traced to the historical events that unfolded due to the power the State and the Church, both of which played important roles in the development of buildings in the state of ruins as well as in the process of reuse or conservation of this heritage. In particular, the Reformation in the 16th and 17th centuries, *"more especially the Dissolution of the Monasteries and the Civil War"* (Thompson 1981, 13) created a tremendous quantity of ruins from the medieval period. In fact, with the Acts of 1536 and 1539, monasteries were dissolved and monastic life ended, leading to the formation of most of the ruins in the history of Great Britain. A modest number of modern ruins, instead, as seen in the historical overviews came from the wartime bombings during World War II. As a consequence of this elevated number of ruins and awareness of their cultural importance, the UK became the cradle of the International Conservation Movement.

41. London, United Kingdom.
The London Wall Place. The Roman city walls are part of public gardens in a new commercial area. The project is designed by Make Architects (2017). It has been awarded as Best New Build in the City of London in 2018.
© Elisa Pilia.

In the late 19th century, the ideas of art critic and theorist John Ruskin and artist and social critic William Morris spawned generations of architectural heritage protection activists who deeply marked future English policy. It was in this period of the romantic and picturesque traditions that the British sensibility for heritage grew, and the concept of Conservation, a key word in UK policy and key contemporary component in architectural and planning practices, developed. Since this time, the UK has been a global leader in both architectural and urban conservation and is currently a model to which many countries lacking strong governmental support for heritage aspire.

Great Britain began to protect its historical heritage very early, with the Ancient Monuments Protection Act of 1882. It consisted of the guardianship of prehistoric monuments but successively become an act to safeguard all unoccupied structures. Ruined structures were also included. This law was regularly amended and extended in the early 20th century so that from 1908 on, an inventory of monuments was initiated. Current legislation is still based on the Ancient Monuments and Archaeological Areas Act of 1979 ad the Listed Building and Conservation Areas Act of 1990 (Kalman 2015, 52). Although this general legislative outline is common to England, North Ireland, Scotland, and Wales, each has distinct heritage agencies, governmental heritage organisations and polices. In general, all heritage questions are administered by 'quasi-non-governmental organisations called 'quango' that report to a particular department – "*an entity midway between a government agency and a non-profit society*" (53). Private and charitable organisations also play important roles as they support the field of architecture, providing advice to owners, architects, and ministers, sometime offering private grants.

Furthermore, even if the English legislation is adopted in Wales and Northern Ireland, the Scottish system is rather different (Larkham 2013, 1). Differences lie not only in the way monuments are listed (different classes) but are also rooted in the historical differences among regions. This is the why England and Scotland are discussed separately.

ENGLAND Historic England, established in 1984 as the Historic Buildings and Monuments Commission for England, is the public body that oversees England's historic heritage. Until April 1, 2015, it was commonly known as English Heritage, but, after this date, a new charity, officially called the English Heritage Trust, took the name of English Heritage. Historic England has the role of championing historic places in order to identify and protect heritage and support change through deep understanding of historic places, providing expertise on the local level (fig. 42). Although 'pure conservation' of monuments is the most extensive trend in England, recently Historic England (2008) has defined its approach to historical heritage as 'constructive'.

This tendency, called 'constructive conservation', has been defined as *"a positive and collaborative attitude to conservation that focuses on actively managing change"*. Its goal is *"to recognise and reinforce the historic significance of places, while accommodating the changes necessary to ensure their continued use and enjoyment"* (English Heritage 2008, 7). In this approach, the relationship between the contemporary and the historical can be well balanced or not, easily using ruins as material for new experiments. Based on Conservation Principles, policies and guidance for the sustainable management of the historic context, it enhances heritage through the assessment of values and implements a 'Heritage at Risk Register', a national registry of historically significant places that are in danger of disappearing. Some cases of ruined structures have been the subject of this approach and the results appear interesting.

The project for the renovation of the ruined Norman West Front Bury St Edmunds Abbey (fig. 43), in Suffolk is one such example. This abbey, characterised by several later additions, was part of one of the most important medieval Benedictine monasteries in England, a building listed as grade I and designated at risk. A series of residences constructed within the structure in the 18th century was neglected and a major project was required to make them habitable again. After archaeological excavation, the ruins were preserved and at the same time converted into five new high-quality dwellings. Nicholas Jacob Architects, the authors of the conservation project in 2008, added contemporary additions together with effective and appropriate conservation solutions for the historic building.

Blancowe Hall in Pernith (fig. 44) is another example of constructive conservation where two fortified medieval towers, both a scheduled monument and grade I listed building, were converted in 2006 into holiday accommodations by Donald Insall Associates Architects, Graham Norman and Charles Blackett-Ord. *"The gash in the masonry that made the ruin so spectacular has been retained, in an eye-catching form. It remains as dramatic a sight as ever but now has behind it inset glazing and balconies"* (English Heritage 2008b, 32). The monument, now reused as luxury holiday homes, is a unique piece of English history. In both the projects, the constructive collaboration of developers, architects, public bodies as well as other partners lead to positive conservation, intended as conversion and re-enhancement of ruins rendered usable again.

On the previous page:
42. Coventry, United Kingdom.
View of Bayley Lane, part of the Hill Top Conversation Area managed by Historic England and Coventry City Council (declared 8 August 1969).
© *Elisa Pilia.*

43. Suffolk, United Kingdom.
Norman West Front Bury St Edmunds Abbey designed by Nicholas Jacob Architects (2008).
© *Fisher Hart Architectu-ral and Interiors Photography.*
In Historic England 2008, 12.

44. Pernith, United Kingdom.
Blancowe Hall designed by Donald Insall Associates Architects, Graham Norman and Charles Blackett-Ord (2008).
© *O. Davies James, English Heritage.*
In Historic England 2008, 32.

SCOTLAND Historic Environment Scotland is, instead, the Scottish executive agency, which answers to the Scottish government's department of Arts, Culture and Sport. Founded in 1991, it is a non-departmental public body and registered Scottish Charity set up to investigate, care for and promote Scotland's historic environment. It is governed by a Board of Trustees appointed by the Cabinet Secretary for Culture, Europe and External Affairs in accordance with the Code of Practice for Ministerial Public Appointments. The Historic Environment Scotland Act 2014 defines its tasks and rules. This legal framework finds its roots in the 19th century when the national identity of monumental Scottish architecture, composed of both monuments and minor buildings built in solid stone-masonry, was preserved according to Geddes' ideology and practices. Religious monuments such as chapels or abbeys (figg. 45–46), palaces, abandoned villages from the period of 'clearances' (18th and 19th centuries), as well as castellated architecture (fig. 47) are the main ruin typologies present in Scotland today. In particular, as Brennan-Inglis (2014, 27) reported, castellated architecture can be considered the symbol from which the sense of national identity arose. Over time, these structures were objects of conservation, restoration and reoccupation because they were very close to people's minds, strictly related to a culture of fighting and independence (Thompson 2006; Brennan-Inglis 2014; Glendinning et al. 2011).

Concerning the protection of Scottish heritage and small traditional buildings, the National Trust for Scotland (NTS), independent charity set up in 1931, played a significant role in the prevention of a possible future state of ruination within the old Scottish towns (dating from the 16th to the 18th centuries).

In the interwar period, in 1930s, with the pioneering campaigns of a group of individuals, a process of recovery (restoration programme) was initiated for these architectures with the aim of renting the properties to local tenants in collaboration with local authorities. It was completely opposed to municipal housing campaign and slum clearance, which, based on the Housing Acts (1930), endangered the existence of the small traditional burgh houses. The most important burgh restoration projects were at Culross in Fife (1932) and Dunkeld in Perthshire (1953), under the auspices of the architect Ian Lindsay. If, initially, the NTS worked with local authorities, in the 1960s it started its own programme called Little House Improvement Scheme (LHIS) as a *"natural development of the previous preservation policy. It was seen, in fact, as an important change in terms of 'cultural ethos, social aims and architectural ideas"* (Watters and Glendinning 2006, 9) as compared to the 1930s NTS preservation pioneers. Now, it focused on safeguarding the small traditional houses for future sale, rather than rental. So, it could bring a possible profit for further restoration.

45. Edinburgh, United Kingdom.
Ruins of St Anthony's Chapel in Holyrood Park.
© *Elisa Pilia.*

In the interwar years, there was a growing international movement to preserve and restore the historic built environment. In each country, different factors and causes drove these initiatives, but all showed a tendency of *"modern dynamism with traditional opposition to modernity"* (12). In Scotland, this ferment and concern for safeguarding heritage stems from 'English domination' but also from the immobility that characterised this period. Both the rural and the traditional built environment were included in the wave of protection. An example is the foundation, in 1927, of the Council for the Preservation of Rural Scotland, an independent charity. All such facts, and particularly the pathos for the small endangered burghs was hugely influenced by the romantic 'Old Edinburgh' cult of the late 19th century. This trend, born from the writings of Robert Louis Stevenson (1850–1894) and conservationist city-planner Patrick Geddes (1854–1932), was widely supported by the middle class in Edinburgh and East Central Scotland. From its beginnings, it was in contrast with the slum clearance practice supported by local authorities with the Housing Acts (1930–1935) that led to replacing the older stock with new housing. This movement for the protection of traditional dwellings stemmed from these events and from widespread clearance. Between 1920s and 1930s, many conservative organisations and initiatives followed one another (15) with a broad range of goals as will be shown. Indeed, the main purpose was to save these historic burgh dwellings (the whole built environment and the ordinary homes), symbols of all Scots, 'rich and poor alike' (16).

In 1932, the NTS started their operative activity by purchasing small proprieties in Culross, restoring properties in Gladstone's Land, Lawnmarket, Edinburgh and, finally, instituting the Old Edinburgh Committee, providing an opportunity to increase interest in the old houses of Edinburgh. This was a true urban renewal process, called by P. Geddes 'conservative surgery', involving both the spiritual and social regeneration of the city.

The first preservation project began in small burghs in Fife, endangered after a long period of neglect but still maintaining their traditional features. The small sixteenth- and seventeenth-century houses were described as having *"walls badly bulged, sagging roof, lacking plasters, scarce ventilation and light, low ceilings"* (19); the Department of Health for Scotland recognised these problems. Even if the Housing scheme (1923) provided financial assistance for rehousing people from slum areas, an important contribution arrived in 1936. This was Bute's pamphlet, Plea for Scotland's Architectural Heritage, privately financed by the aristocrat Bute, an enthusiastic conservationist. The rich and influential man attacked the *"wholesale destruction of Scotland's unique domestic buildings"* (20) and criticised the 1935 Housing Act for demolishing the historical housing stock. He highlighted the importance of raising awareness of the loss that this policy would have caused and, after his active campaign, he designated the young architect Ian Lindsay to carry

46. Melrose, United Kingdom.
Ruins of Melrose Abbey.
© *Elisa Pilia.*

47. Highland, United Kingdom.
Ruins of Urquhart Castle.
© *Elisa Pilia.*

out a systematic survey of traditional and small houses whose goal was to classify them in accordance with the gravity of their problems. Ninety-two burghs and 1047 buildings were classified and declared to the Department of Health. This was a first important step both for the future post-war government-listing programme and for knowledge of existing small-sized heritage.

As a result, in 1950, artistic and social values led to the 'little houses' preservation programme in which Culross was cited as *"an exemplary model for other preservation societies and local authorities to follow" (27)*. It was completed three years later in 1953, *"creating or maintaining visual unity between old houses"* (30).

The programme gained international fame and in 1975, 'European Architectural Heritage Year', it won a European Architectural Heritage Year Award. Little Houses and its successful 'revolving fund' focused on reusing the initial capital many times over, continuing to combine regeneration of historic buildings with the broader aspiration of urban renewal (156).

Currently Scotland has around 40 of the 200 building preservation trusts in the UK and some of the most innovative and important in all the islands, inspired by LHIS. This pioneering Scottish experience signals a clear approach to urban conservation that also includes the small medieval burghs; it was able to avert the obsolescence of the valuable buildings and prevent their possible ruination. With similar conservation and rehabilitation processes, the small abandoned industrial village of New Lanark was restored and listed as a World Heritage site (fig. 48). The village, built in the 18th century by the idealistic Robert Owen and inspired by a model of industrial community based on textile production, continued to manufacture cotton for nearly 200 years until 1968. Its significance as an eighteenth model of industrial settlement led UNESCO to support the rehabilitation project (fig. 49), respecting its integrity and authenticity. In fact, its statement of significance reports that *"when elements are missing or have been replaced, the property is clearly interpreted to reflect this. Where rebuilding or reconstruction have been necessary, this has been carried out to the best conservation standards, based on full historic records. Repair and restoration has been undertaken using appropriate traditional materials and workmanship, following original designs wherever possible, and always respecting existing historic fabric. The original weir, lade and waterways which provided water-power to the mills from the 1780s are still in use today"*.

While in Scotland the approach was mainly one of conservation and preservation, examples of conversion, reconstruction and restoration are not absent. This is what came about in Edinburgh, a mid-size city where a series of integrative interventions in conservation areas contributed to the rehabilitation of buildings in ruination and as a consequence at risk.

48. New Lanark, United Kingdom.
The UNESCO industrial town of New Lanark.
© *Elisa Pilia.*

49. New Lanark, United Kingdom.
Structures waiting for a rehabilitation.
© *Elisa Pilia.*

One example is the project for the urban rehabilitation of Advocate's Close in Edinburgh (fig.50–51). Concluded in 2009 and designed by Morgan McDonnell Architecture, it offers an interesting blend of new and old in the core of the city. The project area consisted of nine listed buildings, built between 16th and 20th centuries, over 11 storeys in height, bridging two closes between High Street, Cockburn Street and Market Street. While many of the buildings were listed, the majority had been greatly altered since their construction. The project won the Best Building in Scotland 2014 Award due to the harmonious combination of traditional building design, such as the crow-step gable, with new building materials and techniques. The rehabilitation project, which created a new 208-room hotel, 50 apartments, bar, restaurant spaces, and office accommodations, increased flows through the area creating a welcoming focal point that encourages visitors to explore and visit, revitalising this key public space (Stewart group 2014).

Sugar Close Project (fig. 52), designed by Oberlanders Architects and rehabilitated in 2012 is another example in which the old and new are combined in a historical area. This was a very large development on a difficult site, combining re-used historic buildings and new-build with ingenuity. Materials, landscaping and scale are all appropriate to the Old Town's fabric (fig. 53). This integrative approach lies in the heart of Edinburgh's Old Town and World Heritage site. The proposal was to reuse and enhance listed stone brewhouses and malt barns while juxtaposing new contemporary interventions. The historic context and urban fabric informs the development strategy, architectural language, heights, scale, and massing. The development comprises a varying mix of accommodations with a pedestrian, car-free, mixed-use development, designed to serve student and tourist (325 beds) demand, aiming to create flexible, high-standard and sustainable (long life/loose fit) accommodations. This project was shortlisted for the 2013 RIAS/RIBA awards.

The site was also of great archaeological interest and the works were coordinated with the keen interest of the City Archaeologist, who established the presence of significant structural and archaeological remains in some parts of the site (2). The Statement of Special Interest reported that the site's exceptional character lay in the fact that it was also one of the few remaining brewery sites in Edinburgh.

The Grassmarket Community Project started in 2002 with the demolition of three derelict industrial buildings near the Kirk house that was involved (fig. 54). An extension was added in a gap space between the walls of the Kirkyard. The extension includes a community hall/theatre, cooking facilities, offices, workshop space, classrooms, and foyer. The aim was to create a strong contemporary addition to the World Heritage Site through a building of exceptional architectural merit. Larger double height volumes benefitting

50. Edinburgh, United Kingdom.
View of Advocate's Close from Princess Street.
© Martina Loi.

51. Edinburgh, United Kingdom.
Old and new inside Advocate's Close.
© Martina Loi.

52. Edinburgh, United Kingdom.
The requalified Sugar Close.
© *Martina Loi.*

53. Edinburgh, United Kingdom.
The contrast between new and old materials.
© *Martina Loi.*

54. Edinburgh, United Kingdom.
Main entrance of the Grassmarket Centre.
© *Martina Loi.*

from skylights are located next to the 8 m high Kirkyard wall with smaller more cellular spaces located around the perimeter. A sedum roof gives the impression of an extension to the kirkyard punctured by the monolithic rooflights using the same metal cladding as the perimeter walls. Overall, these examples of integrative approaches have shown how, in a city like Edinburgh, a World Heritage Site, the preservation and enhancement of historical heritage can be positively supported by means of contemporary additions that emphasise the area's traditional physical and social features.

2.2.2. ITALY

Italian approaches and policies regarding ruined structures, mainly focused on different degrees of conservation and critical intervention, are singular on the European and international panorama. If Italy, thanks to its long tradition of scholarship on built heritage, can be considered a leader in the global field of architectural conservation, education and theory, the same emphasis cannot be found in practice. In fact, this country is so strongly influenced by the 'weight' of its history that transformation processes are slower and less widespread than in other European countries (Levi Montalcini 2002, x). This 'immobility', more common in the smaller Italian cities, has changed the image of the historical centres with inertia and lack of intervention leading to processes of ruination and abandonment. This uncertainty, characterised by insignificant interventions, have determined and increased urban fragmentation due to poor management. Landmark designation has become an element generating stalemate and inertia (Massarente et al. 2002, 8). Carbonara (2011, 35) recognised the problems relating to new interventions on ruins as the results of a lack of quality of projects often caused by the absence of interdisciplinary studies (Varagnoli 2008, 836). Since the 19th century, with the first important restoration projects of the Colosseum by Raffaele Stern and Giuseppe Camporesi (1806–1807) and Giuseppe Valadier's work at the Arch of Titus (1818–1822), Italy demonstrated great sensitivity to and respect for ruins. Indeed, a *"first comprehensive law on architectural conservation"* (Stubbs et al. 2011, 14), the Monument Act, established in 1920, and the political unification of the Kingdom of Italy influenced Italian heritage conservation. Most importantly, noteworthy personalities contributed to the definition of the Italian approaches. Camillo Boito (1836–1914) and his scientific restoration theory focused its attention on the *"discernible difference between old and new work in style and materials used, the visible inscription and documentation of all new restoration work carried out on the historic building, and the display of removed surviving original elements near the restored building"* (16).

Giovannoni's revisions of Boito's principles emphasised the value of minor architecture. The later theories of Brandi and Pane introduced the three *'istanze'* or 'features'– historical, aesthetic and psychological - to stress the value of history, artistic and aesthetic enjoyment, and memory.

From the post-war reconstruction period on, the debate regarding the relationship between 'new and old' began to face the urban scale and issues of planning and legislation, evolving the theoretical debate (Varagnoli 2008, 836). The city began to be considered as a 'consumed resource' and, as Franco Purini stated, the work of the architect was to reconstruct and not construct the existing city, creating a distinctive brand of current architecture which is the result of a different economic and social trends.

55. Pisa, Italy.
Details of the intervention in San Michele in Borgo designed by the architect Massimo Carmassi (1979–2002).
© *M. Ciampi.* In De Vita 2015, 81.

As previously mentioned, Italian interventions are clearly identified by a cultural and formal identity that have their roots in this long-standing restoration tradition. Today, according to the main European tendencies, Italy is also characterised by the same operative practices supported by the principal Italian theorists and contemporary architects in which all interventions are regulated by the administrative law called the Codex for Cultural and Landscape Heritage (art. 10 of the law 137, 6th July 2002). The approach deployed by the architect Marco Dezzi Bardeschi, as already seen, while based on 'pure conservation', considers the distinction and autonomy of the new intervention with respect to the stratified fabric. He thinks of restoration as the sum of two acts: conservation of the existing structure, intended as hereditary value, and the new project that embodies the value of the new (Dezzi Bardeschi 2004, 4–5). His 2016 restoration project for the Augustus Temple Dome in Pozzuoli (fig.56–57), demolished and devastated first by a fire and then by an earthquake in the 20th century, illustrates this approach. It can be understood as linked to the Brandi concept of restoration that should represent itself as a historical event, within the process of transmitting to the future, and consequently, as expression of its time. In the field of reconstruction, supported by the architect Paolo Marconi who claimed the educational and symbolic values of the building, several experiments have been conducted in the architectural and urban fields with different degrees of re-integration. This approach can be seen in the Baroque oratory of San Filippo Neri, in Bologna. The oratory, built in the 17th century and then transformed into barracks in the 19th century, was destroyed during the World War II. In 1999, the designer, architect Pier Luigi Cervellati "*historicised*" the wartime ruins by means of an "*accurate reconstruction of the eighteenth-century Bolognese remains*" (Cervellati 2000, 85–92). Roofs, vaults and ceilings were reconstructed with the use of lamellar timber (fig. 42).

Another important case is the urban typological reconstruction of the mediaeval quarter of San Michele in Borgo in Pisa (figg. 55–58–59) designed by the architect Massimo Carmassi, initiated in 1985. Here, the architect conceived these war ruins as stratified remains that had to be reintegrated by emphasising the layers of time (Carmassi 2007, 63). Two approaches, one of new construction on the old excavated foundations and another of integration with the restored walls, combined the use of modern materials and refined building techniques in complete harmony with the pre-existing fabric. Other creative and allusive reconstructions can be seen in the cases of 'reclaimed memory' of Palazzo di Lorenzo in Gibellina destroyed by the violent earthquake in 1968 and reconstructed in 1987 by the architect Francesco Venezia.

56. Pozzuoli, Italy.
Augustus Temple Dome. Interior of the intervention designed by Dezzi Bardeschi (2016).
© *Caterina Giannattasio.*

57. Pozzuoli, Italy.
Augustus Temple Dome. External details of the intervention.
© *Caterina Giannattasio.*

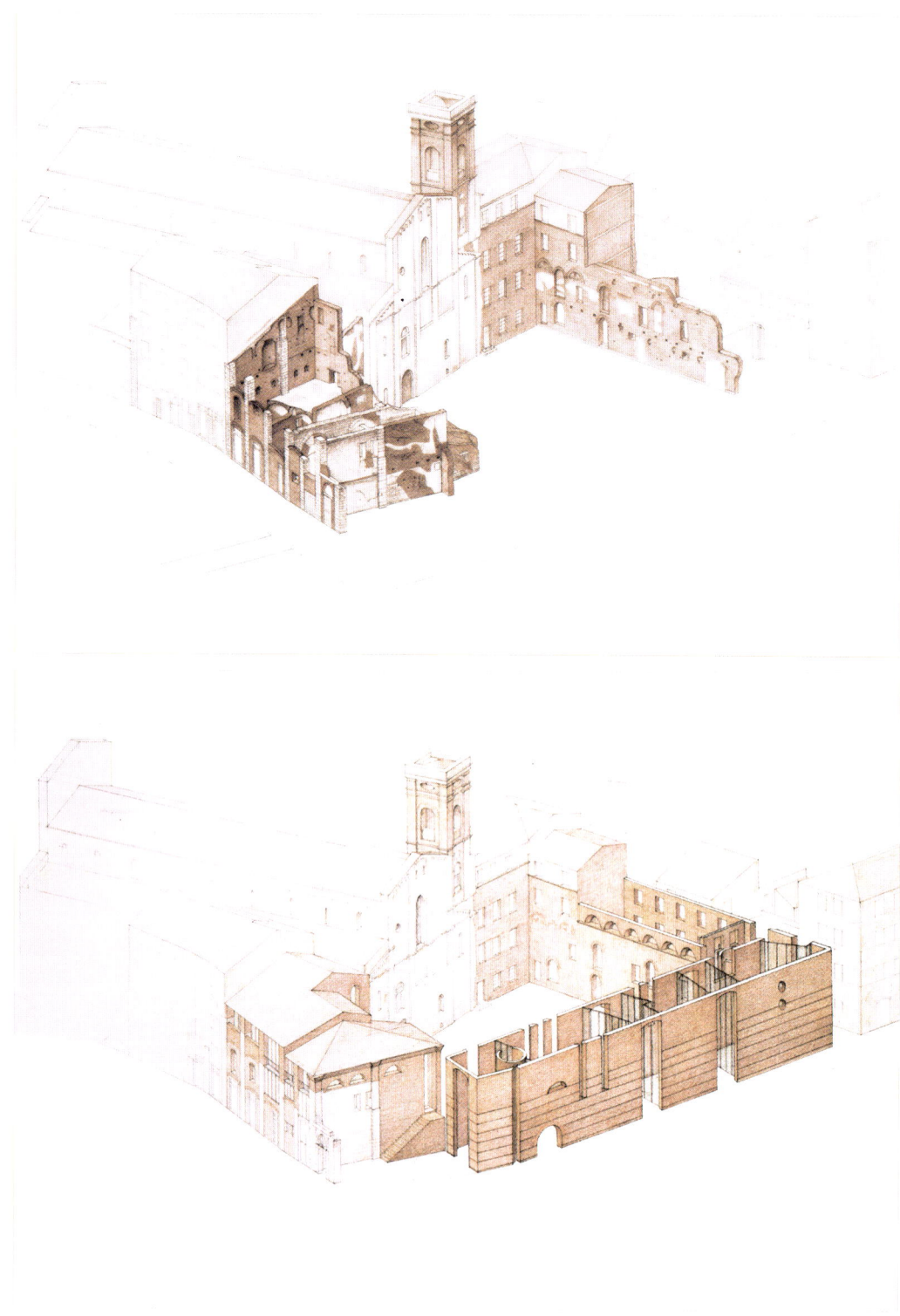

58. Pisa, Italy.
3D renders of the intervention in the Mediaeval quarter of San Michele in Borgo.
© *M. Carmassi*. In De Vita 2015, 72.

59. Pisa, Italy.
Details of the intervention in San Michele in Borgo.
© *M. Carmassi*. In De Vita 2015, 72.

In the project of this House/Museum, the fragment of the façade becomes symbol of time juxtaposing new surfaces with stratified and complex existing structures. Finally, the 'critical-conservation' approach is supported by scholar Gionavanni Carbonara and architects such as Giovanni Bulian, who designed the conservation of the Roman Diocletian thermal baths in Rome between 1983 and 1997 and their outfitting as museum. The integral conservation of the monument and the addition of new reversible elements have shown a great sensitivity in connecting the building's various layers.

SARDINIA The problem of how to preserve and reuse ruins is even more marked in Sardinia where there is a high percentage of heritage in a state of ruins. On this island, ruins differ in typology and origins: an extensive presence of rural artefacts, churches, villages, industrial sites, and defensive heritage (fig.60) lay neglected in the wild landscape. They originated with different events: the slow and progressive decay of disused structures and the violent destructive events produced by natural disaster or traumatic bombing during war. These ruins also vary in their materials, locations and building techniques; they create a variegated heritage and evidence a wide range of problems relating to their state of conservation and to the interventions undertaken for their protection in the past.

Today's advanced state of ruination is due to different factors, such as the frequent poor coexistence of building materials, atmospheric agents as well as difficult access to these structures in their isolated locations. These results may find origins in the long period of neglect and misunderstandings that have characterised Sardinian policy during the 20th century when a new position appeared in Italy for safeguarding ruins. In fact, in 1906, the State issued the circular n.18 signed by Corrado Ricci, historian and general director for the protection of historical heritage between 1906 and 1919. It defined ruins as: all remains from old buildings, archeological fragments, epigraphs and different building elements. Each of them, placed in their original location, has paramount value because it is a document that tells about the history of the building, it conserves the signs of past uses of the structures and it could be useful to reconstruct the general history. Every artistic or historic fragment cannot be changed in position or demolished, but they must be preserved and exposed to the community (Billeci and Gizzi 2010, 183).

In this way, they appeared as monuments to improve but this was only the first step for their real protection; the path for true and effective widespread policy was still remote. In 1964, the Conseil International des Monuments et des Sites – ICOMOS, concerned about the state of abandonment of defensive heritage and in accord with the principles of the Venice Charter (1964), defined seven strategic lines of intervention: 1) castles and ruins are historical documents that should be protected; 2) the maintenance of authenticity is the main goal of every intervention; historical and archaeological studies should be carried out before undertaking any kind of project; 3) the relationship between ruins and the landscape should be preserved through the in situ conservation of every fragment; 4) anastylosis is possible only if carried out with certain historical documentation; 5) minimum intervention and distinguishability should be followed in every reintegration; 6) the integration of the castles and ruined architectures in modern life does not mean their practical reuse: they are valuable elements of cultural life and provide

60. Olbia, Italy.
Castle of Pedres.
© M. S. Pirisino.

us with important information about our past; 7) their reuse is not acceptable if there is a transformation or alteration of their authenticity (Brandi 1977, 29–47). Despite this progress, Sardinia, marginalised and isolated from the dominant mainland intellectual currents, has focused little attention on its heritage. On the island, the first theoretical interest in its ruins began between the end of the 19th and 20th centuries, under the influence of important intellectuals such as Filippo Vivanet, Carlo Aru and Dionigi Scano, landmark commission architects at the time. They worked for the promotion of interventions that redeemed ruins from their wreckage and that safeguarded their picturesque features to guarantee their authenticity. At the same time, in practice, they carried out debatable interventions on ruins with the massive reintegration of new materials. Furthermore, they focused interventions only on the most important sites, neglecting the minor architecture that continued its process of decay. In the island's north east, fortified heritage was involved in an important period of restoration only around the 1960s, with sixty years of delay with respect to the other Italian regions. It was supported by national funding for the south (Cassa del Mezzogiorno) and supervised by the architect Roberto Carità. In this period, the general tendency of reintegration, even if inspired by the ICOMOS and Venice Charter principles, digressed from the limits imposed by the regulations and reached full reconstruction, often undocumented and not historically justified (Cadeddu 2001). 'Della Fava' castle is a clear example of defence heritage in ruins, restored between the 1960s and 80s, with particular attention to the reconstruction of the *mastio*. If non-intervention is the main strategy due to lack of funding, limited cases of integrative approaches can be seen in some Sardinian monuments. This is the case of the medieval convent and church of San Domenico (fig. 61), in the historical core of Cagliari, demolished in the 1943 war bombings. After years of debate, in 1954, a new concrete church designed by Raffaello Fagnoni was inaugurated (fig. 62). Contemporary forms and materials overlapped the ruined walls of the medieval church (fig. 63) while the convent was reconstructed and restored harmoniously with the pre-existing elements. An opposing approach was deployed for the Sant' Ignazio Fort (late 18th century), a military ruin, fallen into decay after its disuse (fig. 64). Here, a conservative approach was used between the 1980s and 90s by the Council. It mainly consisted in the consolidation of the existing structures and in their reintegration with materials found in the area. These integrations were designed 10 cm behind the original wall in accordance with the building's aesthetic value (Pilia 2015, 346–347) (fig. 65). Undoubtedly, designing a conservation or integrative project in the urban or rural Sardinian landscape is complex. It means not only preserving structures and transmitting their values but also designing interventions in stratified, unique settings, in a complex territory like Sardinia.

61. Cagliari, Italy.
Cloister of the convent of San Domenico. On the back, the new volume of the contemporary church.
© *Davide Melis.*

62. Cagliari, Italy.
Aerial view of the Convent of San Domenico in Villanova quarter.
© Elisa Pilia.

63. Cagliari, Italy.
Convent of San Domenico. Detail of the intervention of reconstruction inside the church (1952–1954).
© Davide Melis.

64. Cagliari, Italy.
View of the ruins of Sant'Ignazio Fort.
© Davide Melis.

65. Cagliari, Italy.
The ruins of Sant'Ignazio Fort. Details of the intervention (2012).
© Elisa Pilia.

3. URBAN RUINS: ISSUES AND VALUES

The overview of urban issues in historic areas has established a basic theoretical and practical framework for defining the methodology and for understanding ruins in urban contexts, such as those in the Cagliari case.

A first part examines policies for safeguarding and revitalising historic centres, including the role of ruins. The concept of sustainability currently pervades these polices and concerns economic, social, aesthetic and environmental aspects. All such issues become part of the methodology in light of their importance to the values that will be investigated in part III.

Exploring the transformation processes and policies in our cities is also essential for understanding and defining a correct and balanced project in historic centres; such a project should be respectful of the economic and social questions and maintain intact the place identity of dynamic historic and contemporary cities (fig. 66). While the aim of this book is not to provide a monetary economic evaluation of the costs involved, the study has been focused on the definition and experimentation of a transdisciplinary methodology to assess and define tangible and intangible heritage values. Accordingly, then, it does consider the economic aspects of urban ruins by utilising the concept of non – use value, instead of costs that can be practically estimated by economics in the management of the interventions. Moreover, social, aesthetic and environmental issues are fundamental for rethinking a new set of values that could lead to a holistic view of ruined urban fabrics.

3.1. URBAN POLICY

Different policy trends have defined planning processes in historic centres with ruins. Especially since the 1970s, when heritage protection passed from individual buildings to area-based conservation, inner areas and neighbourhoods took on new significance. Following are the main recognisable phases in the evolution of this change (Tiesdell et al. 1996).

In the 19th century, a first phase of historic preservation policy related to the protection of the individual buildings and artefacts that were the icons of a nation's history or religion as in Britain and in France. Their effects were limited and independent from their urban contexts. New urban needs stemmed from modern living standards relating to vehicular traffic, hygiene and comfort. Consequently, a new tendency of isolating key monuments in vast spaces, as Haussmann did in Paris, brought about widespread demolitions of historic areas throughout all of Europe. In Germany, this radical tendency, called *'Freilegung'* was exemplified in Cologne, Ulm and Regensburg where monumental and residential buildings were sacrificed in order to redefine open spaces (Glendinning 2013, 166). The Haussmann approach also found followers in Italy, where cases of *isolamento and sventramento* (isolation and extensive

66. London, United Kingdom.
Detail of the Western Range at King's Cross Station.
The transformation designed by
John McAslan + Partners (2012) involves different level of intervention: re-use, restoration and new build. In particular, the Northern structures, destroyed by bombing in World War II, have been rebuilt to their original design.
© *Elisa Pilia*.

demolition) were widespread; they are still visible today in Rome in Via della Conciliazione for example (fig. 67), but also in Florence and Bologna. The growing 'cult of the old town' (Glendinning 2013, 165) and the concept of the 'old town as living collective heritage' supported by Darwin's evolutionary theory and Simmel's social thinking, which respectively encouraged an overall vision of the entire city and its social potential, stimulated a new conservative sensibility toward urban protection and the identification of shared values. Thus, at the end of the 19th century, a second phase focused on safeguarding historic townscapes and centres and defining area-based approaches.

VALUE OF PICTORESQUE Camillo Sitte (1843–1903), in Der Stadtebau (1889), provided a significant contribution in the long and complex process of safeguarding historic centres. For the first time, he underlined the paramount importance of considering values in the analysis of the city for its conservation. Furthermore, he introduced a new architectural concept of space: the artistic cityscape characterised by the spatial 'value of the picturesque', meant as aesthetic value (Giambruno 2002, 17–21).
Generally, in clear opposition to the isolation of monuments, he proposed a new way of thinking about and designing the city: old and contemporary cities had to be considered as wholes, planning new areas according to the needs of the old ones and their models. The value of the monument also depended on its context (Ranelucci 2003, 25). Although his philosophy anticipated the theory of values codified by Riegl, the idea of conserving urban areas was still being developed. Protection was conceived only for areas where picturesque characteristics could be maintained while guaranteeing modern comfort (Giambruno 2002, 20).

EVIDENTIARY VALUE The Belgian politician Charles Buls (1837–1914) supported the same opposition to important isolations. He argued that architecture is a reflection of the society that inhabits it; thus, the city is witness to the cultural and educational level of the community that shapes its urban morphology. He proposed a theory of 'freedom' or 'diradamento' (thinning out) for providing an overall cultural, functional and hygienic solution to the problems of transforming old areas while satisfying the needs of modern life (23–40).
At the end of the 19th century, he wrote his studies on the aesthetics of the city in which he saw the chaotic features of old cities as elements of beauty while analysing urban development from three different points of view: technical, aesthetic and archaeological. As already seen in the historic analysis, significant contributions were provided by: Victor Hugo (1803–1885) and his view of the city as 'book of stone'; John Ruskin and his concept of the city as 'witness of material culture' resulting from the stratifications of ages of events;

67. Rome, Italy.
View of Via della Conciliazione from the dome of St. Peter's Basilica. This avenue, designed by M. Piacentini and A. Spaccarelli (1881–1960), is the result of an operation of extensive demolition of the whole '*spina di Borgo*'.
© *Elisa Pilia.*

and Riegl's theory of values which, like the previous theories, emphasises urban and architectural stratifications. Giovannoni extended the concept of monument to 'minor architecture', and the urban context took on a key role in order to confer importance to the singular monument. So, at that time, the concept of conservation moved to groups of buildings and to the spaces around and between them.

In the UK, this phenomenon led to the birth of the concept of the conservation area already present since the 1920s mainly due to Gedde's conservative and intervention approach that emphasised the need to preserve the memory and identity of places with process of modernisation and transformation. The Civic Amenities Act (1967) defined conservation areas as *"areas of special architectural and historic interest the character of which it is to preserve or to enhance"*.

In the Americas, even before the World War II, a series of historic preservation districts already existed in the private realm, such as Williamsburg, Virginia (1926) and Charleston, South Carolina (1931). Only in 1966 was federal legislation signed; it was denominated the National Historic Preservation Act. These concerns and policies were expressed shortly thereafter in most European countries. France and the Netherlands, the two nations that "paid the most attention to cities" (Tallon 2013, 124) approved the '*Loi Malraux*' and the Monument Act in 1961. In 1967, Italy followed the trend with the Urban Planning Act. Finally, in 1973, Turkey issued the Monument and Historical Building Act.

This policy trend had the effect of bringing under protection and control too many buildings, increasing the number of buildings that could be not reused by the community contributing directly to the economy of the area. This drove cities to become open-air museums (Burtenshaw et al. 1991, 157–158). Interestingly, these policies were enacted during a period of economic growth in some countries and in a period of economy stagnation in others. War bombings and the urgent need for the reconstruction of large parts of cities further stimulated the debate about the old/new relationship. In Italy, for instance, urban centres were objects of real-estate speculation due to the absence of codes and regulations. In the 1950s, Pane introduced the need for safeguarding the entire urban territory where historic centres were to be conserved in their volumetric materiality. The environment was conceived of as a 'collective work of art'.

A third phase concerned a new policy which included the management component in the revitalisation of protected dwellings, seeking *"to generate investment and local economic development able to provide the finance necessary to conserve and enhance the quarters"* (Tiesdell et al. 1996, 4). The main goal was to reconcile and find a balance between conservation and regeneration, between economic development and respect for the environment.

68. London, United Kingdom. Covent Garden, the main entrance of the market area.
© *Elisa Pilia.*

69. London, United Kingdom. Preserved historical structures and contemporary additions coexist in Covent Garden market.
© *Elisa Pilia.*

Covent Garden (figg.68–69), the market area in London's West End, can be considered a significant example of this policy. In the late 1960s and early 70s, the site was the object of an important large-scale commercial redevelopment plan promoted by the Greater London Council (GCL). In 1978, the 'Covent Garden Action Plan' recognised this area for its unique character and potential for making an important contribution to central London; over 100 buildings were listed and preserved. Even if highly complex, the revitalisation process brought new uses and functions to historic buildings, maintaining them in good conditions.

In 1960, a conference regarding '*Salvaguardia e risanamento dei centri storico-artistici*' promoted by the architect Giovanni Astengo (1915-1990) in Gubbio (Italy) heralded in a new era for historic centres. The output of the conference, the Gubbio Charter, formally extended the concept of monument to the entire urban context, recognizing that the stratification of the contemporary city was composed of both modern and historic fabric as well as the assessment of values as a starting point for intervening on the existing city: the outskirts as well as the inner areas. Out of this conservative renewal approach grew the necessity for strategic municipal plans, rejecting stylistic restoration as well as demolition, isolation and 'thinning out'. Other important steps were taken to consolidate the concept of reuse and its economic advantages in the Venice Charter (1964) and the Italian Restoration Charter (1972).

A new methodological approach was also delineated at the time: the 'typological approach' proposed by architect and urbanist Saverio Muratori (1910–1973). He considered the city as a work of art that needed to be studied through the idea of 'typology' seen as the modus vivendi of the community who inhabits it (Giambruno 2002, 123). The architect Gianfranco Caniggia (1933–1987) followed this methodology, focusing his research on the identification of tools that might confer architectural dignity upon minor works. Typology became a tool for classifying categories and parameters, useful for the study of prior models and the evolution of building fabrics (in terms of structural elements, architectural features, unification of buildings). The Bologna plan, drafted by architect Pier Luigi Cervellati between 1973 and 1978, was the first plan in which typological restoration and social issues were tested. Conservative redevelopment sought to safeguarding historic values and eliminating incongruous parts. Other plans, like those for Palermo, Vigevano, Monza e Rimini, utilised the same process of analysis starting with the study of historic cadastral documentation to define typological classes of buildings. These were intended as significant models in which the degree of intervention would be based on the value of the building typology, also defined according to authenticity and uniqueness (141–149). From the same study of historical sources and built heritage, Plans of colours, stemming from the idea that colour plays an important role in the perception of the city, were conducted in places like Bergamo.

Similarly, in the same period, the Marais quartier in Paris became an example of mixed-use areas in which the local government worked upon the distinctiveness of their characteristics. In cities such as Birmingham and Glasgow, local plans also identified areas that emphasised local identity. The USA and the UK are especially significant in terms of historic urban landscapes characterised by 19th century industrial features. Their identity, exemplified in the brick and stone houses or early steel and cast-iron frame structures, is unique (Tiesdell et. al. 1996, 7). Furthermore, in 1975, the European Charter of Architectural Heritage also called the Amsterdam Charter, became the new policy regarding the concept of 'integrated conservation' in historic urban neighbourhoods, where conservation and revitalisation were considered to have a symbiotic relationship (Doratli 2005, 751). Studies of the historic centre led to the definition of 'Manuali del recupero' (Handbooks for recovery) that identify standards and procedures aimed at gaining knowledge of the city in terms of its typologies, historic characteristics and the consequent degree and method of intervention. If in Italy the first Handbook was written for Pesaro in 1978, in the same year in the UK, a similar one was published for Edinburgh: The care and conservation of Georgian Houses. A maintenance manual.

All such results, Plans of colours, Manuals for the conservation and typological studies for urban planning, led to only one of the possible readings of the city that became difficult to understand for the next generation. The concept of complexity is important in conceiving a city not merely as a sum of typologies but as complex system of tangible and intangible components: objects-events as the result of centuries of human – nature interactions, strictly relating to a given territory, the society that shaped it and its economy. The intervention on a singular urban/building fabric can change the perception of an entire context. This consideration is the basis for the UNESCO recommendation regarding the historic urban landscape (2011), which recognised that "the city is not a static monument or group of buildings, but subject to dynamic forces in the economic, social and cultural spheres that shaped it and keep shaping it". Furthermore, "*UNESCO's approach to managing historic urban landscapes is holistic; it integrates the goals of urban heritage conservation and those of social and economic development. This method sees urban heritage as a social, cultural and economic asset for the development of cities*" (UNESCO 2013, 5). This approach has been also the basis for defining the study of ruins.

3.2. SUSTAINABILITY

Since the 1970's, the concept of sustainability has become increasingly important for recovering built heritage. Its roots in the conservation movement stemmed from the necessity to find *"ways to design, plan and manage that allow essential or desirable resources to be renewed faster than they are destroyed"* (Matero 2011, xvi). In 1987, the first definition of 'sustainable development' was included in the Brundtland Report. It was produced by the World Commission on Environment and Development (WCED), a United Nations agency chaired by Gro Harlem Brundtland, prime minister of Norway at the time. *"Sustainable development is development that meet the needs of the present without compromising the ability of the future generation to meet their own needs"* (WCED 1987, c.2, p.1). This concept was intended for *"integrating economic and ecologic concerns in a long-term development strategy"* (Throsby 2005, 2). Brundtland represented economic, social and environmental concerns as a set of overlapping circles in which sustainable development is the central area (Jones & Evans 2008, 111). These are the three pillars of sustainability that can be achieved only when social equity, economic development and environmental quality are well balanced (Levy 2011, 294).

The idea of sustainability soon merged with the theory of capital: natural and cultural capital. If natural capital was included in sustainable environmental management discussed by the Brundtland Commission, soon, in the 1990s, another commission, the 'World Commission on Culture and Development' sought to extend this concept to culture in a report entitled Our Creative Diversity (WCCD, 1995). The idea of cultural sustainability and the relationship between culture and the environment garnered increasing interest along with the concept of cultural capital and its application to urban cultural heritage (Throsby 2005, 3). Cultural factors interpreted in this way are a fourth pillar of sustainability. Especially in England and Scotland sustainable development policy has taken on a central role in the National Planning Policy framework (2012) (fig. 70).

3.2.1. CULTURAL ASPECTS – VALUES

The word 'culture' has been used in different contexts with many different meanings. Despite some difficulties in interpretation, most recently of an economic nature, Throsby has given quite a clear explanation in his publication, Economy and Culture (2001). It argued that the term 'culture' could be interpreted in two ways: one anthropological or sociological and the other more functional. In the first view, culture is *"a set of attitudes, beliefs, mores, customs, values and practices which are more common to or share by a group"* (4). This group can be identified by different characteristics that find forms in signs, symbols, texts, language, and so on;

70. New Lanark, United Kingdom.
All the activities in the mill village are developed in an environmentally and economically sustainable way for the benefit of the local community and tourism.
© *Elisa Pilia.*

these collaborate to create the identity of the group itself. The second view considers it *"a set of activities that are undertaken by people, and the product of these activities that the author called cultural industries"*. With this definition, he suggested three kinds of activities: creativity in the process of production; the generation and communication of symbols; and their embodiment as intellectual property (4). Although no universality can be claimed by these definitions because of the different modes of expressions of groups in their activities, these interpretations of culture do converge in the statement that *"culture carries with it a concomitant notion of cultural value"* (Throsby 1999, 6). UNESCO and ICOMOS have provided two other significant definitions. The UNESCO convention for the Protection of the World Cultural and Natural Heritage (1972) generally defined 'cultural heritage' as: *"monuments: architectural works, works of monumental sculpture and painting, elements or structures of an archaeological nature, inscriptions, cave dwellings and combinations of features, which are of outstanding universal value from the point of view of history, art or science:*

- *groups of buildings: groups of separate or connected buildings which, because of their architecture, their homogeneity or their place in the landscape, are of outstanding universal value from the point of view of history, art or science;*
- *sites: works of man or the combined works of nature and man, and areas including archaeological sites which are of outstanding universal value from the historical, aesthetic, ethnological or anthropological point of view"* (10).

'Universal value' clearly confers the adjective 'cultural' upon these three heritage categories.

The Burra Charter, adopted by Australia's ICOMOS in 1979, defined cultural heritage places as *"places of cultural significance"* 1), in other words as places with *"aesthetic, historic, scientific, social or spiritual value for past, present or future generations"* (2).

Culture has also been analysed in economic terms. *"If culture can be thought as a system of beliefs, values, customs etc. shared by a group, then cultural interactions among members of other groups can be modelled as transactions or exchanges of symbolic or material goods within an economising framework"* (Throsby 2001, 10). In functional terms, the concept of *"cultural industries"*, coined by Max Horkheimer and Theodor Adorno in 1947, expressed the idea of the cultural economy as any cultural product; it can be considered in an industrial framework like other economic goods.

CULTURAL CAPITAL To express the idea of culture in economy, Throsby proposed the notion of 'cultural capital'. He added it to the previous three forms of capital already developed in economics: physical, human, and natural (1999, 3). Physical capital is the first type recognised and relates to material goods that can produce other goods such as buildings, in our case. Human capital embodies human skills and practices as they contribute to the production of goods. Finally, natural capital was added in the 90s according to the significant economic effect of environmental issues. It considers both renewable and non-renewable resources and plays an important role in sustainability, forming the basis for ecological economics.

The definition of cultural capital stems from the awareness that heritage buildings are also 'capital assets' just as the cultural phenomena carried out by human practices contribute to economic affairs. Before Throsby's codification, the term 'cultural capital' was already implicitly present in different fields of the academic debate. In 1986, the French sociologist Pierre Bourdieu (1930–2002) introduced the notion of capital defined as the "*potential capacity to produce profits and to reproduce itself in identical or expanded forms*" (1986, 241). In his social study on the way in which society is reproduced, he identified three typologies of capital. Economic capital "is immediately and directly convertible into money and may be institutionalised in property rights". Cultural capital "*is convertible, on certain conditions, into economic capital and may be institutionalised in the form of educational qualifications*". Social capital "*made up of social obligation [...], is convertible into economic capital and may be institutionalised for title of nobility*" (Bourdieu 1986, 242). According to this theory, capital can exist in three forms: embodied, as "*external wealth converted into an integral part of the person, into habits for instance, that cannot be purchased or exchanged*"; objectified, "*as a number of properties which are defined only in the relationships with cultural capital in its embodied form*" (50); and institutionalised as form of academic qualification (Bourdieu 1986).

Overall, while economy and culture find their roots in two different systems of thought, the first in individualism, the second in collective relationships, they share conceptual fundamentals in the notion of value as an expression of worth "*in a dynamic and active way*" (Throsby 2001, 20). Thus, the two fields can be linked through the concept of value. As Throsby stated, values are the "*foundation stones*" for the joint consideration of economy and culture, and these values are the foundation of the methodology for the evaluation of ruins. 'Culture', then, refers to the many attributes and values that distinguish a group, society and so on.

In this context, urban ruins are analysed as assets that embody tangible and intangible cultural values: elements that in the urban settlement are able to stimulate the creativity of modern society – composed of modern artists, architectsy – cas conceived by the American urban theorist Richard Florida. Furthermore, cultural capital was considered of paramount importance in the process of policy formation, insofar as it can shape sustainable models based on the cultural and economic values of ruins.

3.2.2. SOCIAL FACTORS – VALUES

The social dimension in urban historic areas is an essential component that includes not only resident communities but also the population that experiences and visits it. The safeguarding of historic areas, when positively planned, should always include the people upon whom a city's dynamism depends. In the Burra Charter (2013), cultural significance is defined as the social or spiritual values that embrace qualities for which a place becomes a spiritual, national and political focus for a group. As mentioned, social equity and social utility are the two goals of sustainable development. These can bring benefits such as the cohesion of communities, increased public value and thus local identity and sense of place. In contrast, negative aspects can result from unbalanced rehabilitation processes.

For instance, the process of gentrification, even if reinvestment in inner areas that have lost their value improves economic and cultural incomes, discourages social equality.

Gentrification, defined as the transformation of working-class or vacant areas in a central city into middle-class residential and/or commercial areas, has become one of the most prevalent urban questions since its birth in London and in east coast USA cities in the 1950s and 1960s (Lees et al. 2008, xv). In the achievement of social equity and sustainable development, an element of significant importance is the 'creative class', defined by the American economist Richard Florida as talented and creative people who are part of the economy's fourth sector, involved in 'the computer software sector, mathematics, engineering, university lecturing and art, media and design' (Tallon 2013, 126). Consequently, economic success depends on cities' capacity to attract and maintain creative class talent. According to Florida, creatives can drive a city's growth and thus its competitiveness. Diversity, tolerance, openness, and the environment are key factors for the presence of this group in cities. In the US, the most successful 'creative' cities are Washington, Boston, Austin, Seattle and San Francisco while in the UK, they are Wokingham, Reading, Cardiff, London, Brighton and Hove. The definition of this list was based on an analysis that measured the proportion of artists, writers, actors, and painters who live in a city to formulate a *"creative index"* that takes into account technology, talent, and tolerance (Florida 2011, 253).

3.2.3. ENVIRONMENTAL ASPECTS – VALUES

The environmental dimension is a main component of sustainable development. This regards the global concern for climate change and the consequent acceleration of the decay of all building materials as well as the abuse of non-renewable natural resources. On the one hand, environmental matters concern the degradation of local historical building materials, both

71. New Lanark, United Kingdom. Landscape and picturesque values have paramount importance for this mill village also close to the Fall of Cycle.
© *Elisa Pilia.*

natural, like stone, and man-made, such as plasters, mortars and bricks, and their protection from natural processes of decay that increase with high pollution levels. This environmental component is identifiable in nature. Nature, also meant as flora and fauna, is the result of the links among local morphology, climate and materials that are unique to each place. This singular aspect also contributes to the process of community identification with its urban spaces. Due to its undeniable contribution, nature becomes one of the key features to assess, either as an impact or as a risk, for example the destructive effects that invasive roots might have on structures, as well as elements of value (fig. 71).

On the other hand, environmental sustainability can be pursued through the reuse of old buildings instead of constructing new and often expensive buildings, saving energy on demolition and reconstruction. Furthermore, historic masonry buildings are usually constructed with durable materials and building systems and are located in areas with well-developed infrastructure, thus reducing the necessity for construction of new infrastructure (Kalman 2015, 88–89).

Once again, both England and Scotland have produced 'sensible guidelines' that favour interventions of physical retrofitting and proper climate change action plans respectively. Life-cycle costing is one of the methods for assessing the cost of the entire building life meaning the "*total capital and operating costs for acquiring, building/improving, and using a building over its full estimated lifespan*" (93).

In the case of urban ruins, their environmental components are mainly placed in the presence of nature: the preservation of their natural qualities and intended aesthetic and identity features of a specific setting. Overall, they can be assessed in terms of their environmental values.

3.2.4. ECONOMIC ASPECTS – VALUES

Economic questions in the conservation field began to be considered in the 1970s and 80s, with the aim of rendering this sector self-sufficient (Kalman 2015, 95). In the UK and the USA, these events can be tied to entrepreneurial approaches promoted by Margaret Thatcher and Ronald Regan who supported policies with "*private developers in 'quasi-public' redevelopment corporations*" (Tallon 2013, 45). Public-private partnerships became a characteristic of the two policies and since then, the economy has remained a key point in all Western countries.

Considering the previously discussed international policies of conservation and preservation, it is undeniable that the USA is the nation with the highest level of interest in the preservation economy with the foundation of the National Trust for Historic preservation in 1970s and the definition of the Main Street Approach. In the academic world, the first significant study regarding economics in urban conservation dated from 1988 and was penned by the Englishman Nathaniel Lichfield. For the first time, he introduced the concept of the urban system as *"a complex collection of diverse inter-independent resources"* (Lichfield 1988, 39) in which individuals or groups participate in activities; thus these resources need a kind of management to make best use of their life-cycle potential. This was called urban management. The components of this process can be summarised by the following dimensions: property owners, public or private, who have unique characteristics and relationships with their settings, which are geographical and legal and contribute to the definition of the concept of 'proprietary land unit'; the proprietary land unit that can involve a wide geographical area fragmented in several parcels. Thus, the final management decisions for an entire area could be made by the results of the decisions taken in the singular parcels; the properties seen not only in their ownership function but also as a whole concept composed of the community in the broadest sense of the term with their physical, social and economic components; urban amenities and services require specialist and general management strategies by the local government and local authorities; urban and regional planning should guarantee that all decisions are made in accordance with plans and the needs of the community; an extended development planning process and an organised management framework should deal with economic plans and strategies regarding the entire administrative and functional area as well as several fragmented parcels.

In such economic analysis, management and planning activities are strictly interrelated and are, at the same time, different because of the responsible sectorial agencies and the skills and competencies that they require. On the one hand, management is carried out by directors, accountants and administrators whose role it is to translate the needs of the urban system into long-term policies, strategies and plans. On the other, urban and regional planners, working with other skilled figures like developers, conservationists and social scientists, designs plans on the basis of management decisions. The roles overlap in the planning and management process even if they are not exempt from conflicts.

Conservation is a field that must be considered in terms of urban management as it concerns natural, human and man-made resources. While natural assets have been discussed, human resources concern the society that inhabits an urban system and, as a consequence, benefits from the conservation of the tangible and intangible elements that characterise it. Furthermore, conservation means preserving a legacy from the past and at the same time defining new development, which will be linked to and influenced by it.

Development and conservation are not enemies but they must be mutually supportive. Conservation needs both *"continuity and change"* (Lichfield 1988, 56). Built heritage as a resource has a cost and a value. While historic costs cannot be affected by future acts, the values, measured by costs, are profoundly influenced by management policies. For this reason, the manager's role is to increase and make the best use of the possible benefits deriving from these structures. Economic values are essential in order for valuable decision-making for the management of historical places to come about. As already seen, different nations have different approaches and rules for the preservation and conservation of historic urban areas and there is no codified approach in the management and planning of conservation areas.

Two levels of analysis that economists have developed can be related to two planning levels: macro-analysis linked to macro planning and the micro-analysis linked to micro planning (Lichfield 1988; Throsby 2001; Kalman 2015).

MACRO PLANNING ANALYSES The first process in economic analysis is macro planning. It seeks to understand the degree and causes of obsolescence of the overall built heritage. It is important to define whether this obsolescence is static, growing or declining by analysing historical trends, the implication of planning proposals and their effects (Lichfield 1988, 55). This macro level should create an inventory in order to clarify the object of the management process and understand the reasons underlying 'market failure' for which government intervention is required. The inventory can be a tool: an expression of cultural values that contains a preliminary screening of new possible uses, the degree of obsolescence of the structures and possible interventions. This analysis should be carried out in parallel with other urban considerations or questions such as community demographics, in terms of number of residents, and the commercial and industrial activities that are at the basis of the economy of the urban area, as well as how a project can be seen as a resource for the area and the way in which investment can be used to improve the economy. Such issues should be investigated in the previous and current plans, programmes and policies designed for the area, on the national, regional and local levels.

Cost-benefit analysis is a widespread tool used by governments and businesses in decision-making. Every investment regarding the built heritage has the aim of finding the right balance between the amount of resources and services that will be consumed. In other words, it needs to achieve the best 'value for money', a balance between benefits, values for consumers, and costs involved in the project. In this research, while costs are easily estimable because they are quantifiable in terms of resources used, such as time, prices and so on, the values of the benefits are difficult to estimate because of the different capacity of the resources used to create them. This capacity, called 'utility' by Lichfield, has been defined as *"the quality in commodities that makes individuals want to buy them, and the fact that individuals want to by commodities show that they are utility"* (Lichfield 1988, 118). These values could be considered subjective and personal because cost changes according to different perceptions. At the same time, stakeholders are not free to invest incomes as they prefer because there is a government that, in accordance with their programmes and policies, establishes the resources to be spent, how they give them the best value for money and, mostly importantly, where they should be spent.

In this economic calculus, other components are the interests that all subjects involved (public or private) can have in a specific area or building. Interests are the basis for all the decisions that will be made. They can differ in terms of desired goals: not only financial but also profitability or satisfaction with production or consumer services. For that reason, several different interests can bring conflicting decisions that need *"to be balanced by institutional arrangements in the management of the property"* (Lichfield 1988, 121).

Economic impact studies are used in economic macro analysis for measuring the quantitative effects of spending, in other words the amount of money needed for acquiring a building, and the impacts of this cost. This is useful for evaluating a proposed policy. In summary, monetary spending is related to construction costs and property value whereas non-market evaluations that can have important benefits on sociocultural and environmental sustainability are completely neglected (Kalman 2015, 104).

MICRO PLANNING ANALYSES Micro planning analyses investigate in greater detail the current and future condition of the project. This analysis should include: historic-architectonic analysis of the building; assessment of the heritage values for each building and for the buildings that might be affected by the intervention; in-depth analysis of the buildings in their contexts; definition of possible stakeholders and beneficiaries who might be involved in the process; analysis of the neighbouring areas and possible interrelations with future plans. Overall, these analyses have the goal of valorising individual assets and in particular their cultural capital that, as already seen (3. 2. 1.), is composed of economic and cultural values. The problem with this evaluation is that the two components are based on different value systems. If the determination of economic value has been established in the literature, cultural values are still difficult to quantify (Throsby 2002, 105). In this context, urban heritage tourism has been recognised as an activity for increasing both the cultural and economic value of a given area.

URBAN TOURISM Urban tourism has been used in local economy policy as a key element for the regeneration of historic neighbourhoods, taking advantage of their historic character, ambience and sense of place (Tiesdell et al., 1996, 68). This kind of tourism has become a significant economic activity in historic urban areas all over the world, with both positive and negative consequences in terms of authenticity and sustainability. A starting point for this trend can be found in 1975, when the European Architectural Heritage Year (EAHY), born for focusing European attention on the topic of conservation (Delafons, 1997, 110), placed emphasis on the protection and enhancement of buildings and areas. In particular, it stimulated historic interest, the conservation of the features of old towns and fostered a living role for all the ancient buildings in contemporary society (Delafons, 1997, 111). As a consequence, European municipal authorities began to promote the preservation of their historic areas and middle-class residents began to re-think historic centres as desirable places to live (Orbasli, 2000a, 7). In the 1980s, the phenomenon grew considerably with the promotion of tourism in post-industrial cities where the crisis relating to decommissioned industries and to high unemployment gravely impacted the image of inner cities. Local authorities, that saw cultural activities as the heart of future revitalisation supported tourism, perceived as a growing industry (figg.72–73). The reconstruction of this image and the replacement of negative perceptions were pursued, emphasising the distinctive characteristics and specific differences of each place. That process, called 'place marketing', was developed in the USA. It was defined as the activity that *"has been linked primarily to local economic development, the promotion of place and the encouragement of public-private partnerships to achieve regeneration"* (Paddison, 1993, 340). Thus, the main goal of place marketing is not only to promote a city's image but also to make it more desirable for the market through the creation of a distinct place-identity. Inevitably, increased environmental quality encourages the resident community to take pride in their area and consequently, increases economic value. The public and private sectors are usually intricately linked in these types of strategies. While the public sector must protect and preserve the physical and cultural environment, private businesses take part in the creation of a highly competitive market that seeks to promote an urban area with the coordination of local governments. Therefore, a successful tourism strategy can be only achieved through the mutual collaboration of these two parties (Tiesdell et al., 1996, 71). This strategy is even more successful in the US, where the interaction between the public and private sectors involves not only economic and promotional issues in tourism, but also the preservation and re-enhancement of cultural heritage through activities of patronage and philanthropy (Mugayar 2007, 139). Worldwide, urban

72. Manchester, United Kingdom.
The Museums of Science Industry, realised in the Manchester Liverpool Railway in the Castlefield quarter. Brick structures.
© Elisa Pilia.

73. Manchester, United Kingdom.
The steel frame building of the former Manchester Liverpool Railway, now the Museums of Science Industry.
© Elisa Pilia.

tourism gains advantages from the values of cultural heritage that we recognise today. It also influences urban conservation, defining the demand for places that should be valued for their cultural tourism potential. As Aylin Orbasli (2000a, 8) wrote, *"tourism represents a clean economic activity and employment opportunity" for all local authorities that see it as a "potential source of finance and investment"* to preserve and protect both buildings and urban space. Furthermore, it has been defined as a new economy in which history and culture can be considered two valuable commodities (9). Tourism is an indirect financial resource and a strong vehicle for the regeneration of historic cities, as it opens new possible investments through the creation of leisure and entertainment activities. In contrast, the important role of conservation in cultural tourism is undeniable, and this kind of tourism could not exist without it. Several issues emerge from this duality; one, for instance, concerns 'authenticity' (fig. 74). In fact, the sense of place identity driven by the place-marketing trend gave origins to an image-based approach focusing its attention on the 'exterior' conservation and restoration of historic buildings, streetscapes and townscapes. The perception of place assumes paramount importance in visitor expectations; building façades have the task of satisfying tourist needs even if sacrificing an area's authenticity. Tourists focus their experience on the physical and exterior aspects of buildings so that the façade becomes the region on display and the element to preserve and restore through façadism approaches. Several European cities have focused attention on their urban image and particularly deploying façade-based approach. Germany and Poland can be considered two of the countries in which that approach became popular during the second post-war reconstruction. For instance, as we know, Frankfurt and Warsaw (fig.75), based their policies on false historical reconstructions. Authenticity raises significant questions in the USA as well where the general trend in conservation leads to the restoration and reconstruction of a previous heritage image, an arbitrary image of the city. Examples can be seen in Riverside, Georgia, whose history was invented in 1998 for real estate investment ends (Brink, 1998, 61). Another important issue regards sustainability in its different forms. First, in terms of heritage preservation, we might consider environmental sustainability: the increase in numbers of visitors could imply a great risk of decay for the artefacts and for the urban environment, with consequences on both tangible and intangible heritage (Porfiryou 2010, 332). Second, sociological issues emerge when inhabitants raise such tourism problems as vehicular traffic or parking (Brink, 1998, 61). Yet at the same time, tourism could lead to the economic sustainability of historic conservation. Finally, as already mentioned, direct or indirect economic benefits allow greater preservation of cultural heritage and the urban environment, financing protection measures.

74. Stirling, United Kingdom.
View of the Caste. The Great Hall, in yellow tint, is a facsimile reconstruction (1997 – 1998) for touristic purposes.
© *Elisa Pilia.*

75. Warsaw, Poland.
Post-war façadism in the old town Market Place.
© *Francesca Muliiri.*

3.3. AESTHETIC ISSUES. DEALING WITH THE 'LACUNA'

Interventions on urban ruins must also face aesthetic matters both on the architectural and urban levels.

According to Brandi, the conservation of ruins is not only related to an historic value or, but also to their aesthetic value with ruins as a *"piece of art"* (Brandi 1977, 39) with their picturesque surrounds. In fact, aesthetically speaking two are the possible approaches. The first one considers 'rudero' as *"every remains of an artistic work that cannot be recomposed in its potential unity without creating a copy or an imitation"* (39–40). In this view, 'artistic ruins' cannot be reintegrated.

A second approach, on the other hand, is concerned with ruins integrated into an urban or landscape context where they contribute to the general ambiance of the area. In this case, the concept of *rudero* is connected to another artistic element, city or landscape, which is influenced by it and from which the ruin receives its connotation. Ruins can thus qualify urban space as elements not linked to its potential unity but to its mutilated condition that, working with its context, creates a unique 'work of art' (figg.76–79). As Brandi said, over time these monuments have acquired *"an indissoluble facies"* that should be, as in the previous approach, conserved. Giovanni Carbonara (1976, 1996, 2011) also made an important contribution to the debate regarding aesthetic issues of re-integrating the image of fragmented architectures like ruins. He began his observations by taking into account the concepts of *'monument as a document of art and history'* (1996) and the Brandi dualism of the historical and aesthetic approaches for defining this idea of intervention. He considered that if the first assertion, shared by Boito and Giovannoni, was the main feature of scientific restoration thought for the first half of the 20th century, immediately after the war it was no longer universally applicable, as already seen.

The artistic and historical characteristics of the monuments themselves were not significant enough to guide an intervention on a ruin. In addition, the philological approach, careful in understanding evolutionary, stylistic, architectural and artistic aspects, demonstrated that this concept, relating to the historical aspects of the monument, was not sufficient to justify an intervention. As Bonelli said, restoration is not only a critical act but it is also a creative act and pure interest in authenticity cannot be considered to be accepted. He argued, *"an architecture is not only a document but is, above all, an act whose form is the total expression of a spiritual world. [...] For our culture, because of its artistic significance, it represents the highest form"* (Bonelli 1963, 347).

For these reasons, Carbonara argued that the dilemma between conservation and restoration, and between historical and aesthetic approaches should face critical action and choice in each instance.

76. London, United Kingdom.
The ruins of the medieval St. Alphage Church tower are central part of a wider contemporary project in London Wall Place.
© *Elisa Pilia.*

The original monument cannot be resurrected but we can work by reusing its fragments as starting points for a new, original creation that respects the needs of conservation. It can be achieved by creating a *figurative circuit* (Carbonara 1996, 240) when old remains are juxtaposed to new elements. He claimed that *"we would not have the monument of old but a monument that emerges anew – an independent architectural expression, even if fragmentary, that respects the basic integrity of what the past has handed down to us"* (Carbonara 1996, 240). In this way, a new figurative context derives *"from placing the object in a new artistic work, so the object becomes part of the structure into which it is inserted, by maintaining an independent legibility and by joining with other new elements"*. Carbonara compares that process to a museum, where singular objects are presented individually as a part of a new architecture that contains and protects them.

Overall, ruins are aesthetically complicated because of their fragmentary and incomplete nature, not only relating to the fabric in itself but also to a context like the urban one where the skyline as well as the townscape and streetscape contribute to the definition of a distinctive image: the city.

77. London, United Kingdom.
Frontal view of the ruins.
© *Elisa Pilia.*

On page 143:
78. London, United Kingdom.
Ruins and pedestrian connections between buildings.
© *Elisa Pilia.*

79. London, United Kingdom.
View from the elevated walkway.
© *Elisa Pilia.*

"NO, I WOULDN,T CALL THEM RUINS.
I PREFER NOT TO MAKE VALUE JUDGEMENTS".

Cartoon by Handelsman from Punch (3 February 1982),
p. 203. (Ginsberg 2004, 285)

PART III
A METHODOLOGY FOR RUINS

One of the main goals set out for the research project has been to define a transdisciplinary methodology for the study and definition of sustainable interventions on urban ruins, especially those located in historical centres, considering the wide range of issues involved in defining the nature of these artefacts and in understanding their strategic and complex contexts. This goal is pursued based on the preliminary study concerning the historical evolution of the concept of ruin (PART I) and deep investigation into contemporary theoretical and practical urban questions linked to their reuse (PART II). The analysis of policies for the regeneration of historical centres, of the cultural, social, environmental, and economic aspects correlated with sustainable development and of the relative aesthetic issues also contributes to defining methods, techniques and typologies of heritage values. Also important is the comparison and examination of established and significant conservation planning and architectural methodologies in Italy (De Martino 2004; Deplano 2008; Giambruno 2002; Giannattasio 2009; Giannattasio, Grillo & Fiorino 2015; Varagnoli 2005; Zoppi 2001), the United Kingdom (Clark 2001; Historical Scotland 2000; Heritage Brunch 2005; English Heritage 2012), the United States (Mason 2002; de la Torre, 2000, 2002) Australia (Heritage Council of Western Australia 2002; Keer 2013) and other scientific contributions (Stephenson 2008; Freheidman and Kahalaf 2016).

Then, this methodology has been tested and refined in the historical centre of Cagliari in order to identify sustainable guidelines specifically oriented toward conservation, reuse and improvement of ruined architecture on the basis of the values and meanings that they embody. This means proceeding with 'respect' for them, taking into account their features, state of conservation, potential as well as the needs of their neighbourhoods, community opinions and possible compatible re-uses.

A transdisciplinary, holistic and sustainable methodology is presented following a research overview and a critical examination of the current technical and value-based procedures.

1. RESEARCH DESIGN: AN OVERVIEW

The definition of a methodology for the reuse and the preservation of urban ruins in historical urban areas was based on three inspiring principles. It was to be holistic, transdisciplinary and sustainable. A holistic approach is necessary because urban places are characterised by several interconnected theoretical issues that can be explained only when considered in relation to the whole. Thus, the method seeks to face ruins as part of the city, understood as a dynamic organism that should be investigated in its entirety. The transdisciplinary attribute is essential for the wide range of disciplines involved in the approach. Structures should not only be investigated from an architectural point of view but also in relationship to their urban, anthropological and environmental connections, as well as economic aspects and social factors. The method's third key component is sustainability, which, as already seen in PART II (3.2), is a fundamental element in heritage conservation. In this sense, the proposed methodology was designed in order to gear policies toward a new degree of sustainability in reuse and conservation.

In addition, the research considered tangible and intangible values deeply, understanding and emphasising ruins' uniqueness and specificities. Attention to non-material values together with material aspects is a key concept already codified in several UNESCO conventions. Among the many, it is useful to recall The World Heritage Convention (1972), The Convention for the Safeguarding of the Intangible Cultural Heritage (2003), some ICOMOS charters, the Venice Charter (1964), and the Australian Burra Charter (2013b), all characterised by a value-based approach to the conservation of cultural places. If the material values, based on measurable characteristics of built heritage, can be easily investigated by means of well-codified analysis protocols, on the contrary, intangible values are generally less-considered due to the complexity of their identification and codification. But this does not mean that they should be ignored; their importance is essential for the overall knowledge and understanding of ruined urban architectures.

The methodology designed here stems mainly from the union of Italian restoration culture and models deployed in Anglo-Saxon countries: the USA, the UK, Australia, New Zealand and Canada which share the same British legal tradition. The former provides high quality in the knowledge protocol regarding architectural artefacts insofar as it is based on a long tradition in the restoration field and places unique attention on the materials signs, historic symbols and conservation of the authenticity of the building fabric. It generally supports 'authentic conservation', in the Ruskinian sense, preserving the identity of places.

Nevertheless, this often leads to non-intervention practices or demolitions that are unable to face the definition of new uses correctly. Such an approach can be defined as technical because of its specialised protocols based on the accurate analysis of a building fabric.

The latter identifies a more effective process of conservation and preservation intended as sociocultural practices composed of both history and planning. In fact, the *"ultimate goal is not fixing or saving old buildings but rather creating places where people can live well and connect to meaningful narratives about history, culture and identity"* (Kaufman 2009, 1). This approach passes through the maintenance and enhancement of *"the values embodied by the heritage with physical intervention or treatment"* (DeLa Torre 2000, 7). Partially technical in its detailed investigation of the urban context, the approach consists mainly of the so-called 'value – based' method based on deep investigation of the significance and meaning of places. In keeping with these two models, the methodology designed here provides innovative guidelines for the reuse of ruined buildings based on full knowledge and understanding of the urban and architectural questions. Then, it moves to the subsequent assessment of values and analysis of needs, resources, and opportunities by means of, and comparisons with, other case studies.

It also seeks to overcome methodological difficulties in this last phase of the assessment that stem from three main problems: the different nature of values, their continuous variation in relation to their context, and the possible conflicts among them. In addition, heritage values are subjective as they can be seen from the different viewpoints of various stakeholders and professionals (architects, archaeologists, historian, economists, sociologists); they can be interpreted and assessed in different ways and from different perspectives (Mason 2002, 9). Thus, the research might have great impact on the possible solution to the aforementioned issues, offering appropriate methods and tools based on an *ad-hoc* approach to structures in state of ruination. The balanced integration among, and comparison of, the Italian and English traditions might help lead to an innovative transdisciplinary and holistic approach that considers historical ruined structures as key elements to be enhanced through sustainable courses of conservation or transformation.

The two basic research questions regard: 1) how to enhance the meanings of those aspects of the built environment which are often misunderstood due to their fragmentation and incompleteness and, as a result, their perception as places of abandonment and negligence and 2) how to transmit the historical values embodied in these ruins to the future by means of contemporary conservation and preservation projects. These questions have been resolved through a combination of technical and value-based approaches, specifically designed for urban heritage in state of ruins in which abstract concepts relating to immateriality, sensuality, memory, absence, and power are part of their complex heritage values. Ethnographic methods and tools supported the identification and assessment of these values by investigating social and economic questions.

2. FROM CURRENT METHODOLOGIES TO A NEW PROTOCOL FOR INTERVENTION

The proposal for a new methodology began with a critical analysis and evaluation of the methodologies currently used for the investigation of urban and architectural assets and for the assessment of their tangible and intangible values. As already mentioned, the method seeks to explore different aspects and issues relating to ruined structures in urban contexts. This involves several scientific and disciplinary areas like urban and architectural conservation, archaeology, anthropology, sociology, and economy, which need to be understood and analysed in keeping with their specific methodologies. The Italian and the English approaches are merged to reach a final, multidisciplinary 'blended approach'.

2.1. TECHNICAL APPROACHES

This approach defines the analyses focusing on the knowledge of the context and building structures. Intervening on existing architecture always implies studying its context. Every building project needs background knowledge and understanding of the existing urban spaces and structures (Schwalbach 2008, 9) insofar as it deals with a historical but, at the same time, contemporary and dynamic environment in continuous development: the city.

The study of the urban layers has developed greatly since the 1960s with the definition of a proper urban conservation methodology. This area-based approach is extremely important for the definition of a context's spatial evolution, its existing overall image, planned development and future trends. Furthermore, it is important for the investigation of different factors or issues regarding historic places, as previously noted. Spatial, social, economic, and aesthetic factors define a context and shape design. Urban analysis involves different levels of studies that investigate both what is visible and invisible in the city from the aesthetic and scientific points of view (Schwalbach 2008). This means considering not only its morphology, but also its visual perception through the lens of the local community. According to the Italian and Anglo-Saxon approaches and experiences, analyses usually include the following steps: morphological description of the context; analysis of the historical development of the areas; study of the urban stratigraphies for the comprehension of the evolution of the built environment and the analysis of their construction; street networks; plot system; analysis of land use structures, open and green spaces; understanding of historical and current functions; analysis of social space. Urban analyses create a figurative representation of an area for future urban planning measures or specific building intervention. However, they cannot properly investigate social and economic aspects that should be taken into account as bases for planning in historical urban contexts. Consultation and collaboration with the community, local authorities and other parties involved in urban life are of paramount importance for correct sustainable urban development. Analyses focused on the urban context constitute the premises for analytically studying the buildings that will be the objects of design.

The Italian approach, mainly focused on the conservation of the building's historical materials, contributed significantly to this phase of analysis. In the 20th century, different schools of thought defined knowledge protocols that comprise the combination and interoperability of different disciplines focusing attention on architecture's dimensional, material and constructive aspects.

The long tradition of architectural conservation studies defined a sectorial and detailed protocol for the study of structures, beginning with measured drawings. Therefore, the urban fabric is explored according to a knowledge protocol that comprises historic and documentary examinations, analysis of materials, decay and building techniques, and structural and diagnostic investigations. These steps can have different degrees of detail according to the importance of and interest in the work of architecture; they are the bases for designing the project.

In Sardinia, the School of Architecture in Cagliari has recently defined a transdisciplinary process of investigation according to the different cultural heritage typologies present in the local context. As for heritage in state of ruination, this methodology was tested on three types of ruins: coastal towers investigated in the ForAccess project (Giannattasio and Grillo 2001; Giannattasio, Grillo and Murru 2017); defence heritage (Fiorino and Pintus 2015; Giannattasio, Grillo, Pilia and Pirisino 2016; Pilia and Pirisino 2016); and rural churches, examined in the project Ecclesia Fabbrica in collaboration with the Province of Nuoro (Fiorino and Concu 2013; Fiorino, Giannattasio and Grillo 2015; Fiorino, Grillo and Pilia 2015, 2016). Today, urban and building analyses are well-codified and provide the technical bases for the definition of the design, which should take into account the results of such analyses.

2.2. VALUE-BASED APPROACHES

The value-based approach has increased in popularity since the 1990s. It was theoretically investigated by several international committees and authors: (Riegl 1902; Australia ICOMOS 1979, 2013; Lipe 1984; Darvill 1995; Carver 1996; Frey 1997; Ashley-Smith 1999; Pye 2001; Throsby 2001; Mason 2002; Feilden 2003; Keene 2005; Appelbaum 2007; English Heritage 2008; Orbasli 2008; Stephenson 2008; Stubbs 2009; Gòmez Robles 2010; Szmelter 2010; ICOMOS New Zealand 2010; Lertcharnit 2010; Fredheim & Khalaf 2016); and practically adopted for a wide range of heritage typologies such as historical buildings, archaeological sites, and the urban and rural landscape, in order to identify, sustain and enhance their significance (Fredheim & Khalaf 2016, 466). The method is based on the identification of the values embodied in the heritage and in their final assessment. Here 'values' are intended as the real and potential positive qualities and characteristics (de la Torre & Mason 2002, 7). Orbasli defined 'values' as *"the qualities and characteristics that different users and different societies place on the cultural heritage at different times"* (2008, 38). In fact, they can change according to historical events and groups of people.

Values define the significance of heritage (de la Torre 2000, 7) suggesting possible future uses and benefits. In some contexts, values have been formalised; in Australia, the ICOMOS Burra Charter (2013) was the result of several years of reviews; in England, the guide for assessment written by Heritage Collection Council (2001) became the English Heritage in 2008 defining precise categories. While ratified only in Australia the former has become a guide for practice throughout the English-speaking world. Its innovation is expressed in the new concept of cultural significance associated with places. It is meant as *"aesthetic, historic, scientific, social or spiritual value for past, present or future generations. It is embodied in the place itself, its fabric, setting, use, associations, meanings, records, related places and related objects"* (Burra Charter 2013, 2). Furthermore, it emphasises the concept of pluralistic values in places of all cultures and values to be preserved without distinction (art. 5.1).

The Burra Charter process is a series of investigations, decisions and actions made up of understanding the meaning of place and its cultural significance, the development of policies and management in keeping with these policies. It defines conservation processes and practices.

The latter is the English value-based model. It focuses on sustainable management of the historic context, *"set out an approach to making decisions and offering guidance about all aspects of the historic environment, and for reconciling its protection with the economic and social needs and aspirations of the people who live in it"* (English Heritage 2008a, 13). It identifies six conservation principles and focuses on understanding values divided into four categories: evidential, historical, aesthetic, and community-based. The assessment of these values leads to the management of change and possible interventions. Overall, both processes enunciate Conservation Principles for maintaining cultural significance. Even if widely used, these approaches have recently received criticism from scholars (Rudolff 2006; Poulios 2010,2014; Walter 2013; Fredheim and Khalaf 2016) for the weaknesses both in the classification of the typologies of values, impossible to define and apply universally, as well as in its theory, which seems to define decisions through an incomplete understanding of heritage values.

Criticism of the typologies of values stems from an inability to grasp the full range of factors that characterise the heritage, leading to incorrect conservation decisions. Recently Fredheim and Khalaf proposed an interesting alternative (2016). They asserted that conservation should be a holistic method that evaluates every aspect of the object under assessment. They argued that none of the current approaches (Burra Charter, English Heritage) considers values as qualities which should be recognised in a specific context like an urban environment in continual change, while taking into account the dynamism of places.

Moreover, the meaning that economists and cultural experts give to the term 'value' is different. On the one hand, economists claim that values are benefits generated by use. On the other, different cultural professionals support the idea that heritage should have a value even if not in use, such as ruins. This can be considered a 'potential value' that cannot be quantified. Starting from these critiques and from the consideration that the classification of values is inevitably a failure, they proposed a holistic values-based approach, which overcomes the previous theory stating that values are often based on incomplete interpretation of heritage. It is composed of three steps: 1) identification of the *features of significance* in order to understand what heritage is; 2) definition of aspects of values for understanding why this heritage is important; 3) identification of degrees of significance according to qualifiers of values. Having analysed the previous theories based on the identification and assessment of values, this model, tested on heritage in general, based its cornerstones on Stephenson's (2008) previous study of landscape heritage using The Cultural Value Model.

As the author wrote it *"offers an integrated conceptual framework for understanding the potential range of values that might be present within a landscape, and the potential dynamics between these values"* (127), considering how heritage is perceived by both experts and non-experts alike (Fredheim and Khalaf 2016, 462). In that method 'form, practice and relationships' are the three heritage features that are continuously changing in a landscape. While form represents the tangible and material aspect of a building, relationships and practices are the two aspects that embody intangibility or immateriality. The landscape is seen in its dynamism in which present values, called 'surface values' are the result of 'embedded values' that come from the past. Thus, time takes on overriding importance in the assessment of values.

Fredheim and Khalaf added other *aspects of values:* associative, sensory, evidential, and functionary (2016, 473) in order to define how values become important. Regarding the associative aspects, all values that express connections between people, events, places, and practices represent 'traditional values', which, due to their associative properties such as those tied to history and memory, can be recognised by expert and non-experts. Sensory aspects derive from aesthetic considerations and subjective concepts of beauty. Evidentiary aspects consist of evidence from the structures in order to highlight singular features that could be useful for further scientific and other research. Finally, functional aspects are considered *"crucial for justifying preservation"* (474). With no proper function, archaeological remains are associated with educational value, in other words they are tools that benefit the field of knowledge. The last three aspects can only be assessed by experts.

In this way, heritage 'fabric' consists of forms, relationships and practices broken down into four value categories. There is no category reserved for 'social' or 'common' values, because, while appearing to include non-expert values, *"the inclusion of these categories has tended to separate and marginalise these values in practice"* (474). In general, these categories are excluded because it is held that significance should be indicated by someone who can fully understand the interpretations described above. *Qualifiers* are defined to identify which aspects of such values are the mostly significant. Authenticity, rarity and condition are examples of qualifiers that *"are not sources of significance, but they can cause perceptions of significance to increase or decrease"* (475) and can determine degree of significance.

In summary, this method mainly focuses on why heritage is significant, rather than understanding how heritage is identified, perceived, experienced, and used and by whom. At the same time, *"it is based on a broad, dialogical and symmetrical understanding of heritage"* according to Stephenson's Cultural Value Model and it once more recognises the identification and interpretation of values as basic actions in the decision-making process.

2.3. CRITICAL NOTES

With their strengths and weakness, all such models were the theoretical bases of the methodology designed for urban heritage in a state of ruin. The concept of value expressed by De la Torre (2002) and Orbasli (2008a) was considered fundamental in the analysis of ruins due to their uselessness and disuse. In this sense, ruins play a plural role. They can be not only material and documentary objects but also powerful symbols for society, on the same level as other monumental cultural heritage. The multifaceted nature of ruins leads the methodology to consider values through two different viewpoints: anthropological, environmental and economic. The definition of the typologies of values seems, in this context, the most effective way to characterise these 'apparently unmeaning' ruins and to steer stakeholders toward the best sustainable approach. The different languages and viewpoint of the various disciplines and investors imply conceptual and practical difficulties linked to the consequent subjectivity of interpretation. Again, this subjectivity requires the codification of values that should consider all aspects: associative, sensorial, evidential, and functional as systemised by Fredheim and Khalaf (2016). It should also consider their dynamism and temporality, their features such as form, relationships and practices that evolved in the past, but are deeply-rooted in the present and must be preserved and transmitted to future generations. Moreover, all expert and non-expert parties involved should be taken into account, as well as all their interests, with the aim of overcoming possible social and economic conflicts. The technical and value-based approaches provided the theoretical background for the definition of my methodology. On the one hand, on the urban and building levels, the technical approach delineates the historic and scientific (tangible) framework for the definition of the practical guidelines for intervention. On the other hand, the value-based approach also considers intangible aspects tied to the ruined buildings.

The three influential valued-based approaches taken under consideration for the definition of the method were mainly the American research reports compiled and edited by Marta de la Torre for The Getty Conservation Institute (2000; 2002); the Australian Burra Charter; and Ruins, a guide to conservation and management edited by the Australian Heritage Council (2013) and the English Heritage model (2008). Other studies also influenced the protocol. In fact, Stephenson's value-based approach can also be applied to this particular category of heritage (meaning ruins, and not only landscape heritage) insofar as dynamism and temporality are two key features that characterise ruins, structures that, even if at the end of their cycle of life, are in continually changing within historical centres. Relationships between community and 'these forms' should be investigated while taking into account the 'practices' supporting their abandonment such as the creation of illegal parking, places of rubbish/waste and so on.

The Fredheim and Khalaf model can only partially be accepted for this category of heritage. If, on the one hand, they include features of values and aspects that state why these features are significant, on the other hand, they totally neglect the role of the community and its participation in the process of reuse and redefinition, as well as the ways in which this can be carried out. Following the Stephenson Cultural Values Model, this holistic understanding of ruins' values involves the participation of communities as well as tools and methods from different disciplines. 'Intangible' values are difficult to analyse. For this reason, they are often not considered. But they do play an important role in assessment, improving the identity and the value of often forgotten heritage categories. An interesting concept is the value qualifier that can contribute to quantifying the degree of significance supporting the understanding of the most important values to enhance, and could help define the extent of intervention and the degree of urgency in the final proposal.

3. PROPOSAL FOR A HOLISTIC AND TRANSDISCIPLINARY APPROACH

This research project seeks to transcend the weaknesses of the approaches examined, considering the tangible qualities and characteristics of urban heritage in state of ruins, emphasising the role of the intangible aspects that cannot be quantified, as well as considering the entire urban context and its far-ranging issues. For these reasons, the method proposes a 'transdisciplinary approach', intended not only as the integration of knowledge of a specific research topic but also as the assimilation of reciprocal bodies of knowledge, overcoming the concepts of multidisciplinary and interdisciplinary work (Marzocca 2014, 22). In such an approach, there are no boundaries between sectorial disciplines, but exhaustive and complete comprehension of the ruin. The methodology is conceived on three levels. The first 'macro level' considers the ruin as an 'urban piece' that metaphorically composes the city's whole 'puzzle'. It faces urban issues and investigates the urban context. It studies all aspects relating to that context; ruins are considered the results of human and natural events and practices after years of implementation policies and urban dynamics. Their new role within sustainable strategies can only be defined after in-depth analysis of the features and issues that characterise the local context.

The second 'micro level' considers the ruin as a 'document in stone' according to Hugo's previously mentioned definition of the city as 'book of stone'. It analyses the architectural, material, chronological, and structural aspects and is strictly related to the investigation of the building fabric in its historic, morphological, material, and technological aspects through an archaeometric approach that seems to be the most suitable for the anatomical knowledge of the structures. This line of inquiry, consisting of traditional and innovative tools, considers ruins as educational and benchmarking instruments that, through their study, can bear important information both for understanding how a structure is made, and consequently for defining a correct conservation and design project. Moreover, this approach identifies possible typological and dimensional constants referring to a specific geological context and period. Thus, these constants might also be useful tools for comparing and dating coeval structures, such as other *"minor works of architecture"* that are difficult to date (Fiorino and Pilia 2015; Giannattasio et al, 2016; Pilia and Pirisino 2016). This is relevant to the case of Cagliari where all urban ruins are stratified sites dating from before the 19th century and built with local materials and building techniques.

These two levels of investigation, typical urban and architectural conservation methodologies, are followed by a third level, a value-based analysis that assesses the significance of ruins, called 'ruin as treasured urban element'. After the analyses of the context and the structures, the method proposes

TRANSDISCIPLINARY METHODOLOGY

STEP 1 MACRO LEVEL ANALYSIS / RUIN AS 'URBAN TILE'

1) Analysis of urban morphology and history.
2) Urban surveys. Geometric knowledge and localisation.
3) Study of planning legislation, strategic plans, and urban analyses.

STEP 2 MICRO LEVEL ANALYSIS / RUIN AS 'STONE DOCUMENT'

1) Indirect analysis:
- Consultation of archival, bibliographic and iconographic sources, memorials of uses, traditions, and changes and practices.
2) Direct investigations:
- Geomatic survey;
- Archaeometric analyses (stratigraphic analysis, minero-petrographic analysis of natural and artificial materials, study of building techniques);
- Digital investigations for sensitive knowledge.

STEP 3 ASSESSMENT / RUIN AS 'TREASURED URBAN ELEMENT'

1) From the analysis of the fabric.
2) From the stakeholders point of view.
3) Individuation of characters-defining elements and assessment of values.
3) Statement of significance.
4) SWOT analysis.

STEP 4 GUIDELINES FOR NEW USES / RUIN AS 'OPPORTUNITY'

1) Identification of local current approaches.
2) Definition of new contemporary values.
3) Definition of compatible interventions and new uses.

80. Scheme of the transdisciplinary methodology.
© Elisa Pilia.

the identification of heritage values. They are conceived according to the Cultural Values Model previously illustrated and assessed through a transdisciplinary process that also takes into consideration the participation of stakeholders that contribute to sustainable conservation planning and management within a holistic process. Theoretically speaking therefore, this can be divided into two strictly interconnecting views: the anthropological, the environmental and the economic, considering the assessment of these values as a *"socially constructed phenomenon and the identification of values and hence of prices cannot be isolated form the social context in which they occur"* (Throsby 2000, 27).

A SWOT analysis and comparison of local proposals and international experiences grant objectivity to constructive discussions for reaching a definition of balanced guidelines. In this fourth step ruins have been considered as opportunities for the historical core. Starting from the identification of local current approaches, all the previously investigations allow not only at the definition of compatible interventions for the case study considered but also at the definition of a general range of new contemporary values for this kind of structures.

All the data is acquired and investigated by means of indirect and direct analyses. The indirect analyses consist of the analysis of all the documents regarding the object of study. Bibliographic, archival, cartographic, iconographic, and archaeological studies are extremely important for recreating the ruins' construction, history and evolution providing important information about building materials and techniques as well as possible past interventions.

Direct data was collected through the analysis and survey of the structures and community by means of archaeometric and ethnographic techniques. The first concerns dimensional, material, stratigraphic and diagnostic data from architectonic analysis, stratigraphic surveys, diagnostic laboratory investigations on materials (mortars, plasters, stones), and the use of digital analysis to understand the ruins' nature and state of conservation; the second concerns community opinions constituting the anthropological data collected for the analysis of heritage values.

Generally, the approach, based on tools and methods used in technical and value-based approaches, follows a rigorous procedure in which sectorial methods produce a wide range of data from different sources that can be triangulated, allowing a holistic, comprehensive and transdisciplinary analysis that explores all aspects (fig. 80).

3.1. MACRO LEVEL. THE RUIN AS 'URBAN TILE'

This phase is focused on the knowledge of the historic integrity and cohesion of the neighbourhood contexts identifying the characteristics of the spaces in which the ruins are located, including physical and functional dimensions (Tiesdell, Oc, Heath 1996, 11). This means studying the area and considering its historical development both in terms of urban evolution and legislation, the analysis of its morphology, materials and state of conservation, community analysis, the distribution of uses and the current government plan. The areas of analysis are described in the following paragraphs.

MORPHOLOGY AND HISTORY This analysis investigates the area's forms, urban development and evolution in order to reach an understanding of the overall urban cultural landscape intended as the result of centuries of interaction among human activities and natural processes. The support of indirect data such as historic cartographies, maps, iconographic and archival documents were investigated in order to reconstruct the historic development of the inner centre and of the case studies investigated.

URBAN SURVEYS. GEOMETRIC KNOWLEDGE AND LOCATION Urban surveys are important for the study of ruins, as for any cultural heritage. Such geometric knowledge allows us to clarify the global location of the assets involved as well as to provide information useful for understanding both the context and the building. GIS tools and urban investigations and surveys offer clear evidence of the urban voids in terms of areas and volumes occupied by ruined structures. Moreover, they allow us to locate the ruined building in a global system of coordinates that can be catalogued in a georeferenced map of the historical centre. This phase was important to survey the ruins in Cagliari, create an urban map of ruined structures and analyse their context. This part of the research was carried out with QGis software.

PLANNING LEGISLATION, STRATEGIC PLANS AND URBAN ANALYSES Current and historical plans must be consulted in order to reconstruct the planning policies and development of the historic centre as well as to identify urban and architectural constraints that are determining factors in the choice of approach. Furthermore, urban typological and demographic information can also be deduced from the planning instruments, giving a general overview of the historical neighbourhoods. Overall, this urban analysis allows the definition of the context in which a work of architecture, in this case ruins, is located and to better understand and assess the research topic: the historical urban landscape of Cagliari. Furthermore, it defined the architectural case study on which the second part of the method has been tested: the ruined convent of Santa Chiara in the Stampace neighbourhood.

DIGITAL DESIGN TECHNIQUES Contemporary digital design techniques can be helpful in exploring ruins on both the urban and the architectural scales.

This approach, in the public sphere, seeks to emphasise collective interaction while simultaneously revealing and activating latent spatial connections within historical contexts on the metropolitan scale. It proposes new ways through which to reorganise, reframe and augment the collective experience of urban spaces, especially those with the presence of ruined structures. For that reason, the use of digital techniques is focused on activating the environment surrounding ruins, so that ruined structures are both inputs and outputs of human interaction that can describe, articulate and renovate specific urban phenomena within the fabric of the city.

This investigation can be carried out by using different parameters. One concerns the accessibility to public urban space by recording and digitalising the routes or paths that people usually take through the city. This analysis, using simple GPS recorders, can reveal the preferential ways that people experience and perceive the city as well as to understand how and where they prefer to pass for crossing nodal points in the city. The recorded data can be georeferenced by creating sensing maps in order to understand the main paths in the city.

Furthermore, such Android apps as AndroSensor, installed in our mobile phones, can record and manage important physical parameters for defining new possible uses for the building or, as in this case, ruins. In detail, this app acts as a physical sensor to provide accelerometer readings, (including linear acceleration and gravity sensors), gyroscope readings, light sensor value, ambient magnetic field values, device orientation, proximity sensor readings, pressure sensor (barometer), relative humidity sensor, temperature readings and sound level meter (decibel). The data can be processed with 3D rendering software like Rhinoceros and Grasshopper.

Overall, these experimental investigations confirm the increased exposure of the use of digital technologies in architecture consenting the use of data from these mutual exchanges of innovative practices, paying particular attention to architectural interventions in the context of historic urban settings.

Moreover, the investigations increase awareness of the particular dynamics of public space within the historic urban fabric through an understanding of the basic workflows of digital sensing and parametric design, and the development of a critical position regarding data-based design practices in the context of the public domain. This experimental field of investigation was tested on the Cagliari case study thanks to the collaboration of the Edinburgh School of Architecture and Landscape Architecture – College of Art of the University of Edinburgh.

3.2. MICRO LEVEL. THE RUIN AS 'STONE DOCUMENT'

This phase focuses on acquiring knowledge of the building through a detailed and consolidated scientific and transdisciplinary protocol of investigation specifically designed for buildings in a state of ruin. The protocol, already partially codified and tested on rural ruins in the project 'Accessit – Accessibility for the ruined religious structures in Sardinia' (Fiorino and Concu 2013) aims to recognise their archaeological and documentary importance and involves methods, techniques and tools from different scientific areas: architectural history, geomatics, petrography, materials diagnostics, archaeology of architecture, and digital techniques. It includes such architectural surveys as the photographic, geometric and structural, archaeological graphic restitution, architectural analyses, stratigraphic surveys with the classification of masonry typologies, and diagnostic laboratory investigations regarding natural and artificial materials (mortars, plasters, bricks) to understand their nature but also their state of conservation.

This analysis consists of two phases of knowledge gathering, indirect and direct. As already seen, all information linked to the history of the building and its construction can be indirectly investigated through the consultation of all the documents regarding the object of study. Bibliographic, archival, cartographic, iconographic, and archaeological studies have paramount importance for reconstructing the building's history and evolution, providing important information about the building materials and techniques as well as possible previous interventions. Also, prior geometrical surveys can help in this phase of knowledge. This analysis was conducted through the consultation of National, Civil, Ecclesiastic and Council Archives, the documentary, photographic, iconographic archives of the Superintendence for Architectural, Landscape, Historic, Artistic and Ethno-Anthropologic Heritage, and the Archaeological Superintendence.

This examination seeks to: reconstruct the building's history with the identification of the early structures and building phases from the foundation to the actual state of ruination; reconstruct the static history of the structures, identifying possible problems of instability; identify the owners and the builders who designed and built the structures and their building techniques; reconstruct the uses and functions of the buildings and the reasons for their abandonment. All the changes, both structural and aesthetic, need to be carefully identified in order to understand the building's evolution. According to the availability of the sources, historic drawings such as plans, sections, photos and pictures play a valuable role in acquiring knowledge of the building.

Direct analyses are based on the study and interpretation of directly acquired data and from the analysis and survey of the structures. This phase can be divided into the following steps:

3.2.1. GEOMATIC SURVEY

Geomatic surveying techniques are essential for the knowledge of a building because they help provide in-depth understanding of the structures in their dimensional, geometric, material, constructive, and structural aspects. Furthermore, they provide 3D models of the site from which take measurements both directly from the point cloud or from the restitution of single orthophotos. Thus, they offer general and detailed graphic drawings and renderings that show the dimensions and forms of the ruined building in every detail. This means not only illustrating horizontal and vertical structures and decorative components, if they exist, but also provide accurate sections and construction elements, such as masonry samples. The general goal is achievable through the combination and integration of the geomatic methods, technologies and tools.

As widely discussed, ruins are complex structures that raise different issues concerning the investigation and understanding of their irregular and incomplete forms. Also, geomatics supports the interpretative phase of the archaeological study of the building (Russo et al. 2011, 169) such as those carried out for the knowledge of the ruin, as in this research. Finally, and most importantly, these surveys are important bases for defining the significant elements to preserve and enhance in a reuse project. Different survey methods can be chosen in relationship to the scale of representation, and desired accuracy and precision from photogrammetry and terrestrial laser techniques. Indeed, the combination and integration of data, photos and point clouds from these techniques offer great potential for the knowledge of cultural heritage (Guidi et al. 2003, 2009; El-Hakim et al. 2004; Guarnieri, Remondino 2011; Remondino and El-Hakim 2006).

PHOTOGRAMMETRY Photogrammetry is a science that allow us to obtain precise measurements starting from pictures with terrestrial, aerial and satellites sensors (Russo et al. 2011, 181) useful for creating 3D models. Starting from different similar points identified in photos, this technique allows us to determine metric and dimensional information of an object as well as its form and location.

Photogrammetric instruments such as cameras and software are not expensive and can be easily used. This method, based on the metric elaboration of photos, can be of three types: monoscopic when only one photo is used, stereoscopic with the elaboration of two photos and, lastly, multi-image or bundle-block adjustment with more than one photo. This technique, today less used because of the development and the potential of the laser scanner, can offer great benefits to straighten out archival photos, reconstructing the forms of structures that no longer exist or are damaged (Gruen et al. 2004). Certainly, this operation can be very useful in case of ruins

81. Photogrammetric restitution of an archival photo. Sacristy masonry of the Convent of San Domenico in Villanova. Cagliari, Italy. Before and after the reconstruction. Chronology of the masonry.
© Elisa Pilia.

On page 163
82. Location of the rural church of San Giovanni Battista in Bortigali, Italy.
© Elisa Pilia.

Photographic survey of the ruined structures:
© Elisa Pilia.

83. The gate of access to the church.
© Elisa Pilia.

84. The main façade.
© Elisa Pilia.

85. Southern view of the roofless structure.
© Elisa Pilia.

86. The middle nave of the church.
© Elisa Pilia.

to identify the previous state of conservation or a lost configuration or possible new reconstructions. Fig. 81 shows the applicability of this elaboration carried out for the study of reconstructed parts of a Sardinian wartime ruin reconstructed immediately after the war: The Convent of San Domenico in the Villanova neighborhood. As can be noted, the archival photos taken immediately after the war allowed us to understand the entity of the reconstructed parts and the consequent level of authenticity of its masonry. As widely discussed, ruins are complex structures that raise different issues concerning the investigation and understanding of their irregular and incomplete forms.

TLS – TERRESTRIAL LASER SCANNING These issues have been resolved in recent times through the use of laser scanning techniques (TLS), that can reconstruct three-dimensional geometries in short time frames and with high accuracy. Furthermore, this technique offers the opportunity to achieve new ways of representing and visualizing a site with the goal of creating a better metric description. Therefore, these are powerful tools not only for the analysis of sites, allowing us to deeply examine and identify the masonry techniques and possible structural deformations, but also, to support both conservation or design activities (Vacca et al. 2012, 589; Deidda and Vacca 2013, 23).

In particular, in this research protocol strictly aimed at the study of ruins, the laser scanner survey was indispensable when it is possible to access the site. In fact, to understand a building's architectural evolution, irregularities, stratigraphies, and discontinuities, only an accurate tool like the laser scanner can provide the proper level of information. Finally, GPS readings allow us to locate the investigated sites within a universal system of coordinates (UCS). Regarding the tools, the laser scan Focus3D (fig. 87) produced by Faro was used to perform scans in the case study. This is a light and versatile instrument designed to obtain high potential for documenting internal and external applications for architecture, restoration and industry. In detail, it is a high-speed scanner with a contained size (24 cm x 20 cm x 10 cm) and weight (5 kg). It is equipped with WLAN (WiFi) that allow technicians to start, stop, and download scans even at a distance from the site. Concerning its characteristics, it can scan up to 120 m with an error of linear distance equal to ±2 mm for a distance between scanner and object included in a range from 10 to 25 m. The noise (standard deviation of the values from the best-fit plan) of this instrument is variable from 0.6 mm to 10 m with a 90% reflectivity and from 2.2 mm to 25 m with a 10 % reflectivity. It also has a vertical visual field of 305° and a horizontal one of 360°. Both horizontal and vertical resolution is 0.009°. Furthermore, the Focus 3D laser scanner has a scan speed of 976.000 dot/sec. A colour digital camera with a resolution of 70-megapixels is integrated in the laser

87. Laser scanner Focus 3D.
© Elisa Pilia.

88. 3D model of the church of San Giovanni Battista, a section of the main nave.
© Elisa Pilia.

89. 3D model, northern view of all the complex.
© Elisa Pilia.

90. Point cloud from top.
© Elisa Pilia.

91. Point cloud of an interior.
© Elisa Pilia.

scanner and it is possible to generate directly a 3D rendering of the model. The activities of surveying and data processing can be divided into five steps: project scan; scan acquisition; data elaboration; extraction of geometric information; graphic output. The software used to manage the cloud of points produced by the scanner is produced by Gexcel and is called JRC 3D Reconstructor 2 and is used to manage, build and investigate the 3D model of the site. Through the processing of the points, it is possible to obtain high-density three-dimensional clouds of points that, thanks to the integrated camera, takes their colours from the RGB of all the structures. The protocol for the application of TLS technique is shown in figg. 88–91. This method was previously codified on another ruined structure: a rural church in Bortigali (Sardinia) (figg. 82–86). This case, although located in the countryside, offered a valid basis and starting point for this research. From its results, in fact, more detailed structural analyses of the point cloud and the 3Dmodel was carried out. Overall, this step-in knowledge acquisition investigates the building's tangible features illustrated here in its forms and geometries.

3.2.2. ARCHAEOMETRIC AND ARCHAEOLOGICAL ANALYSES

Based on detailed surveys such as those conducted with TLS techniques, this phase of the methodology seeks to analyse the building according to protocols deriving from the archaeological sciences, called archaeometry. These investigations represent the cooperation of different scientific methods that involve physical and biological sciences with archaeology and art history. Their helpful combination and the use of dating methods, detailed studies of the artefacts, remote sensing techniques, and studies of state of conservation offer an accurate investigation of materials, building techniques, technologies, and chronologies that are fundamental for the identification of tangible values such as those defined by functional and documental aspects, as well as intangible values with associated features linked to historical practices and relationships.

In the present research, this archaeological approach, applied in the architectural context on ruined structures, focused on three specific lines of inquiry: stratigraphic analysis, material investigation, and the codification of building techniques, each characterised by specific methods, tools and techniques. In some Counties and especially in Sardinia, this kind of study is often more difficult than in the others due to the continual use of local materials in different centuries. Additionally, the research is complicated by the reuse of materials from other minor or monumental works and the involvement of non-specialised workers simply recruited in situ, as already confirmed by studies of other local structures such as coastal towers and fortified architectures (Giannattasio and Grillo 2011; Giannattasio and Pintus 2013; Fiorino 2014; Giannattasio, Grillo and Murru 2014; Putzu 2014; Giannatttasio, Grillo and Pirisino 2015; Fiorino, Giannattasio and Grillo 2015; Pirisino and Pilia 2016; Giannattasio, Grillo, Pirisino and Pilia 2017). Consequently, in this local context, the combination of these analyses is of great importance. For instance, often the identification of the different stratigraphic units could be insufficient from just the macroscopic analysis of masonries: they are apparently similar, but hugely different under the microscope. In that case, the mineral-petrographic and geochemical analysis of mortars can provide useful data to define and characterise the stratigraphic units. Therefore, it is important to investigate ruins according from the archaeological point of view, not only in order to study their structures and architectural values deeply but also to find urban chronological, technological and typological correlations, useful for identifying holistic values that link the building to its context and for designing the best suitable interventions. Lastly, the preliminary results of these investigations allow us to elaborate chronological syntheses which facilitate the understanding of the different construction phases, and the association of each masonry technique with an historical phase. Overall, the investigations carried out for the Santa Chiara case study concern: stratigraphic analyses, material investigations, and identification of chrono-typologies. Figure 92 exemplifies these steps in the ruined church of San Giovanni Battista in Bortigali.

STRATIGRAPHIES Stratigraphic analyses, focusing on the archaeological investigation of the building, supported the research on ruins intended as 'archaeological buildings' or the results of a series of positive and negative layers *(strati)* derived from building and demolition actions respectively. The methodology, based on archaeological and geological concepts and applied to buildings from the 1970s has had considerable widespread use in architecture with the formation of schools of thought over the last thirty years. The concept of Stratigraphic Unit (US) in the architectural field identified as Masonry Stratigraphic Unit (USM), veneers (USR) and negative features or cuts (USN), is intended as the result of human actions linked to each other through different stratigraphic relationships: anterior, posterior, earlier and innermost. The main goal of these studies is to reconstruct the history of buildings not only related to the medieval periods but also to the modern and contemporary ones guiding future interventions toward safeguarding of all stratigraphies. Thus, this study was carried out in order to have clear and deep knowledge of all the material and historical interfaces or discontinuities that, supported by the analysis of materials and building techniques, can emphasise the documental aspects and values to enhance and preserve in the future. An example can be seen in fig. 93.

Facade

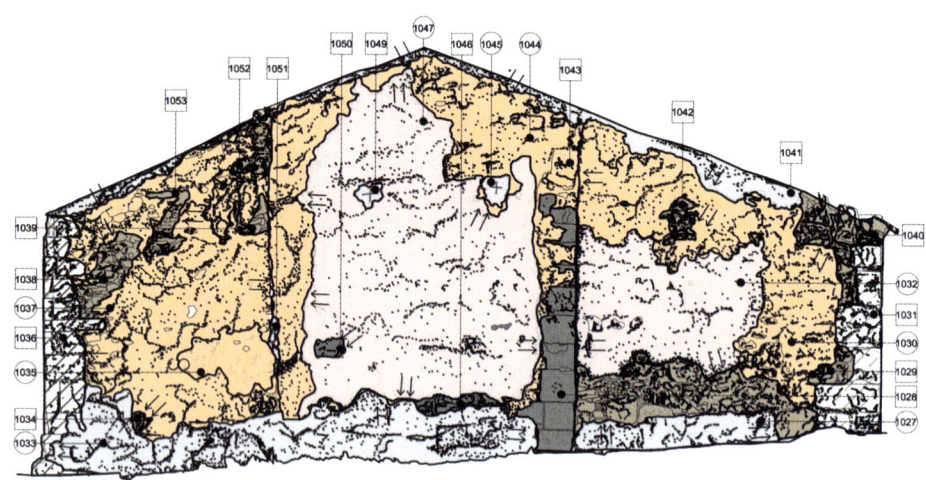

West facade

Masonry typologies and cronologies

Phase 1. XIII - XIV cent.

- Bearing header bond with double coursed ashlar of rhyolit and basalt. Mansory type 1
- Canton in rhyolit and basalt
- Rubblework in rhyolit and basalt

Phase 2. XVI - XVIII cent.

- Arcade in rhyolit and basalt
- Decoratives elements
- Bearing coursed ashlar with the internal side in rubblework and the external in framework of rhyolit and basalt. Mansory type 2
- Rubblework in rhyolit and basalt. Mansory type 3
- Canton in rhyolit
- Canton in reused ashlar of rhyolit and basalt
- Lime plaster

Phase 3. XVIII cent.

- Lime plaster

Phase 4. XX cent.

- Concrete plaster
- Roof

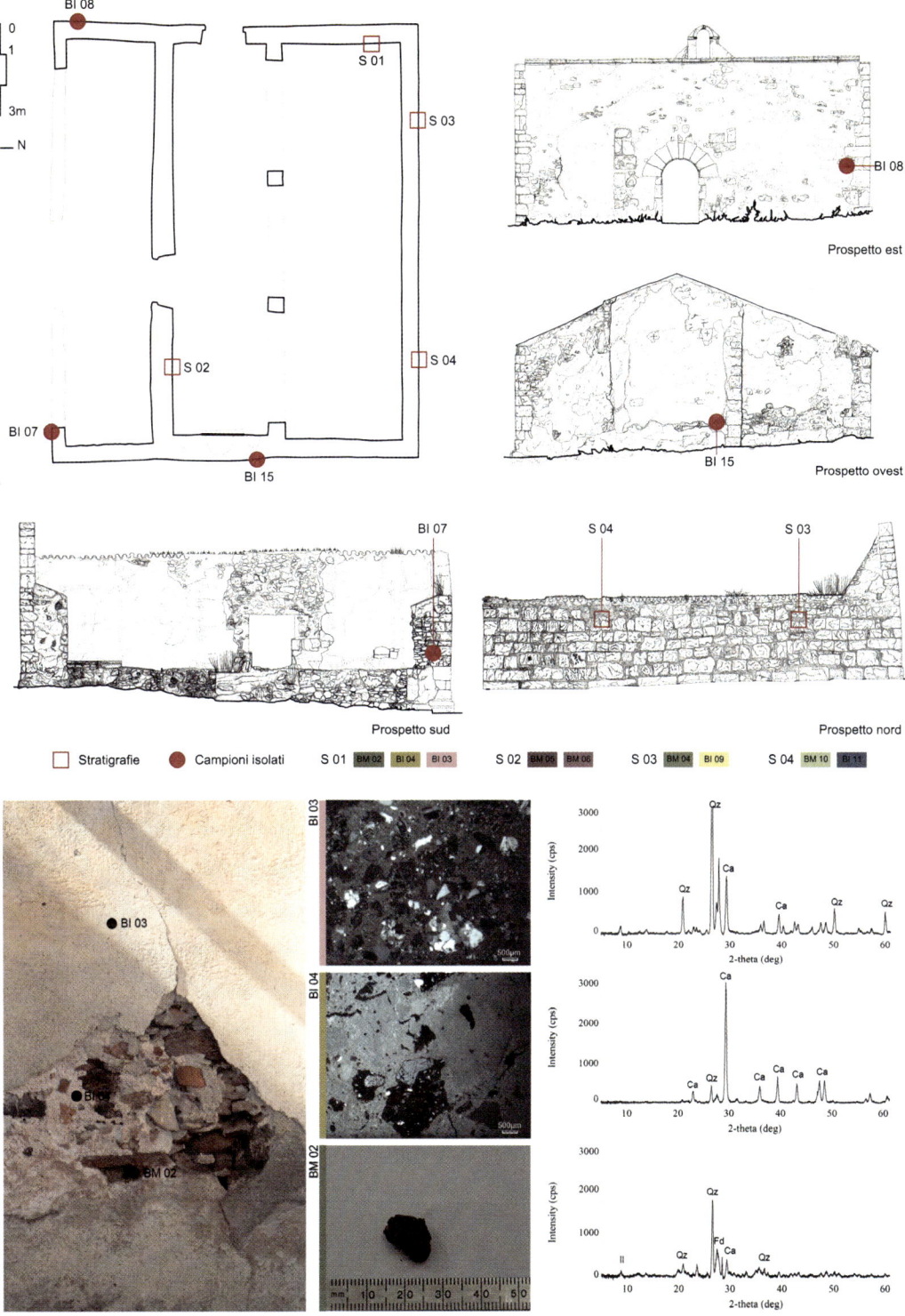

169

MATERIALS Material aspects were studied through a detailed diagnostic protocol due to the poor consideration that materials often have in the analysis of historical contexts. The issues relating to the poor study of materials, especially mortars, increase in the case of ruins. They are potential elements of knowledge of their state of conservation but are frequently neglected due to their lack of use and consequent insufficient consideration. Thus, the research also considers ruins as a powerful historical links between humans and their territory through materials, territorial signs of a place (Grillo 2015, 142–145). In fact, materials can also clearly represent topography and the interaction between nature and builders' skills and abilities (Acocella 2004, 113).

Also, as Gionata Rizzi (2007, xix - xxiii) said, ruins differ from other kind of buildings due to the fact that their anatomies reveal how they are built. Their missing finishes unmask their entrail – the materials of which they are built, the structural principles that determine their design and the techniques that made their construction possible (Rizzi 2007). Mortars, mixtures of aggregates and binder, are an integral part of historical masonry with the functional role of bonding or protecting. They combine with masonries throughout their life cycle and, in the most cases, allow them to survive. Mortars strictly relate to construction techniques and local materials. In this light, the present step of the research illustrates the importance of the characterisation, the identification of historical mortars and the analysis of their state of conservation, especially for buildings in a state of ruin. For various reasons, mortars have been considered the most important material to be analysed.

First, they are precious records that permit us to understand the building's materials and the traditional techniques, understanding the composition of historical products in relation to different workforces. Second, they are valuable bases to identify new repair layers designed with chemical, physical and visually compatibility with the existing structure (English Heritage 2011, 202). Moreover, the analysis of old mortars is fundamental in determining the origin of decay or failure of old mortars, evaluating the stability of the structures and proposing appropriate and compatible new mixtures, whether for conservation or for re-use. Finally, they can be used as dating elements to support the study of chronologies especially when historical archives do not provide documentary or photographic evidence. In these cases, analysis reveals great information about the samplings chosen; factors such as site conditions, position, time, and method of application can change the results. For this reason, after a careful sampling of natural and artificial stones, the protocol for material investigation sought to define the mineralogical-petrographic nature of stones and mortars, identifying their binder and aggregate.

On page 168:
92. Stratigraphic analysis and chrono-typological study carried out for the church of San Giovanni Battista.
© Elisa Pilia.

On page 169:
93. Sampling project and minero-petrographic analyses of the stratigraphy S01.
© Elisa Pilia.

94. Analysis of the building techniques for the church of San Giovanni Battista.
© Elisa Pilia.

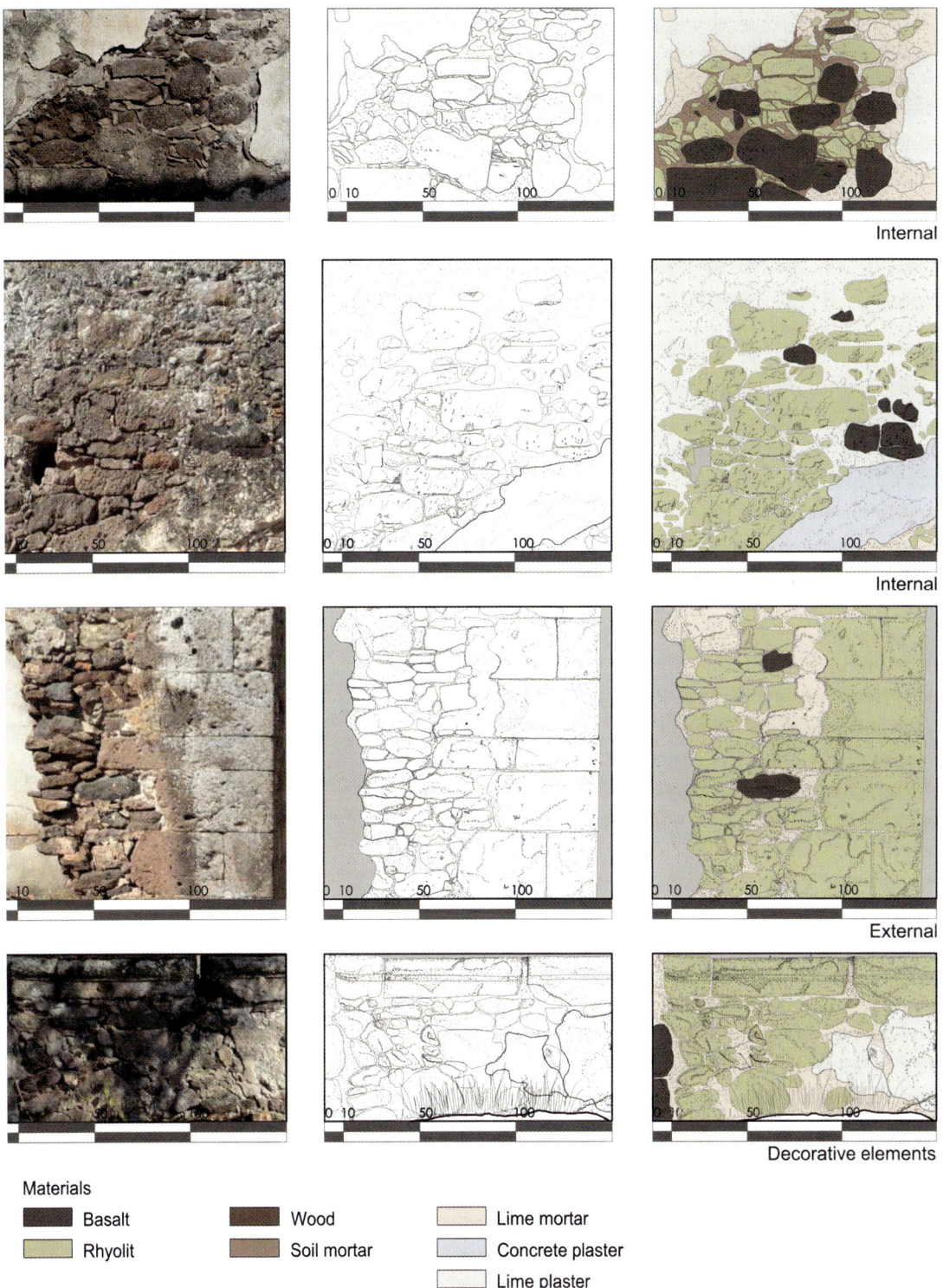

Then, the study of alterations or decay defined the material state of conservation. Macro assessment allowed us a first general identification of the composition and the structure of mortars whereas archaeometric analysis such as microscopic analyses on thin sections, diffractometric and fluorescence X-ray, microscopy and micro analyses, permitted a complete understanding and characterisation of building materials, defining not only the mineral-petrographic characteristics and state of conservation but also the monument's chrono-typologies (Grillo 2015, 147) (fig. 94).

BUILDING TECHNIQUES Parallel to the previous archaeological analyses concerning stratigraphies and materials, the masonries can be 'typologically' investigated for the identification of building techniques (fig. 95), highlighting their possible period of construction and construction peculiarities strictly connected to the territory and the builders. Masonry techniques, differently realised in relationship to their function, can be structural indicators as well as chronological benchmarks due to their dimensions and technologies.

3.3. ASSESSMENT. RUIN AS 'TREASURED URBAN ELEMENT'

Once knowledge of the urban context and the structures has been acquired, the next analyses regard the understanding of embodied values, also considering the intangible components of ruins. As stated earlier, the research considered prior experiences of technical and value-based approaches as the bases for the elaboration of a protocol seeking to assess and enhance the significance of ruined structures.

This step is directed at defining *"the importance of a site as determined by the aggregate of values attributed to it"* (De la Torre, Mason 2002, 3). Values have always had a great importance in the history of conservation, from Riegl to Brandi and today they are considered as *"reference points"* (Mason 2002, 3). They involve numerous fields of heritage knowledge and again bring into play the transdisciplinarity of the methodology. Starting from the consideration that the conservation approach is not only technical but also sociocultural and that values can be of different types, their analysis can suggest additional considerations regarding a building's usefulness and benefits. According to the definition of values (Orbasli 2008; Mason 2008), they can only be understood in reference to social, historical, and even spatial contexts.

For this reason, the definition of the typologies of these values for the local context are of great importance; in this study, the historical centre of Cagliari, they want to both guarantee the preservation of the memory of the ruins and, at the same time, highlight the need for redemption from their negative conditions. This research starts from the conservation principles listed by the English Heritage (2008): evidential, historical, communal, aesthetic and by the Getty institute (2002) which defines the typologies of value relevant for ruins through multidisciplinary assessment. It was considered as the combination of values that came from two different explorations: the first from the overall analysis of ruins in their context, the second instead, from the point of view of the stakeholders involved. These contributions define the aspects and elements of significance, useful for SWOT analysis and the definition of guidelines. Following this classification, the assessment of significance, or rather *"the application of a systematic and consistent process, which is appropriate and proportionate in scope and depth to the decision to be made, or the purpose of the assessment"* (English Heritage 2008, 35), can be undertaken. The criteria to define these values were based on an integrated 'top-down'/'bottom-up' approach. In fact, if the top-down model considers values established by a dominant group of society such as experts and professionals through technical studies, in the bottom-up model, the less technically educated local community might be able to interpret and define their own values in a more direct way. This analysis summarises the anthropological and economic values currently attached to the building and how they inter-relate. In addition, it explains the importance of the values identified and possible tensions among potentially conflicting values. The assessment, also based on values as social constructs, defines the statement of significance and identifies the characteristic features and values that require intervention or preservation.

Finally, the Strength-Weaknesses-Opportunity-Threats analysis (SWOT) supports the definition and the degree of intervention identifying positive and negative future trends.

FROM THE BUILDING ANALYSES After the analyses of the context and of the ruined architectures, the method proposes the identification of heritage values – anthropological, economic and environmental. They are conceived according to the Cultural Values Model (Stephenson 2008) and evaluated through multidisciplinary assessment. In that method, heritage values derive from the analysis of three features: 'form, practice and relationships' that are continually changing in the urban landscape. While form represents the tangible and material features of a building that can be directly investigated, relationships and practice are the two aspects that embody the intangibility or immateriality considering history, traditions and past uses of ruins. These are considered in their dynamics in which present values, the result of 'embedded values' from the past, stand for their physicality and perception. From these features, connoted by associative, sensory, evidentiary, functional aspects, the analysis of features leads towards the identification of attributes and character-defining elements. These elements represent the features of values that are embodied in the structures and can be considered key features to protect and preserve for the enhancement of the building's significance.

In this way, values are established from the deep knowledge of structures as parts of a cultural urban landscape where human and natural interactions and relationships are makers of the sense, memories, and meanings of a place and that establish their cultural identity. In this research, values were divided into three main classes: anthropological, environmental and economic. The anthropological class includes all values that derive from the social, cultural, historic, aesthetic, and semantic analysis of ruins. The environment class is composed of all the aspects that link structures with their territory and landscape. Finally, the economic class was considered an essential and useful tool for understanding the possible future benefits for the overall historical area and for planning the sustainable rehabilitation of these ruined structures. These values are the sum of monetary and land values, obtained by analysing the real estate market together with their non-use value. Especially in this case, non-use values were considered fundamental as ruins do not have a function but do have significant potential economic value.

FROM THE STAKEHOLDER POINT OF VIEW After the identification of values from the overall building analyses, through the support of anthropological and ethnographic methods such as semi-structured interviews and focus groups, the research investigates the opinions and points of view of the community in the urban area.

In the process of identifying heritage values and in the value assessment of ruins, stakeholders are essential because of their direct or indirect involvement in conservation or reuse. They can be identified as insiders and outsiders, divided into four groups.

The first group is composed of stakeholders with 'planning and administrative power' such as the landmarks commission, council policy makers, conservation experts and developers. They are the three levels involved in the decision-making and planning process also including the expert group of stakeholders. They have a high level of education and knowledge of the process and are directly involved in assessment.

The second group is made up of people who do not have great knowledge of this kind of process. They are not professionals but citizens that often are not involved in assessment due to their lack of specific knowledge of the sector. Here, they have been identified as residents, people who live in the four historic neighbourhoods; they represent community opinions. They were interviewed in their role as outsiders whose opinions are just as important as those of insiders because of their spontaneity and knowledge strictly relating to daily life. Citizen participation, as already mentioned in part II, is a matter of politics that should always pursued in order to have a high level of approval of a final proposal.

Within the community, a third insider group was interviewed: the business classes, people who represent the commercial and economic interests of the neighbourhoods. They are retailers and business owners. Finally, a key role was played by another group of outsiders: the students of the Architecture School, involved as the educated future generation and creative part of society who live and spend the most part of their time in the historical centre.

The 'statement of significance' was used in the present protocol as a powerful decision-making tool from value-based approaches based on descriptive analyses, heritage and economic values assessment and character-defining elements for urban ruins. It aims to reflect contemporary values or 'embedded values' of ruined structures considering their forms, relationships and practices. It also seeks to define the significance of each, identifying which part of history they represent, how and why their values are important today and the need to preserve them in the future.

This important tool is also an assessment of values that community members and investors, previously consulted, associate with ruins.

STATEMENT OF SIGNIFICANCE This step in the methodology ensures the participation of all stakeholders involved directly or indirectly ensuring the design of the proper level of intervention whether conservation or integration. This statement could also be useful for providing key information to the local municipal and governmental institutions involved in the protection of these urban ruins and in the definition of conservation policies. For these reasons, the results of the previous analyses are considered background information, both on the macro and micro levels, of fundamental importance in this phase of synthesis and assessment. Furthermore, the analysis can be considered a step in creating better understanding of the historic context in which the structures are located.

The sum of background information contributing to the identification of characterising aspects and elements of ruins with the community point of view resulted in the statement of significance. In fact, from this data stems the hierarchy of heritage values - anthropological, environmental and economic - important for past, present and future generations, and difficult to quantify. The result of this assessment is shown in the matrix of 'cultural significance' (fig. 95).

	FEATURES	ASPECTS	CHARACTER - DEFINING ELEMENTS	
TANGIBLE	**FORMS**	FUNCTIONAL	SPATIAL, HISTORIC, ARCHEOLOGICAL ELEMENTS	**HIERARCHY OF VALUES**
		EVIDENTIARY		
INTANGIBLE	**PRACTICES**	EVIDENTIARY AND SENSORIAL	HISTORIC EVENTS - BUILDING PROCESSES	
		SENSORIAL		
	RELATIONSHIPS	ASSOCIATIVE	HUMAN - NATURE PROCESSES / CULTURE INTERACTION	

3.4. THREATS AND OPPORTUNITIES: SWOT ANALYSIS

Having identified the cultural significance through the combination of technical (urban and architectural) and ethnographic methodologies, this step was useful in determining issues or conflicts and opportunities relating to the identified anthropological and economic values for future interventions as well as the future success of the planned transformations (Low 2002, 34). The issues to consider include site condition, the actions needed to preserve or restore the setting of the site, the identification of any development issues and opportunities, any public access requirements or limitations, available resources, both immediate and in the future.

Specifically, SWOT (strengths, weaknesses, opportunities and threats) analysis is a strategic tool used in business that can be applied to ruined structures for deciding the best way to achieve optimal renewal. In detail, strengths and weaknesses can be identified as elements with an internal origin such as: physical condition (use, position, structure, material), management context (legislation, political will and resources), public awareness (community identity, education). Threats and opportunities regard changes in meaning and value judgment dependent on external factors, for instance social, cultural, political forces, as well as physical factors, such as the environmental and the social/cultural phenomenon of gentrification.

All prior analyses and deep investigations of form, design, material, techniques, traditions, past uses, stakeholder opinions and so on, allow us to understand the level of authenticity of a place and, through SWOT analysis, aid us in assessing the elements that have been altered and those that are still intact. Here authenticity is an essential qualifying factor (Nara Document 1994) that cannot be judged using fixed criteria but through the deep knowledge of the building as proposed in this protocol.

Thus, SWOT analysis identifies the threats that must be managed through a project that, according to the previous macro and micro investigations, should be respectful of the values assessed. On the other hand, intact elements should be protected since they are essential for preserving the site's authenticity.

The dynamic nature of heritage is a key concept in this methodology; this type of analysis applied to the heritage values embodied in ruined structures permits us to evaluate which values are in danger and require future intervention and which are still alive and need to be preserved.

95. Matrix of 'cultural significance'.
© *Elisa Pilia*.

4. APPLICATION OF THE METHODOLOGY IN CAGLIARI

This protocol of investigation is defined in its application on urban ruins in different historic contexts. Nevertheless, it has been tested in a special case study: the city of Cagliari, a walled coastal city situated at the centre of the Mediterranean Sea, on the southern coast of Sardinia (Italy) chosen for its complexity and uniqueness (fig. 96). Here, the ruins left by the aftermath of the bombardment by the Allies during the World War II, represent something of a blight on the landscape beyond the mere presence of fallen masonry and overgrown vegetation. They also represent an absence, a series of voids located in nodal points of the historic centre that have neither a current function nor any plans for future use. This is largely the result of ineffective planning characterised by a tendency toward non-intervention.

After the careful analysis of Cagliari's historic urban landscape, attention focused on a representative case of ruins that could synthesise the urban issuesand potentials of this context; this was the medieval monumental Santa Chiara convent, a ruined structure in the city's historic core, greatly damage during the World War II but previously fallen into ruination due to its disuse after the abolition of the monastic orders.

4.1. MACRO LEVEL ANALYSES | THE HISTORICAL URBAN LANDSCAPE

The strategic geographical location between seven hills and the sea conferred upon the city of Cagliari an important role in history. From Phoenician occupation on, various dominations transformed its landscape, creating the modern city as an *"extraordinary result of several mixed cultures and architectural styles with an outstanding dominance of bright colours, from ancient to modern buildings, due to different stones and plasters used over time"* (Fiorino and Grillo 2015, 113). Throughout history, while several modern changes were designed in order to improve and transform the urban fabric, the city's medieval form and configuration remained intact, conferring a special and unique aspect upon the city composed by four historical districts: Castello, Stampace, Villanova and Marina whose layout recalls the iconography of a golden eagle with a cross on its chest, recurrent in medieval pro-imperial cities such as Pisa (Cadinu 2009, 52).

On the left:
96. Cagliari, Italy.
View of the historical centre from the sea.
© *Caterina Giannattasio*

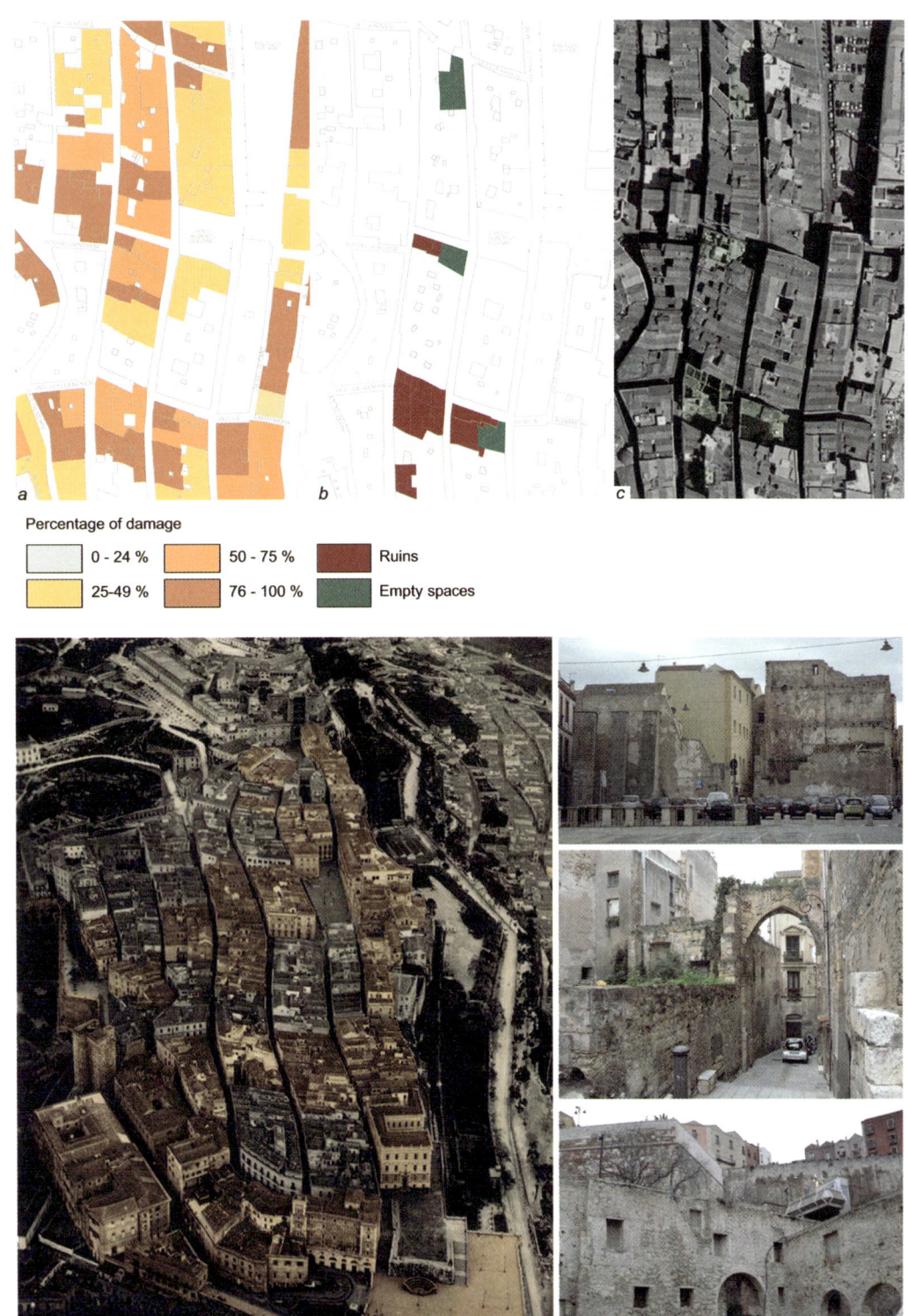

Percentage of damage

- 0 – 24 %
- 25-49 %
- 50 - 75 %
- 76 - 100 %
- Ruins
- Empty spaces

FORM, HISTORY AND URBAN PLANNING The analysis of its ruins has started from documents of the end of the 19th century, when Cagliari was a growing city that had to face the unhealthy slums of its historical centre and was also characterised by numerous ruins. Several authors began to represent these local memories surrounded by the natural landscapes in pictures. Panoramic views showed the ruinous conditions of the Phoenician-Punic archaeological remains like the Tuvixeddu necropolis as well as the Roman amphitheatre and the medieval defensive walls and towers. Eduard Delessert and the English Dominican priest, Peter Paul Mackey, were only two of the several authors of these picturesque and poetic views that joined aesthetic melancholy contemplation of ruins with condemnation of their state of abandonment. These ruins were not the only ones which characterised the city of Cagliari. In fact, the World Word II and its devastation marked the cityscape deeply.

Monumental, archaeological, residential and public spaces from different historic periods are objects of ruination. Their origins can be mainly identified in the destructive wave of the World War II and in ongoing processes of obsolescence that have led, year by year, to the formation of true fragmented structures and empty spaces or, in other terms, place of waste. For these reasons, an in-depth study has been focused on the understanding of this war destruction for the whole historical centre, its percentage of damage (figg. 97–98), the post war interventions arriving at identifying and cataloguing the current ruined structures using Gis tools according to their origins and typologies (fig. 99).

These urban investigations have been supported by innovative design technologies and techniques that have allowed the study of the accessibility around urban ruins and their connection by means of paths, for emphasising collective interaction and revealing latent spatial connections between ruins within the local historical context. This was also an experimental way through which to reorganise, reframe and augment the collective experience of the urban spaces. The elaborations of this analysis revealed movement map (fig. 101) of the city with the preferential paths through which people experience the city during the day and, most importantly, has permitted to understand how (in terms of speed) and where the participants crossed the centre.

Furthermore, it has also allowed to individuate urban nodal points where ruins are placed, and to establish an architectural ruined case study for testing the experimental methodology: the medieval ruined Convent of Santa Chiara, a representative case that might sum up all the urban issues and potential in this context.

97. Particular portion of Castello quarter:
a) re-elaboration of the Genio Civile post-war cartography with the percentage of damage;
b) current survey showing the presence of ruins and empty spaces from bombings;
c) orthophoto with highlighted the neglected areas.

98. Castello quarter view from a dirigible in the 19th century with highlighted the bombed areas. On the right, three current ruined spaces: Piazza Palazzo (Palace Square), Vivaldi-Pasqua Portico, S. Chiara convent.
© Elisa Pilia.

On page 182:
99. Typological analysis of ruins.
© Elisa Pilia.

On page 183:
100. Wartime ruins of Aymerich Palace.
© Elisa Pilia.

101. Movement map above the 3D model of historical centre of Cagliari.
© Elisa Pilia.

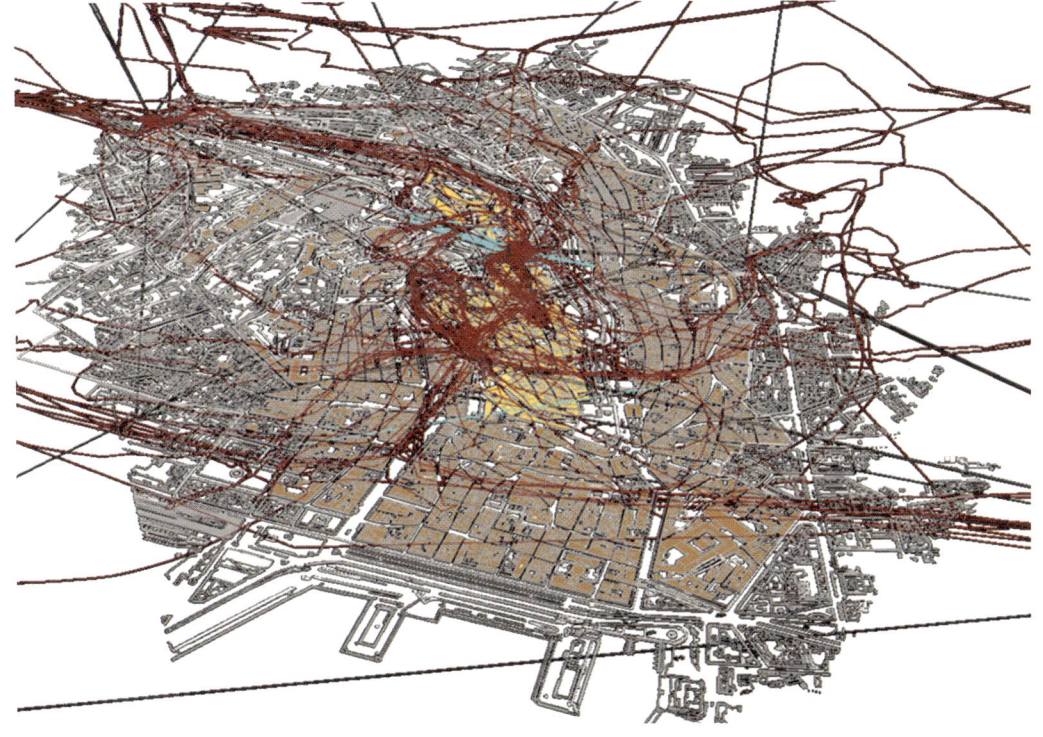

4.2. MICRO LEVEL ANALYSES | THE CONVENT OF SANTA CHIARA

The convent ruin is located in Stampace on the western side of the Castello hill in a flat area between the Santa Croce Bastions, Via Santa Margherita, and Piazza Yenne, a nodal urban space connecting the three historic quarters of Stampace, Castello, and Marina. It is part of a more extensive monumental complex that also included the baroque Santa Chiara church and the local Santa Chiara market built in the modern era (fig. 102).

INDIRECT | INVESTIGATIONS Starting from indirect analyses, supported by archival (cartographies, documents, photos, and iconographies) and bibliographic sources it has been possible to reconstruct the history of this fabric, starting from its origins to its decline, the restoration works and current state of ruination. The monument, assigned to, and occupied by, the order of Clarisse nuns, was built in the 14th century on an existing church dedicated to Santa Margherita outside the city's medieval defence walls and isolated from the urban context. During the 17th century, the baroque church was built in its current form and the convent was probably enlarged during some restoration works. Indeed, relationships changed with its surroundings as it began to play a significant role in the city's urbanisation and economy. At the end of the following century the convent was described as an unhealthy place, especially the dormitory due to its location near the humid embankment. As a consequence of its structural obsolescence, the order sharply declined in the 19th century closing definitely its activities in 1864. In the meantime, the engineer Gaetano Cima designed a new urban plan (1858) for the city in which the Santa Chiara complex became a nodal point of connection between neighbourhoods through the design of a monumental staircase on the rocky and wild uphill path to Castello from Piazza Yenne.

With the closure of the Convent in the 20th century and its consequent desertion, the area lost its central role to become a neglected place. In 1943, WWII bombing destroyed part of the structures and the consequent cleanup returned a ruined shell of masonry with no roofs and floors. Then, in 1957, a temporary local market was installed inside the convent transforming the space with new roofs, floors, and partitions. At the time, the area became important again, although in a different way from its previous religious role, having been a point of convergence for Castello, Stampace, and Marina.

Due to this significant role, and the convent's importance, the Council moved the market close to the Church access stairs where, in 1984–1985, the Superintendence carried out important archaeological excavations on the structure; it also performed some structural renovations and repairs with compatible materials. In the 1990s, the decision to install a lift in the space between the church and the convent, the original location of the confessionals and oratories, raised additional issues in terms of the legibility of the structures,

102. Cagliari, Italy.
View of the Santa Chiara Convent from the Elephant Tower.
© Elisa Pilia.

perceived as two different buildings. Today's disuse of the lift has intensified the abandonment of this place and, notwithstanding the recent restoration and integration work by the Superintendence (designed by Architect Paolo Margaritella), nobody can access these structures.

DIRECT INVESTIGATIONS / TLS SURVEY After this historical study on the origins and transformation of the fabric, a more detailed protocol of investigation has been based on detailed geomatics surveys. The presence of different levels and macroscopic structural anomalies as well as the numerous stratigraphies discovered during the several surveys, led to the decision to support geometric knowledge with the greater accuracy provided by laser scanner techniques (TLS) and GPS survey (fig. 103). During the phase of restitution and editing, a more accurate study of the geometric characteristics of the vertical and horizontal structures was prepared. In fact, the aim of the TLS survey was not only to provide the graphic documentation to support design such as plans, sections, and elevations but also to investigate possible anomalies or stratigraphies of the building. For that reason, a series of graphic outputs were extracted from the convent's 3D model. Specifically, horizontal sections were performed every 10 cm from the lower level of the convent (34 m above the sea level) to the highest point of the walls.

ARCHAOMETRIC AND ARCHAOLOGICAL ANALYSES In addition, vertical sections were used for analysing the depth of the cisterns (fig. 104) as well as for studying the verticality of some walls. Starting from the restitutions of these surveys, archaeometric investigations were carried out with the goal of better defining forms, materials, practices, and technologies.
Precisely, they were carried out with an archaeological approach consisting of stratigraphic analysis, mineral petrographic investigations of historic materials, and the identification and analysis of building techniques. Stratigraphic analysis of the ruined Santa Chiara complex followed two lines of inquiry aimed at reconstructing its relative chronologies. On the one hand, stratigraphic analysis of the interfaces and layers, conducted for all masonry, offered the first evidence of hypothetical chronologies. On the other, accurate plan analysis carried out with the support of the horizontal sections performed with the TLS technique provided the opportunity to identify significant plan sections that help to define the ruin's more detailed chronology and evolution. Overall, this analysis was carried out both on the elevations and in plan.
Following stratigraphic analysis and understanding of the relative chronologies, a visual assessment of the materials, such as mortars, was fundamental for the in-depth investigation connecting the different phases.

103. The laser scanner Faro Focus 3D in the cloister.
© Elisa Pilia.

104. Some of the results from the TLS survey: on the left top the 3D model of the convent, on the right the plan with the position of the stations; on the left bottom plan sections for the analysis of the fabric (sections were performed every 10 cm from the lower level of the convent in order to arrive at the restitution of the plan at 35 m above the level of the sea (1.5 m above the quote 0), on the right: final restitution of the plan.
© Andrea Dessi, Elisa Pilia.

CONTEMPORANEITY

◯ is linked to

LATER

↓↓ Cover

↕↕ Cut

STRATIGRAPHIC UNIT

▢ Masonry (USM)

◯ Covering (USR)

△ Negative or cut (USN)

BORDER

— USM
— USR
— USN

A_M01

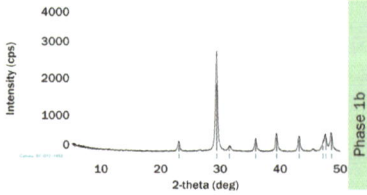
Phase 1b

The protocol considered a rational sampling in view of the different kinds of mortars used, where and how they were placed, also taking into account the previous stratigraphic investigations. In detail, the sampling was made according to specific goals: the qualitative characterisation of the materials due to their compatible reintegration and the identification of their chrono-typology to support the building's overall chronology given by the stratigraphic analysis of the masonries. It concerned only mortars and consisted of 20 samples. An analysis was compiled for each, indicating significant information for the correct interpretation of the results (fig. 105). The stratigraphic and minero-petrographic analyses of the building ultimately led to the classification of specific masonry techniques, widely influenced not only by economic and cultural factors, but also by local geological features and native materials with their mechanical and technological properties. All these investigations, supported by the analysis of the state of conservation, were also fundamental for defining a relative hypothetical chronology of the ruined structure, never defined before, and to find interesting comparisons and connections of this fabric with other structures of the wider historical centre in terms of materials, forms, decorative elements and building techniques.

4.3. ASSESSMENT OF VALUES

Indeed, starting from these transdisciplinary analyses, it can be asserted that the convent certainly bears witness to the forms, relationships, and practices developed from the medieval age to the present.

FROM THE BUILDING ANALYSES Overall, tangible values were identified through the analysis of the building forms, meant as all the material and measurable elements of the structures that can embody functional and evidentiary aspects. They are conceived as the material aspects of the landscape like all historical and archaeological features, and man-made architectures: stones, mortars, and building techniques. This investigation highlighted how the monument, built with the same traditional techniques and materials as other nearby residential buildings as well convents, can allow, though comparisons, possible indirect dating among coeval structures lacking archival sources. The character-defining elements of the functional aspects can be recognised in the spatial importance of the sites, first due to the development and growth of the city, as a point of expansion of the walled Castello district; then, as element of connection between quarters, a role evidenced by the stairs and by the presence of the unused lift and finally as central market and social meeting point for Cagliari's entire historic centre. These functional aspects, founded on the geometrical extensions, forms, accessibility, and location, still recognised as a preferential point of connection

105. Example of stratigraphic analysis of a masonry of the convent and the mineral-petrographic analysis of one of the twenty sample of mortar (5A_M01). From the left: sampling localisation, macroscopic and microscopic view (2.5×), and diffractometry.
© Elisa Pilia.

to the Castello hill, led to the definition of environmental values, linked to the panoramic view of the site, as well as to economic values related to the presence of market. They were considered essential and useful tools for understanding possible future benefits for the entire historic area and planning the sustainable rehabilitation of these ruined structures.

Considering the long abandonment of this complex, a potential or non-use value can be recognised as the sum of three economic values: existence, option, and bequest values that emphasise the area's great potential.

Evidentiary aspects were instead based on the building's legibility as an 'open book' about itself. Forms, materials, stratigraphies, and techniques evidenced the role of this monument as a document that can also be related to Cagliari's entire historic built heritage. Cultural, historical, and aesthetic values can be assessed based on these character-defining elements rich in historic evidence and technological and material testimonials. Cultural values can refer to craft because they are linked to the skills and crafts of the medieval builders. Not only building techniques but also the compositions of materials such as mortars and plasters, referring to a particular way of building, are significant benchmarks for all historic structures. Strictly related to this concept of benchmark for dating buildings, forms also embody historical values expressed as educational values. Considering intangible values, practices are determined by historic events and building processes and can express evidentiary, sensorial, and associative aspects, also present in relationships.

On the one hand, the convent is associated with historic events embodied in its forms. These can be identified in the establishment and goals of the Mendicant orders and their activities, the in the transformation of the city in the 20th century evidenced by the construction of the monumental stairs. It has also played an important role in the urbanisation and development of the neighbourhoods. From all these evidentiary and sensorial aspects, the convent ruins embody socio-psychological values such as identity, due to the area's specific characteristics and memory, due to the historical role that this complex played in the city's history.

On the other hand, building processes express achievements in terms of concepts, design, technologies (building techniques) and planning of a given period. Both come from inter-cultural relationships and exchanges that, on the local and European levels, developed and defined specific building characteristics and particularities in terms of technique, material and form. As a consequence, these can be considered key components that link not only the past to the present but also different cultures and territories. In fact, as already noted, several testimonials of Aragon domination can be read in the convent structures. These stylistic elements also relate to relationships throughout the entire historic centre (fig. 106). As already stressed, the convent not only bears witness to a war scar like other

106. Other masonry-technique samples that show the same building technique M01, found in Santa Chiara. These can be found in other monumental and residential cases inside the historical centre of Cagliari.
© *Elisa Pilia.*

urban ruins, but it has also clear relations with other local Franciscan and Dominican convents. Human and natural interactions and relationships emphasise the established social values in terms of identity and memory, widely embodied in these structures and that define the cultural identity of places. These concepts refer to the different roles played by the convent during history. As evidence by the sources, it was a religious and funerary centre for the community of Stampace for a long time. Then, it became marketplace from the 50s to 80s growing in the community as symbol of religious and social life. These factors led to other cultural values: commemorative, spiritual, religious and symbolic.

FROM THE STAKEHOLDER POINT OF VIEW The final hierarchy of values is the result also of investigation of the stakeholder's point of view through semi-structured interviews with citizens, tourists, and business owners, as well as a focus group with students. The opinions of local experts instead, were taken into account by analysing the strategies of intervention proposed in the recently provided local strategic urban plan concerning the protection and the possible interventions on the analysed ruined structures. Generally, stakeholders stressed the negative connotations of this ruin but with contrasting points of view. These were related to the controversial situation regarding the lift installed in the convent, non-functional since September 2015. Consequently, the impossibility for people to move easily through the city and to support the local economy, nowadays in crisis for the ongoing abandonment of the market area. Indirectly, all people recognised an economic value to this ruin asserting that they could afford a tax if the intervention could be aimed at a collective reuse and restoration of the fabric even if expressing a distorted concept of authenticity.

Looking at the urban plan, the level of intervention for this ruin is classified in the class of value I, for which is established the conservation and partial reconstruction recomposing the old dimensions and spaces of the area such as the memory of the nuns garden in place of the present market.

At the same time, not all the parts of the ruined convent have same importance in the urban plan as, for instance, the areas of connection between church and convent are still not listed and so lacking in protection. The weaknesses and threats related to the current urban policies, and all the potentialities mainly placed in the central position and accessibility of the site have been highlighted in the SWOT analysis, leading towards a holistic understanding of the fabric and of its heritage values.

All these values, embodied in the fabric according to the before-mentioned cultural values model, divided in tangible and intangible, and organised in a hierarchy, because of the difficulty of interpretation and the possible quantification of the intangible aspects, are mainly representative.

4.4. INSTITUTIONAL CURRENT APPROACHES

The historical centre of Cagliari is recently provided by a strategic plan concerning the protection and the possible interventions on traditional buildings. As concerns ruined structures, these have been divided in monumental and residential and different levels of interventions have been defined.

Looking at the monumental convent of Santa Chiara, the level of intervention is classified in the 'class of value I' for which is established the conservation. In particular, only the part of the ruined convent consisted of the old courtyard and portico as well as the church are in class |A1. Instead, the area in past used for the connection between church and the convent are considered 'parts of contour' *(sezioni a contorno)* not listed.

This class A1 consists of all the built heritage dated back before the war with a public function or of public interest that has to be conserved in its artistic, architectural, cultural, typological, morphological and technological parts. The aim of this class is to: conserve the original fabric persevering the external and internal characters of its spaces, delete the modern alterations that compromise the fabric, enhancement of the built heritage.

In general, the strategic plan recognises the urban role of the structure and its spatial and historical values as well as the current negative connotation of this place, that, for its mutilated appearance is considered a detractor of the urban landscape.

The proposal suggests: the preservation and enhancement of the structures by means of their reuse; the reconstruction of the volumes around the patio emphasising the enclosure character of the structures and recomposing the old dimensions; the restoration of the structures according to the conservation principles of authenticity, distinguishability, minimum intervention and reversibility; the demolition of the actual market and its transformation in garden as memory of the monk gardens; the addition of elements of connection with Castello quartier integrated into the structures. As the figures 107 and 108 show, the intervention suggests to build new structures and volumes on the archaeological remains of the old masonries now lost, respecting the height of those already existent. The other ruined structures should be conserved and volumes could be reintegrated addictions.

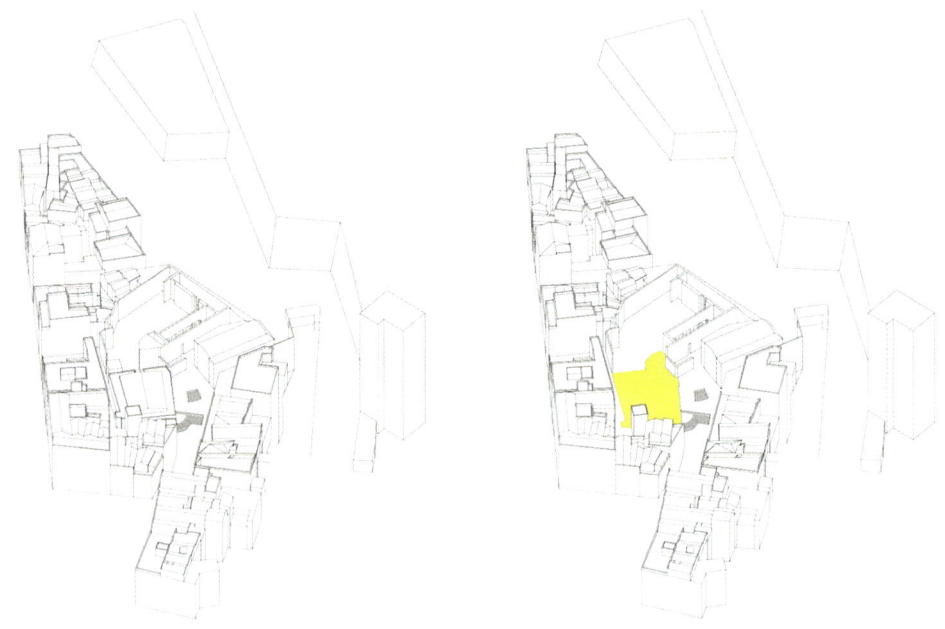

Stato di fatto

Demolizioni

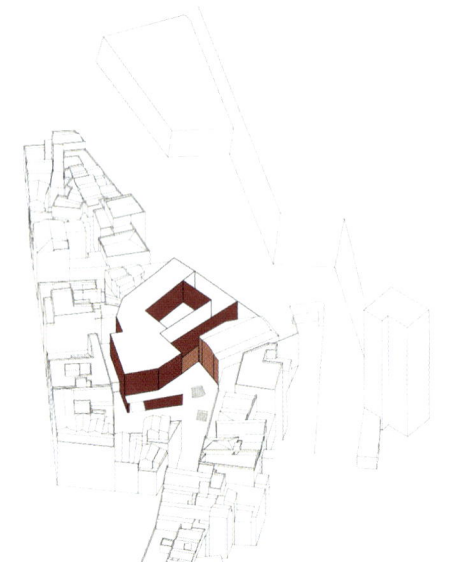

Ricomposizione volumetrica

Spazio pubblico e verde

107. Views of the state of places, demolitions, reconstructions and green areas.
PPCS Etg. 017.

108. Rendering of the project.
PPCS Etg. 017.

109. Detail of juxtaposition of the stairs and the historical wall. Point cloud not structured.
The concrete stairs block has level of authenticity 0.
© Elisa Pilia.

110. The main entrance wall has shown a high level of authenticity for the presence of two decorative elements clearly dated to the Aragon period. Cagliari, Italy
© Elisa Pilia.

4.5. COMPATIBLE INTERVENTIONS AND NEW USES

All the studies considered, the protocol associates to the character defining elements identified, meant as constructive elements or stratigraphic units that bears values of the fabric, a level of transformability according to the qualifiers of authenticity that strongly influence the values embodied in the ruin. Authenticity is here intended as a qualitative qualifier that drive towards the intervention. It is a character of what still intact has been preserved from the several historical layers of the ruin. As the Nara Document claimed, this concept is rooted in the different sociocultural context and it is not possible to base judgements of authenticity within general fixed criteria. Nevertheless, the present research has tried to establish an approach for evaluating possible degrees of authenticity based on the knowledge of the fabric following a growing scale starting from the absence of authenticity towards the maxim level.

Authenticity is absent when an element has not relations with the original fabric. It is realised in modern shapes and modern materials incompatible with the historical one.

In the Convent of Santa Chiara this level of authenticity can be associated to all the new modern elements realised in materials incompatible with the historical structure. This is the case of the new stairs built in reinforced concrete (fig. 109). Furthermore, the lift and the supervision room are other two negative values of this fabric. Here, the new elements have been built again with incompatible materials touching the historical material and compromising the readability of the original configuration of spaces. Concrete plasters are also considered lacking in authenticity. In this case the demolition and the restoration or addition with compatible materials are possible.

A low/medium degree of authenticity can be instead assessed when masonry stratigraphies are late addition to the original fabric. They can be divided in additions realised in modern materials and techniques, or new elements added according to traditional or historical technologies. In this case can be considered also all the masonries that have been cut and repaired in the last fifty years. These two cases can be visualised in the Convent in all the addition aimed to close openings: in bricks and concrete mortars or in Cantone stones and lime.

The comparison with the state of place in 1908 clarifies these additions and, visually they are still visible in the site. Finally, the highest level of authenticity is associated to all the character defining elements that embodied the value of the fabric, its historical configuration and uses. These elements must be preserved or conserved in their intact forms and materials. The convent of Santa Chiara is rich of these examples that remind the medieval or Aragon fabric. The bell towers, the stoup, the decorated openings as well as all the stratigraphies are all elements

that have a high level of authenticity that consider all the phase of historical development of the fabric (figg. 110 – 112). At these levels of authenticity can be associated degrees of transformability that will grow as less is the authenticity of the element. Indeed, the highest level of authenticity corresponds at the maximum protection, preservation or conservation of the element.

By contrast, all the disturbing and incompatible elements can be demolished and reconstructed according to some guidelines later presented. Concerning the elements with a low/medium level of authenticity these can be object of different consideration. Thinking to a reuse of the fabric, all the masonry additions in the closed opening could be removed justifying a pre-existent historical function. In the other case, they should be maintained. The concrete beams could be removed and replaced with compatible materials. The archaeological remains instead conserved for their undeniable memory. All these degrees of transformability lead to different possible interventions (fig. 113).

Generally, all the authentic elements such as historical structure that remind the history and the evolution of the previous building must be conserved and enhanced in the fabric. Additions can be considered compatible if aimed at reconstructing original volumes with compatible solutions detached from historical materials (figg.114 – 119). Any other new volume build on structures should be assessed and respectful of the historical boundaries (figg. 120 – 122), avoiding the creation of new shapes that could compromise the heritage values evaluated. All the historical masonries, as in the local case, must be protected with compatible plasters or mortars according to composition highlighted with the mineral-petrographic analysis. Indeed, for its strategic position and role in the urban context, the convent of Santa Chiara needs an intervention that could mix the tradition with the contemporaneity.

111. One of the two examples of historical plasters still in place.
© *Elisa Pilia.*

112. A detail of the historical stoup to conserve.
© *Elisa Pilia.*

On page 199:
113. Possible interventions according the level of authenticity.
© *Elisa Pilia.*

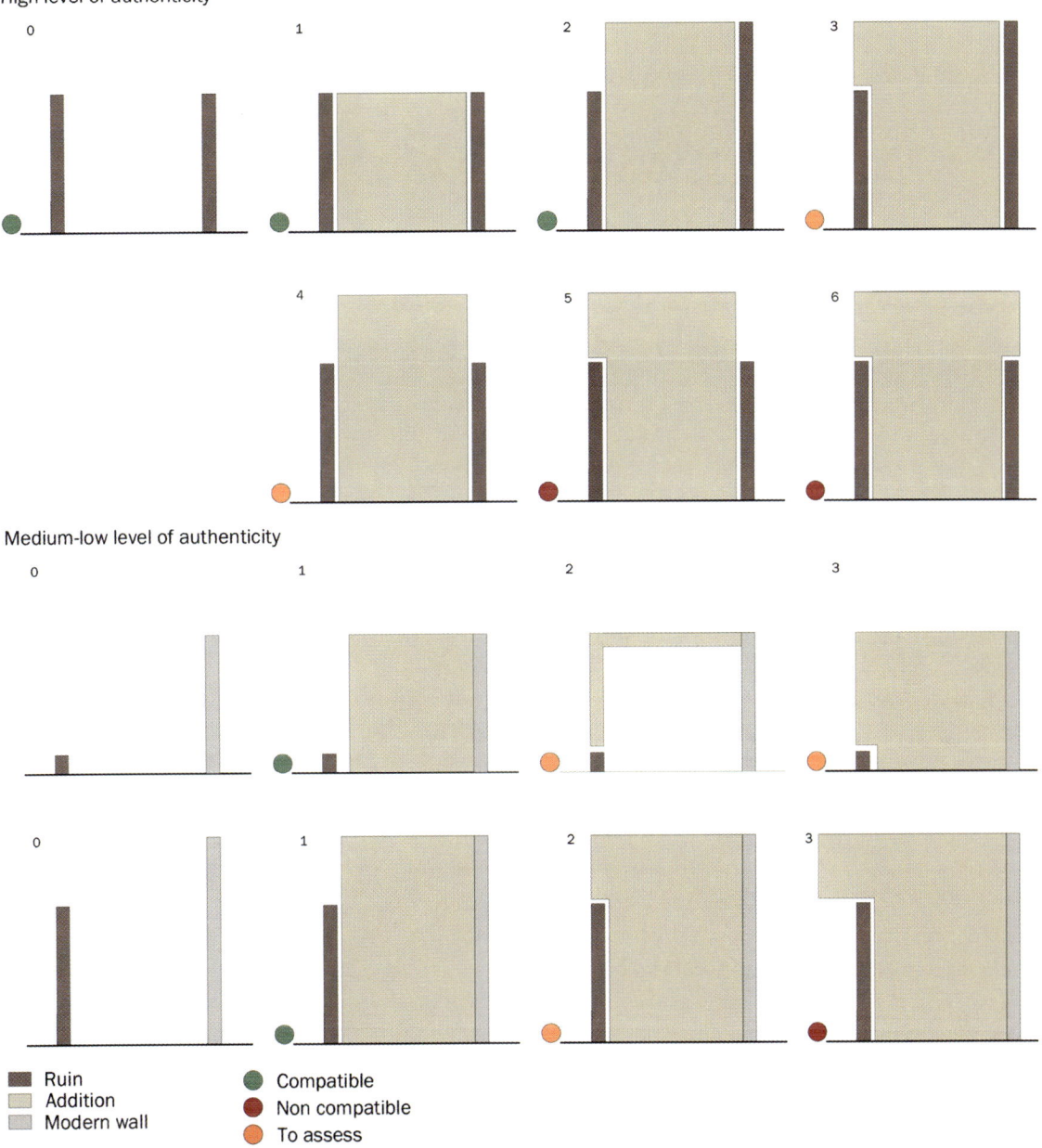

114. Edinburgh, United Kingdom.
Advocate's close. The new addition is clearly identifiable and detached from the historical material.
© Martina Loi.

115. Edinburgh, United Kingdom.
A detail of new and old materials in Advocate's close.
© Martina Loi.

116. Edinburgh, United Kingdom.
Sugar close project combines re-used historic buildings and new-build clearly identifying the new addition in compatible materials.
© Martina Loi.

117. Edinburgh, United Kingdom.
A detail of new and old materials in Sugar close.
© Martina Loi.

118. Suffolk, United Kingdom.
Decovete Studio. An 'endoparasite' of wood and Corten has taken place in the ruin respecting the historical stratigraphies.
© Philip Vile.

119. Suffolk, United Kingdom.
Detail of interiors in Decovete Studio.
© Philip Vile.

120. Lisbon, Portugal.
The archaeological site of Praca Nova. A new structure has overcome the archaeological remains, untouching them.
© Mattia Canetto.

121. Lisbon, Portugal.
Detail of the sovrapposition new-old.
© Mattia Canetto.

5. DEFINITION OF NEW CONTEMPORARY VALUES

The analysis of the historical evolution of the concept of ruin and its correlated values, the critical investigation of the main issues in the contemporary context and the experimentation of the methodology on the historical centre of Cagliari and specifically on the ruined Convent of Santa Chiara has driven the study towards the categorisation of values that are deeply rooted in some important considerations evidenced during the research.

Ruins must be considered in their dynamicity and temporality. Although this is important for cultural heritage in general, it is especially significant for ruins, artefacts that have lost their original image and use. Thus, values have to face to structures that are result of long, often traumatic historical processes; they have to consider their origin, evolution, development, old uses and cause of ruination; in other terms, they have to mirror their past. At the same time, the present state of ruination has to deal with a contemporaneity that require new wills, habits and standards; a contemporaneity that connoted by a strong nihilism has often deleted the past for giving space to a new modernity defined by Bauman as 'liquid'. A modernity in which current ruins are often the reflection. But, as Fiorani asserted, this contemporaneity consists past as well as of future (Fiorani 2016). This future is the third temporal component that have to lead toward a consideration of ruins as opportunities for their potential economic values. Furthermore, values are rooted in the cultural, social and physical context where the ruin is placed. The same context that has 'shaped' ruins and still contribute to the definition of their meanings and perception that the society experiments.

All that considered, the codified tangible and intangible values, result of an in-depth analysis of context, fabric and society can be summarised in three main classes: anthropological, environmental and economic.

ANTHROPOLOGICAL VALUES

Values that come from came from social, cultural, aesthetic, semantic and evidentiary features related ruin have been considered under the class of 'anthropological values'. This is because they depend from the human nature in terms of skills, abilities, technologies, ways to perceive, think and interpret these artefacts. They consist of historical, cultural and social values.

HISTORICAL VALUES

They are rooted in the past of the fabrics, its origin, evolution and start of ruination. They can be divided in:

Artistic values. They consider the artistic aspect of the fabric, the presence of particular style or designed following some artistic trends. This has been evidenced also in the Santa Chiara convent rich of clear stylistic elements linked to the Aragon tradition.

122. Pozzuoli, Italy.
View of interior ceilings in the Pozzuoli Dome where new parts face to the old ones.
© *Caterina Giannattasio.*

Educational value. Ruins are powerful element of knowledge about the past. This educative value stems in the possibility to use them as instrument from which learning about past practices and relationships for future reuses.

CULTURAL VALUES

These values are those values linked to a specific culture of a community and related to the cultural capital.
Political/civic values. They are related with the concept of power of ruins. In fact, they are always connected with a politic choice. It can be related with the origin of that ruins (wars) or with policies after its dereliction such as politics of non-intervention.
Craft/work-related values. They are linked to the methods and techniques used to build the structures. They are values related to the process of making and building.
Commemorative, spiritual, religious and symbolic values. These are related to the deep historical and religious aspects of each society.
Social values. These values are connected with the society who live and experiment ruins and are linked to the social capital. They include the place attachment aspects of heritage values (de la Torre & Mason 2002, 12) such as concepts of: identity, memory, sensory.

AESTHETIC VALUES

These values are those connected to the perception and the experimentation of ruins. This can be attributed according to the notions of sublime, artless beauty, creativity and authenticity.

ENVIRONMENTAL VALUES

This class of value gives importance to the context where ruins are place. Both urban and rural contexts transmit and connote these artefacts. Furthermore, their location in these environments have great contribute in the definition of future intervention. The *Landscape and nature values* embody these context aspects that often remains not considered. As also seen, nature is a powerful feature of the ruin, the state through which a fabric goes back to its original state.

ECONOMIC VALUES

This class of values, already prospected in the analysis of economic issues, are considered essential for ruins in order to achieve their sustainable reuse and to design balanced interventions. Furthermore, they can be useful tools for understanding the possible future benefits of these interventions for the whole historical area. As already said, ruins are structure that for their disuse

123. Matrix with the summary of values.
© *Elisa Pilia.*

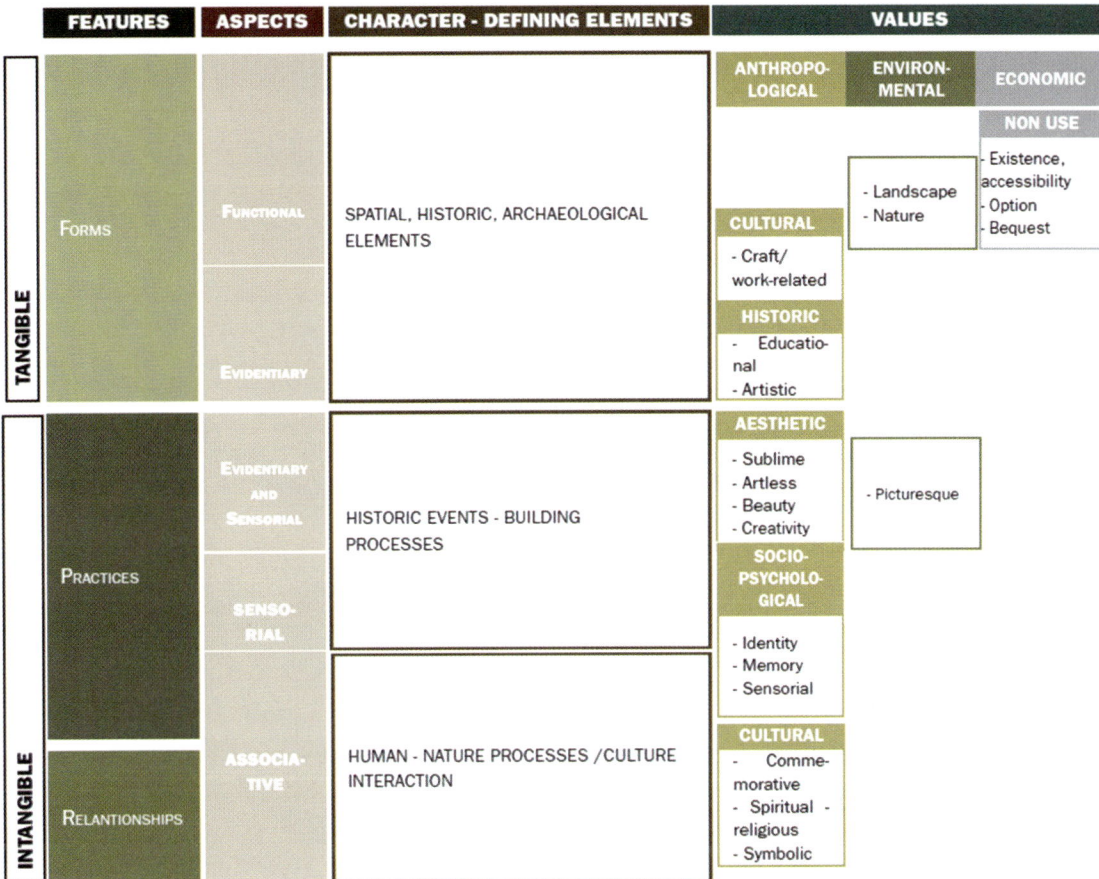

cannot have a market involvement. For that reason, their economic value is the sum of their physical values, obtained following the estate marketing plus their non-use value. This category of values differs from the previous one because it is related to the utility and the price of things.

For that they are divided into two classes: use and non-use values. Considering the disuse of ruined structures, it seems considerably important to evaluate especially their non-use values, in other terms the values that depends from a condition of no market, more complicated and critical to evaluate in comparison with the use value.

Existence value regards the mere existence of an asset. People could recognise a value in a ruin also only for its existence.

Option value is related to the possibility that this good could have a new use in the future because the policies and the legislation allow that.

Bequest value stems from the will of the society to bequeath to the future generation ruins as witness of past times.

"THE LATTER GLORY OF THIS HOUSE WILL BE GREATER THAN THE FORMER, SAITH THE LORD OF HOSTS AND IN THIS PLACE I WILL PROVIDE PEACE"

(Haggai 2.9)

CONCLUSION

124. Coventry, United Kingdom.
The inscription in Coventry Cathedral wishes immoral glory to these ruins.
© *Elisa Pilia.*

With an international perspective, this book has illustrated the contemporary relevance and complexity of the debate on the reuse of ruins, highlighted by the rich literature in several fields of research ranging from architectural conservation to the urban field, and involving economic, politic and social issues. First, the difficulty of intervening on ruins stems from the complex meaning and subjective interpretations of the concept of ruin according to different cultural contexts. This is especially true in Italy where the debate is rendered even more complex because of the existence of the two terms, *rudere* and *rovina,* that both mean 'ruin'. These words are frequently misunderstood and improperly used, creating problems of interpretation that can have consequences on the design project. As seen in the various dictionaries, although they have different roots, they mean the same thing while the other definitions examined are personal interpretations of the term. This terminological specification has underlined the difference between ruin or *rovina/rudere* with other words. Generally, while *rovina* is linked to positive connotations, all the others: *frammento*/fragments, *resti*/remains, *relitti*/wreckages, and *vestigie* tend to be negative, focused on absence thus giving a derogatory meaning to ruins often in order to justify extensive interventions on the building fabric.
This focus on terminology and on the differences between the Anglo-Saxon and Italian terms was also crucial in understanding the consequent differences between the design approaches in the two countries that were the subjects of a comparative analysis. This complexity can also be considered to be rooted in the long historical development of the concept of ruin. A historical overview has shown the underlying reasons, thus providing a clear framework for understanding contemporary practical approaches. In general, a widely accepted theoretical and practical framework for approaches to urban ruins cannot be found; this is due to the fact that theoretical orientations are deeply related to the historical events and the value system of each country.

Analysis of this debate evidenced two main lines of inquiry: theoretical and practical ones.

The first deals with ruins in their dual existence as absences, as element of reflexivity, of vacuity, loss and, at the same time, of creative interpretation of modern society, elements of memory, identity and place-attachment with psychological implications for observers; they are rich in political and economic implications. Ruins are also spaces for experimentation, opportunities for imprinting power on the city, symbols of failure or of rebirth. Indeed, ruins can be considered places of great creative potential, key components in regeneration and in the consolidation of place identity. The practical debate, instead, faces to two main approaches: conservation and integration, each of which is characterised by varying degrees of intervention. A wide-ranging analysis of different projects illustrated their 'driving elements' in terms of origin, function of the original building, location, degree of ruination, and integrity. Certainly, it can be asserted that the strongest justifying component is the origin. As shown, ruin from rapid events such as natural events and war bombings have shown huge differences in intervention based on the contrasting poles of overcoming or neglection of the trauma.

In this broad context, the United Kingdom and Italy have significantly contributed to the issues surrounding the question of ruins. Both have been and still are characterised by strong conservation approaches, albeit in different ways. Although the British tradition, founded on a value-based approach, offers a wide range of ruin heritage, it is carefully enhanced and managed by the two main national institutions, Historical England and Scotland. Here, the long tradition of protecting ruins and urban conservation areas has placed special attention on well-codified conservation planning policies. In particular, Scotland and Edinburgh have offered virtuous examples of interventions on ruined structures today absent in its conservation areas. This is also a result of the existence of a proper registry: 'Buildings at Risk', regarding listed buildings and buildings in conservation areas that were vacant and had fallen into a state of disrepair.

The Italian conservation approach is strongly influenced by the 'weight' of its history to the point that transformation processes are slower and less common than in other European countries. Here, the lack of design quality is often caused by the absence of interdisciplinary studies, a fact also widely recognised by the academic community.

Furthermore, the analysis carried out on urban issues regarding policy, sustainability, cultural, social, environmental, aesthetic and economic aspects, has provided a general framework for understanding the dynamics of ruins. Moreover, it highlighted the tools and methods, the typology of values to reconsider, and possible strategies and key concepts for reflecting upon the debate on ruins.

These considerations and the awareness of the topic's complexity has provided the framework for seeking answers to the research questions. The first asks what is the possibility of enhancing the meanings of those aspects of the built environment that are often misunderstood due to their fragmentation and incompleteness and consequently perceived as places of abandonment and negligence? Second, what kind of methodologies can be deployed to reach an appropriate degree of intervention that can intelligently relate ruins to their surroundings? Moreover, is there a way to transmit the historical values embodied in ruins to the future through contemporary conservation and preservation projects? Eventually, what new functions can be attributed to ruins in cases of intervention and reuse?

From these questions and the historical and contemporary outline, the study sought to define and codify an *ad hoc* methodology, based on the sharing of the value-based and technical methods that are respectively Anglo-Saxon and Italian. This method should reconsider urban ruins from a holistic view of their architectural issues and potential, intimately interconnected and explicable only if related to the broad urban context and its community. It should also be an approach having no boundaries between sectorial disciplines, but the assimilation of reciprocal bodies of knowledge, each indispensable to and supporting further investigation and the final project. In other words, it would be a methodology that is transdisciplinary and at the same time sustainable for the cooperation of scientific sectors and the research of compatible interventions in ruined structures. The value-based approach, which, in the present protocol, supports the technical investigation of the built urban fabric, is here focused on understanding the 'character defining element' of the fabric, meant as that key element that bears the values that should be transmitted to the future. The parallel definition of the level of authenticity and integrity of these elements and consequent values led to the defining the level of transformability of the fabric. Three main investigations were undertaken: a macro analysis on the urban level, a micro analysis on the architectural scale and a final assessment of their significance, guiding the research towards the definition of new possible degrees of intervention.

This methodology has found its application in Cagliari, the starting point of the general discussion because of the great concentration of urban ruins. Cagliari was an interesting case study both due to the singular post-war debate that is still influential as well as to the high degree of tangible and intangible values embodied in the city's stratified historical urban landscape. This context is still rich in those scars of war which, due to lack of funding or a sense of urgency, were left abandoned to their ongoing process of ruination. Critical analysis has suggested that the city, after a first wave of attention to the emergency of post-war reconstruction, saw decreasing interest contributing to the growing significance of the problem. Nevertheless, such urgency has not found any answer in modern policies, and non-intervention approaches have lead to the current state of decay and abandonment of structures that have become ruins.

Concerning the architectural level of investigation, the ruin of the convent of Santa Chiara offered a valid case study in light of its good accessibility and legibility, allowing the full application of the method on all levels including its unresolved local issues.

Overall, these case studies have offered general findings such as the reconsideration and codification of a set of values largely present in all ruined structures; such values enable the definition of a series of degrees of transformability and, consequently of intervention for the enhancement and protection of their tangible and intangible values. This enhancement finds its roots in the awareness that the profound comprehension of a such a complex and misunderstood artefact like a ruin is based on the deep knowledge of its features, here considered in terms of three key concepts: forms, practices and relationships, seen in their associative, sensory, evidentiary, and functional aspects. These features and aspects can be identified only from a series of analyses such as those proposed in the ad-hoc methodology proposed here. Subsequently, the case study provided interesting findings on the local urban and the architectural scale such as the reconstruction of the chronology of the site's evolution, knowledge of it in terms of dimensions, forms, materials, techniques and relationships within the city's entire medieval urban fabric. Therefore, local ruins can still contribute to the regeneration of the historical centre which, after a sharp decline in population, is trying to regain new life through the enhancement of its cultural layers. This is clear in two strategies: the 'Historical Urban Park' and 'The Museum City' designed in the new plan for the historic centre, still in the approvals phase, along with the 'guideline projects' which include ruined structures. Nevertheless, a strategy for defining a proper level of intervention based on the holistic assessment of values is still remote.

On this topic, the English and Scottish experience, based on a different model through which heritage issues are administered and stewarded by private and charity organisations, is based on a model which might provide inspiration. For instance, the English positivist approach of constructive conservation sponsored by English Heritage and defined as a *"collaborative attitude to recognise and reinforce the historic significance of places, while accommodating the changes necessary to ensure their continued use and enjoyment"* (English Heritage 2008, 7) and the National 'Heritage at Risk Register' of historically significant places that are in danger of being lost are, indeed, two valid models for managing and preventing more damage to structures in state of ruins.

First, the constructive approach seeking to define a new use could allow also local ruins to reinstate their life cycles, contributing to the reuse of urban voids and to the repopulation of historic neighbourhoods. Also, given the high percentage of ruined structures in Sardinia as well as in Italy, a Registry of buildings in various stages of ruination might be a valid tool for the management of these structures.

At the same time, the National Trust for Scotland, founded immediately after the war, offered another positive example based on the prevention and the management of buildings in state of ruination. Here, immediate postwar attention and urgency for protecting buildings at risk as evidenced by the Little House programme, was aimed at 'long term' programmes focused on increasing awareness and promotion of the education of the community regarding the preservation and transmission of vernacular features of the bombed cities. The systematic survey and classification of the damaged buildings as well as the 'revolving fund' strategy set a model for management and social growth still deployed in modern British policies. Furthermore, the contemporary interventions appear to be fully respectful of the memory and history of the fabric and, at the same time, positively supported by contemporary additions that emphasise the city's traditional physical and social features.

Nevertheless, the methodology also demonstrated some limits to its application. The role of non-expert stakeholders in the phase of assessing values resulted difficult and controversial.

If the creative society of experts and students showed interest and a positive attitude, understanding the concept of value and especially of memory and history, the local community (residents and business owners) was not able to understand and define the concept of value. Residents were sceptical and uncertain in expressing their opinions. Finally, tourist perceptions of ruins were always negative and proposals were focused on the enhancement of a distorted concept of authenticity like the reconstruction of the original forms. At the same time, their opinions were important in the SWOT analysis and in understanding the weaknesses and threats.

Overall, the research investigated and emphasised the origins of the local urban issues at the basis of the creation of these ruined structures as well as possible contemporary questions. These cannot be seen only in the controversial pragmatism of a post-war plan focused on reconstruction which in the end resulted in some unrealised cases, perhaps fortunately, but also in the context of today's overly complicated bureaucracy. Furthermore, these ruins, today sites of neglect and abandonment, degrading elements in the medieval urban core of the historical centre, while memories of destructive events, need to be reconsidered in a positive light. The sorrow of war that defines these architectures as wounds and absences still widely perceived negatively by the community, should be overcome and the loss of the original artefact should be accepted. These negative wreckages, remains, fragments, *ruderi* and *vestigia* should instead be seen in a positive way as ruins, 'rovine', taking advantage of their valuable presence as historical testimonials to forms, materials, technologies. In other words, they should be symbols of collective memory and especially of place-identity whose tangible and intangible values must be preserved, protected and transmitted to the future. The designed and tested transdisciplinary methodology, also applicable in other similar contexts, has proposed a way ahead to achieve this that goal. In conclusion, memory and contemporaneity are the two key words that this research would like to emphasise and stress when considering ruined artefacts. Memory, in this context meant as 'collective memory', should be considered as the cornerstone for connecting the past and the present. All things considered, ruins are elements that embody the temporality of existence; they can construct unique contemporary 'memoryscapes' (Edensor 2005), where memory and relationships with the past can materialise. Thus, memory is a key value that should be highlighted and, at the same time, should drive the contemporary project as a feature of connection between old and new and from which to define new compatible uses. As Edensor (2015) asserted, memory is an opportunity to give to ruins a new narration, a new contemporary life.

BIBLIOGRAPHY

Abis A. and Ladu, M. 2015. *Il paesaggio della città pubblica. Il patrimonio immobiliare e il sistema del verde in Paesaggio storico urbano. Progetto e qualità per il Castello di Cagliari.* In Paesaggio storico urbano. Progetto e qualità per il Castello di Cagliari edited by Abis, E. 266–299. Roma: Gangemi.

Abis, E., ed. 2015. *Paesaggio storico urbano. Progetto e qualità per il Castello di Cagliari*, Roma: Gangemi.

Accardo, A. 1996. Cagliari. Series of *Storia delle città italiane*, Bari: Laterza.

Acocella, A. 2004. L'architettura di pietra: antichi e nuovi magisteri costruttivi, Firenze: Alinea.

American Merriam-Webster dictionary. 2017. (on-line).

Andreassen, E., Bjerck, H.B., and Olsen, B. 2010. Persistent Memories: Pyramiden – A Soviet Mining Town in the High Arctic. Trondheim: Tapir.

Andrews, D., Bedford, J., and Bryan P. 2015. Metric Survey Specifications for Cultural Heritage, Historic England.

Appelbaum, B. 2007. Conservation Treatment Methodology. Oxford: Butterworth-Heinemann.

Area – Addition, n. 148. 2016.

Armstrong, J. 2010. *Every day afterlife: Walter Benjamin and the politics of abandonment in Saskatchewan, Canada.* Cultural Studies 25: 273–293.

Artizzu, F. 1974. L' Opera di Santa Maria di Pisa e la Sardègna, Padova.

Ashley-Smith, J. 1995. *Definitions of Damage.* Accessed March 28 2016. http://cool.conservation-us.org/byauth/ashley-smith/damage.html.

Ashurst, J., ed. 2007. Conservation of ruins, Oxford: Taylor & Francis.

Ashworth, G.J. 1991. Heritage Planning: Conservation as the Management of Urban Change. Groningen: Geo Press.

Aston, M. 1973. *English Ruins and English History: the Dissolution and the Sense of the Past.* Journal of the Warburg and Courtauld Institutes, Vol. 36: 231–255.

Augé, M. 1999. Disneyland e altri nonluoghi. Translated by Salsano, A. Torino: Bollati Boringhieri.

Augé, M. 2004. Rovine e macerie. Il senso del tempo. Translated by Serafini,
A. Torino: Bollati Boringhieri.

Augé, M. 2009. Non-places: Introduction to an Anthropology of Supermodernity. Translated by Howe, J. New York: Verso.

Augé, M. 2010. Che fine ha fatto il futuro? Dai non luoghi al nontempo. Translated by Lagomarsino, G. Milano: Eleuthera.

Australia ICOMOS. 1979. *The Australia ICOMOS Guidelines for the Conservation of Places of Cultural Significance ('Burra Charter').''* Accessed March 17, 2016. http://australia.icomos.org/wp-content/uploads/Burra-Charter_1979.pdf.

Australia ICOMOS. 2013. The Burra Charter: The Australia ICOMOS Charter for Places of Cultural Significance. Burwood: Australia ICOMOS.

Australian Heritage Council. 2013. Ruins, a guide to conservation and management.

Avent, J. 2011. *Conserving and Stabilizing Masonry Ruins.* Journal of Architectural Conservation. Volume 17, no. 1: 29–57. Accessed January 16, 2014. http://dx.doi.org/10.1080/13556207.2011.10785081.

Baldick, C. 2012. Literature of the 1920s: writers among the ruins, Edinburgh: Edinburgh University Press.

Banerjee, T. and Southworth, M., eds. 1990. City sense and city design. Writings and Projects of Kevin Lynch, Cambridge and London: The MIT Press.

BAPSAE Superintendence of Naples. 2012. Confronti. L'architettura allo stato di rudere, Quaderni di restauro architettonico della Soprintendenza per i beni architettonici, Napoli: Arte'm.

Barbanera, M. 2013. Metamorfosi delle rovine, Milano: Electa.

Barbanera, M. ed. 2009. Relitti Riletti. Metamorfosi delle rovine e identità culturale, Torino: Bollati Boringhieri.

Bartolomucci, C. 2009. *Sistemi informativi geografici per la conservazione della città storica.* In Antiche ferite e nuovi significati. Cagliari e la città storica edited by **Giannattasio, C.,** 87–96. Roma: Gangemi.

Bauman, Z. 2000. Liquid Modernity, Cambridge: Polity Press.

Bauman, Z. 2007. Liquid Times: Living in an Age of Uncertainty, Cambridge: Polity Press.

Beckmann, P. and Bowles, J. 2004. Structural aspects of building conservation. Oxford: Elsevier Butterworth-Heinemann.

Bell, D. 1997. The Historic Scotland guide to International Conservation Charters. Edinburgh: Historical Scotland.

Bell, D. 2008. Edinburgh old town: the forgotten nature of an urban form, Tholis Publishing.

Bellini, A. 2011. *La ricostruzione: frammento di un dibattito tra teorie del restauro, questione dei centri antichi, economia.* In Guerra Monumenti ricostruzione. Architetture e centri storici italiani nel secondo conflitto mondiale edited by de Stefani L.,14–65. Venezia: Marsilio.

Bevan R. 2006. The Destruction of Memory: Architecture at War. London: Reaktion.

Billeci, B. and Gizzi, S., eds. 2010. Cesare Brandi e la Sardegna. Archeologia
e paesaggio, Roma: Gangemi.

Billeci, B., Gizzi, S. and Scudino, D., eds. 2006. Il rudere tra conservazione
e reintegrazione, Roma: Gangemi.

Bloszies, C. 2012. Old buildings, new designs. Architectural transformations,
New York: Princeton Architectural press.

Boato, A. 2008. L'archeologia in architettura. Venezia: Marsilio.

Bollack, F. and Frampton K. 2013. Old Buildings, New Forms. New directions in architectural transformation, United States: Monacelli Press.

Bonelli, R. 1963. Voce *Restauro-restauro architettonico*. Enciclopedia Universale dell'arte, vol. XI.

Boriani, M. 1996. *Complessità del costruito e qualità del progetto.* 'Ananke. Cultura, storia e tecniche della conservazione, n. 15 (September):64–65. Firenze: Altralinea.

213

Bourdieu, P. 1986. *The forms of capital.* In Handbook of theory and research for the sociology of Education edited by Richardson, trans Nice, R. 46–58. New York: Greenwood.

Brandi, C. 1977. Teoria del restauro, Torino: Enaudi.

Brennan-Inglis, J. 2014. Scotland's Castles: Rescued, Rebuilt and Reoccupied, Gloucestershire: The History Press.

Brink, P. 1998. *Heritage Tourism in the U.S.A.: Grassroots Efforts to Combine Preservation and Tourism.* APT Bulletin 29, no. 3: 59–63.

Cadeddu, B., Cocco, G.B., Sau F. and Siddi, C. 2015. Castello Toolkit. Cagliari, patrimonio storico vs usi contemporanei, Roma: Gangemi.

Cadeddu, M.E., ed. 2001. Studi storici sulle istituzioni della Sardegna nel Medioevo, Nuoro: Ilisso.

Cadinu, M. 2001. Urbanistica medievale in Sardegna, Roma: Bonsignori.

Cadinu, M. 2009. Cagliari. Forma e progetto della città storica, Cagliari: Cuec.

Cambridge Dictionary. 2017. Cambridge: Cambridge University Press.

Calvino, I. 2002. Invisible cities. Trasleted by Weaver, W. London: Vintage books.

Capuano, A., ed. 2014. Paesaggi di rovine paesaggi rovinati. Landscapes of Ruins Ruined Lands, Macerata: Quodlibet.

Carbonara, G. 1976. La reintegrazione dell'immagine. Problemi di restauro dei monumenti, Roma: Bulzoni.

Carbonara, G. 1996. *The integration of the image: problems in the Restoration of Monuments.* In Historical and philosophical issues in the conservation of cultural heritage edited by Melucco Vaccaro, A., Stanley-Price, N. and Kirby Talley, M., 236–243. Los Angeles: Getty Conservation Institute

Carbonara, G. 1996–2008. Trattato di restauro architettonico, vol. I-XI, Torino: Utet.

Carbonara, G. 1997. Avvicinamento al restauro: teoria, storia, monumenti, Napoli: Liguori.

Carbonara, G. 2011. Architettura d'oggi e restauro. Un confronto antico-nuovo, Torino: Utet.

Cardi, M.V. 1996. *Architettura con rovine: immagini del mondo artistico nordeuropeo tra Cinque e Seicento.* 'Ananke. Cultura, storia e tecniche della conservazione 15, (September):30–37.

Carmassi, M. 1999. *"Restauri e architettura d'interni".* In Del restauro, quattordici case edited by Carmassi, G., 15–37. Milano: Electa.

Carmassi, M. 2007. Conservazione e architettura, Venezia: Marsilio.

Carver, M. 1996. *On Archaeological Value.* Antiquity 70 (267): 45–56.

Casiello, S., ed. 2011. I ruderi e la guerra. Memoria, ricostruzione, restauro, Firenze: Nardini.

Casiello, S., Pane, A. and Russo, V. 2007. Roberto Pane tra storia e restauro: architettura, città, paesaggio, Venezia: Marsilio.

Clark, K. 2001. Informed Conservation: Understanding Historic Buildings and Their Landscapes. London: English Heritage.

Cocco, G.B. and Giannattasio, C. eds. 2017. Misurare Innestare Comporre. Architetture storiche e progetto / Measure Graft Compose. Historical architectures and design. Pisa: Pisa University Press.

Colavitti, A. M. 2005. *La topografia antica e l'impianto urbanistico della città nuova.* In Il quartiere di Marina a Cagliari. Ricostruzione di un contesto urbano pluristratificato, edited by G. Deplano, Milan: Edicom Editore.

Colavitti, A. M. 2015. *Città pubblica e rigenerazione urbana nei nuovi strumenti di piano. Il caso di Cagliari.* In Infrastrutture blu e verdi, reti culturali, virtuali e sociali. Green and Blu infrastructures, Virtual Cultural and Social Networks, edited by Moccia F. D. and Sepe M. Naples: Planum

Colavitti, A. M. 2003. Cagliari: forma e urbanistica, Roma: L'Erma di Bretschneider.

Colletta, T., ed. 2013. *Città storiche e turismo culturale. Città d'arte o città di cultura? Marketing urbano o turismo culturale?.* In Proceedings of the workshop organised by Centro Europeo Universitario per I Beni Culturali, Villa Rufolo, Raviello, 24–23 Marzo 2012, Napoli: Gangemi.

Colquhoun, I. 1995. Urban regeneration. An international perspective, London: B.T. Batsford Ltd.

Conway, H. and Roenisch. R. 1994. Understanding Architecture, London: Routledge.

Conzen, M. R. G. and Whitehand, J. V. R. 1981. The urban landscape: historical development and management. London: Academic Press.

Corti, E. 2004. *Identità storiche e priorità progettuali.* In. Cagliari tra passato e futuro, edited by Ortu G. G., 355–375. Cagliari: Cuec.

Crinson, M., ed. 2005. Urban Memory. History and amnesia in the modern city. London and New York: Routledge.

Croci, G. 2001. Conservation and Structural restoration of architectural heritage, Southampton, Wit press.

Cruciani Fabozzi, G. *Valore di novità e progetto per l'esistente.* 'Ananke. Cultura, storia e tecniche della conservazione, n.15 (September):62–63. Firenze: Atralinea.

Curl, J. S. and Wilson, S., eds. 2015. Oxford dictionary of Architecture (3 ed.), Oxford: Oxford University Press.

Darvill, T. 1995. *Value Systems in Archaeology.* In Managing Archaeology, edited by M. A. Cooper, A. Firth, J. Carman, and D. Wheatley, 40–50. London: Routledge.

Davis, S. 2008. *"Military landscapes and secret science: The case of Orford Ness".* Cultural Geographies 15: 143–149.

Dawly, S. L. 2010. Clockpunk Anthropology and the ruins of Modernity in Current Anthropology, vol. 51, no. 6 761–793.

De la Torre, M. and Mason, R. 2002. *"Introduction".* In Assessing the Values of Cultural Heritag, edited by The Getty Conservation Institute, 3–4. Los Angeles:
The J. Paul Getty Trust.

De la Torre, M., ed. 2002. Assessing the Values of Cultural Heritage. Los Angeles, CA: Getty Conservation Institute.

De Martino, G. 2004. *L'edificio allo stato di rudere: aspetti teorici e metodologici.* In Il monumento e la sua conservazione: note sulla metodologia del progetto di restauro, edited by Romeo E., 73–100. Torino: Celid.

De Martino, R. 2011. *Le ricostruzioni in Francia nel secondo dopoguerra.* In I ruderi e la guerra. Memoria, ricostruzione, restauro, edited by Casiello, S., 77–99. Firenze: Nardini.

De Stefani, L., Coccoli, C., eds. 2011. Guerra monumenti ricostruzione. Architetture e centri storici italiani nel secondo conflitto mondiale, Marsilio.

De Vita, M. 2015. Architetture nel tempo: dialoghi della materia, nel restauro, Firenze: Firenze University Press.

Deidda, M. and Vacca, G. 2013. *Tecniche di rilievo Laser Scanner a supporto del progetto di restauro conservativo dei beni culturali. l'esempio del Castello di Siviller e del campanile di Mores*. Bollettino SIFET n. 4 del 2012 23–39 ISSN 1721–971X.

Delafons, J., 1997. Politics and Preservation: A Policy History of the Built Heritage, 1882–1996, Oxford: Alessandrine Press.

Delogu, R., 1946. Letter to the Ministero della Pubblica Istruzione, Direzione Generale Antichità e Belle Arti di Roma, Cagliari, in Archive of superintendence BAPPSAE for the counties of Cagliari and Oristano.

Deplano, C. 2008. Laboratorio del paesaggio urbano. Analisi storico morfologica del quartiere di Castello a Cagliari, Gorizia: Edicom.

Deplano, G., ed. 2004. Politiche e strumenti per il recupero urbano, Gorizia: Edicom.

Deplano, C. 2009a. Antropologia urbana. Società complesse e democrazia partecipativa, Gorizia: Edicom.

Deplano, G. 2009b. La pianificazione urbanistica partecipativa nella società dell'informazione, Gorizia: Edicom.

Deplano, G., ed. 2009. Analisi del paesaggio urbano: Cagliari ed il suo centro storico, Gorizia: Edicom.

DeSilvey, C. 2007. *Salvage memory: Constellating material histories on a hardscrabble homestead*. Cultural Geographies 14: 401–424.

DeSilvey, C. and Edensor, T. 2012. *Reckoning with ruins*. Progress in Human Geography 37, n. 4: 465–485. Manchester Metropolitan University, UK.

Desrochers, B. 2000. *Ruins revisited: modernist conceptions of heritage*. The Journal of Architecture 5, no. 1: 35–46. Accessed Febraury 18, 2011. http://dx.doi.org/10.1080/136023600373673.

Dezzi Bardeschi, M. 1996. *Amate l'architettura: valore di novità degli antichi e valore storico dei moderni*. 'Ananke. Cultura, storia e tecniche della conservazione 15, (September):58–60. Firenze: Altralinea.

Dezzi Bardeschi, M. 2004. *Il restauro: una nuova definizione per un'antica (ambigua) disciplina*. 'Ananke. Cultura, storia e tecniche della conservazione, n. 41, (marzo): 2–5.Firenze: Altralinea.

Di Blasi, V. and Robbiati, C. 1996. *Rovine, testimoni del tempo*. 'Ananke. Cultura, storia e tecniche della conservazione, n. 15 (September): 22–29.

Dillon, B. 2006. Fragments from a history of ruin. Cabinet Magazine. Available at: http://www.cabinetmagazine.org/issues/20/dillon.php.
Dillon, B., ed. 2011. Ruins (Documents of Contemporary Art), London: Whitechapel Gallery.

Dillon, B., ed. 2011. Ruins. Documents of Contemporary Art, London: Whitechapel Gallery.

Dillon, B., ed. 2014. Ruin Lust. New York: Harry N. Abrambs.

Docci, M. and Maestri, D. 2009. Manuale di rilevamento architettonico e urbano, Roma: Laterza.

Doglioni, F., ed. 1997. Stratigrafia e restauro, tra conoscenza e conservazione dell'architettura, Trieste: Lint.

Doglioni, F. 2008. Nel restauro: progetti per le architetture del passato, Venezia: Marsilio.

Dokmeci, V., Altunbas, U. & Yazgi, B. 2007. *Revitalization of the Main Street of a Distinguished Old Neighbourhood in Istanbul*. European Planning Studies 15, no. 1: 153–166.

Doratli, N. 2005. *Revitalizing historic urban quarters: A model for determining the most relevant strategic approach*, European Planning Studies, vol. 13 no. 5, 749–772, DOI: 10.1080/09654310500139558.

Douglas, G. and Gray, I. 1992. *Notes on surveying techniques*. In Materials and traditions in Scottish building; essays in memory of Sonia Hackett edited by Stell, G. in Riches, A., Edinburgh.

Douglas, J. 2002. Building adaptation, Oxford: Butterworth Heinemann.

Dvorak M. 1972. Catechismo per la tutela dei monumenti, (1916). In Paragone, Rivista mensile di arte figurativa e letteratura founded by Roberto Longhi, n. 257 Firenze : Sansoni, stampa (Officine Grafiche Firenze)

Edensor, T. 2005. Industrial ruins, space, aesthetics and materiality, Oxford: Berg.

Edensor, T. 2007. *Sensing the Ruin*. Journal of The Senses and Society 2, issue 2: 217–232. Accessed April 16, 2015. http://dx.doi.org/10.2752/174589307X203100.

Edensor, T. 2008. *Walking through ruins*. In Ways of Walking: Ethnography and Practice on Foot, edited by Ingold, T. and Vergunst, J. L., 123–142. Aldershot: Ashgate.

El-Hakim, S.F., Gonzo, L., Girardi, S. Picard, M., Whiting, E. 2004. *Photo-realistic 3D reconstruction of castles with multiple-sources image-based techniques*. Proceedingsof ISPRS XXth Congress, 2004, Istanbul, Vol. 35(B5), 120–125.

English Heritage. 2008a. Conservation principles. Policies and guidance for the sustainable management of the historic environment.

English Heritage. 2008b. Constructive Conservation in Practice.

English Heritage. 2012. Enabling development and the conservation of significant places regeneration in the UK, London and New York: Routledge, Taylor.

Ercolino, M. G. 2006 *Il trauma delle rovine. Dal monito al restauro*. In Semantica delle rovine, edited by Tortora, G., 137–166. Roma: Manifestolibri.

Ercolino, M.G. 2014 *Le rovine 'dimenticate'. Identità, conservazione e valorizzazione dei resti archeologici nella periferia romana*. Il capitale culturale, Studies on the Value of Cultural Heritage, Vol. 10: 439–469.

Farci, S. & DICAAR. 2015. Etg 015. Cagliari *città della cultura*. Progetto strategico il museo città. Piano Particolareggiato del centro storico, Cagliari Council.

Farley, P.and Roberts, M. 2011. Edgelands: Journeys Into England's True Wilderness. London: Jonathan Cape.

Fawcett, R. 2001. The Conservation of Architectural Ancient Monuments in Scotland, Guidance on Principles. Edinburgh: Heritage Policy, Historic Scotland.

Featherstone, M. 2005. *Ruin Value*. Journal for Cultural Research 9, no. 3: 301–320. Accessed July 2, 2016. http://dx.doi.org/10.1080/14797580500179634.

Feilden, B. M. 2003. Conservation of historic buildings. Amsterdam, London: Architectural Press.

Ferlenga A., Vassallo E. and Schellino F., eds. 2008. Antico e nuovo. Architetture e architettura. Proceedings of the Conference, 31 March–3 April 2004, Padova:
Il Poligrafo (voll 1–2).

Ferlenga, A. 2014. *Tra i muri del tempo*. Archeologia dell'architettura XIX: 90–97.

Ferri, S. 2015. Ruins past modernity in Italy, 1744–1839, Oxford: Voltaire foundation, University of Oxford.

Fiorani, D. 2009a. *Architettura, restauro, rovina.* In Relitti Riletti. Metamorfosi delle rovine e identità culturale edited by Barbanera M., 339–355. Torino: Bollati Boringhieri.

Fiorani, D. 2009b. *Restaurare la città storica: strategia e casi d'intervento in Europa.* In Antiche ferite e nuovi significati. Cagliari e la città storica edited by Giannattasio, C., 121–134. Roma: Gangemi.

Fiorani, D. 2013. The other shore. Preservation and the past in the United States. Loggia 26: 8–37.

Fiorani, D. 2015. *Architettura storica e contemporaneità in Europa. Scenari operativi, prospettive culturali e ruolo del restauro".* In Architor, anno III, no. 6: 107–141.

Fiorino, D. 2009. *Stratigrafia urbana* In Proposte per Stampace.Idee per in piano di conservazione del quartiere storico di Cagliari edited by Giannattasio, C., Scarpellini, P., 69–74. Roma: Gangemi.

Fiorino, D., Concu, G. 2014. Il progetto Accessit: L'accessibilità ai ruderi degli edifici di culto della Sardegna. La Metodologia Ecclesiae Fabrica.

Fiorino, D. and Pilia, E. 2014. *Il rudere come Time-Landmark del paesaggio storico.* In the International and Interdisciplinary periodical. Agribusiness Paesaggio & Ambiente, XVII no. 2: 108–114.

Fiorino, D. 2015. *L'onda lunga della ricostruzione: restauri a Cagliari nel secondo dopoguerra.* Palladio, vol.55, 95–124

Fiorino, D.R., Giannattasio, C. and Grillo, S.M. 2015. *Interpretazioni stratigrafiche di malte e intonaci nelle chiese rurali della Sardegna: S. Giovanni Battista a Bortigali (NU)".* In Materiali e Strutture. Problemi di conservazione. La materia del restauro, edited by Fiorani, D. Serie IV, no. 8., 21–30 , Roma: Edizioni Quasar di Severino Tognon s.r.l.

Fiorino, D and Grillo, S.M. 2015. *Coastal cities and Cultural Heritage: problems of conservation and management. The case of the ancient walled city of Cagliari (Sardinia, Italy).* In Coastal Cities and their Sustainable Future edited by Rodriguez, GR; **Brebbia, CA,** 111–148, WIT Press.

Fiorino, D. R., Grillo, S. M. and Pilia, E. 2015. *Interdisciplinary Knowledge for Conservation of Ruins: Stratigraphic Investigations of San Giovanni Battista Church (Sardinia, Italy),* Athens: ATINER'S Conference Paper Series, No: ARC2015–2123.

Fiorino, D., Giannattasio, C. and Grillo, S.M. 2015. *Fortificazioni e cronologie. Protocolli conoscitivi per la conservazione.* In Verso un atlante dei sistemi difensivi della Sardegna, edited by Fiorino, D. & Pintus, M., 128–172. Napoli: Giannini.

Fiorino, D.R., Giannattasio, C. and Grillo, S.M. 2015. *Interpretazioni stratigrafiche di malte e intonaci nelle chiese rurali della Sardegna: S.Giovanni Battista a Bortigali (NU).* In Materiali e Strutture. Problemi di conservazione. La materia del restauro, edited by Fiorani, D. Serie IV, no. 8., 21–30, Roma: Edizioni Quasar di Severino Tognon s.r.l.

Fiorino, D.R., Grillo, S.M. and Pilia, E. 2016. *Historical mortars as record in the knowledge of ruins.* In Proceedings of the 4th Historic Mortars Conference – HMC 2016. 10–12 October 2016, Santorini, Greece, edited by Papayianni, I., Stefanidou, M. & Pachta V., 779–256. Laboratory of building Materials, Department of Civil Engineering Aristotle University of Thessaloniki, ISBN: 978-960-99922-3-7.

Fitch, J.M. 1990. Historic Preservation: Curatorial Management of the Built Environment, Charlottesville: University Press of Virginia.

Florida, R. 2011.The rise of the creative class, revisited, New York: Basic book.

Forsyth, M. 2007. Structures & Construction in Historic Building Conservation. Oxford: Blackwell Publishing Ltd.

Fowkes Tobin, B. 2005. Colonizing nature: the tropics in British arts and letters, 1760–1820, Philadelphia: PENN/University of Pennsylvania Press.

Franck, K. A. and Stevens, Q. 2007. *Tying down loose space.* In Loose Space: Possibility and Diversity in Urban Life, edited by Franck, K. A. and Stevens, Q., 1–33. Abingdon: Routledge.

Franco, C., Masserente, A. and Trisciuoglio M. (eds.). 2002. L'antico e il nuovo. Il rapporto tra città antica e architettura contemporanea. Torino: Utet.

Freud, S. 1930. Das Unbehagen in der Kultur, Germany: Internationaler Psychoanalytischer Verlag.

Frey, B. 1997. *The Evaluation of Cultural Heritage: Some Critical Issues.* In Economic Perspectives on Cultural Heritage, edited by M. Hutter and I. Rizzo, 31–49. Basingstoke: Palgrave MacMillan.

Gazzola, P. 1967. *La difesa del rudere.* Castellum no. 5, Roma: Istituto Nazionale dei Castelli.

Gelsomino, L. 1984. *La progettazione del recupero, del restauro, del rinnovo urbano nell'esperienza di alcune città italiane.* In Intervenire sull'esistente negli anni '80: documenti e riflessioni, edited by Ballandi, R., 55–79. Bologna: Ente autonomo per le fiere.

Giambruno, C. 2002. Verso la dimensione urbana della conservazione, Firenze: Alinea.

Giambruno, M. ed. 2007. Per una storia del restauro urbano. Piani, strumenti e progetti per i centri storici, Torino, Citta Studi.

Giannattasio, C. (ed.) 2009. Antiche ferite e nuovi significati. Cagliari e la città storica, Roma: Gangemi.

Giannattasio C. and Scarpellini, P., eds. 2009. Proposte per Stampace. Idee per un piano di conservazione del quartiere storico cagliaritano, Rome: Gangemi.

Giannattasio, C. and Grillo, S.M. 2011. *The Mezzaspiaggia tower (Cagliari-Italy): the dating of structures by the metrological-chronological analysis of masonry and the petro-geochemical stratigraphy of building materials.* Proceedings of the 37° ISA., 489–494. Siena, Berlin-Heidelberg: I. Turbantini Memmi, Springer.

Giannattasio, C. and Pintus, V. 2013. *Il complesso claustrale di San Francesco a Stampace in Cagliari.* Arkos fifth series no. 3–4: 47–68.

Giannattasio, C., Grillo, S.M., Murru, S. 2014. The Western Sardinian coast defensive towers (16th–17th century): an interdisciplinary approach for the chronological definition of masonries, in G.T. Papanikos (ed), Proceedings of 4th Annual International Conference on Architecture (Athens, July 7–10), Athens Institute for Education and Research, Atene, pp. 3–17.

Giannattasio, C., Grillo, S.M., Vacca G. 2014. *The Medieval San Francesco Convent in Cagliari: from the architectural, materical and historical-stratigraphical analysis to the information system.* International Journal of heritage in the digital era. Vol. 3 no. 2: 413–429. ISSN 2047-4.

Giannattasio, C., Grillo, S. M. and Pirisino M. S. 2015. *The Rectorate Building of the University of Cagliari (18th–20th century): Archaeometric Analysis of Masonries.* Arkos fifth series no. 9–10: 30–52.

Giannattasio, C. & Pinna A. 2016. Ancient architecture and new meaning in the New World. Current tendencies in the USA. Proceedings of the 10th International Conference of the European Association for Architectural Education (EAAE) and the Architectural Research Centers Consortium (ARCC), Lisbon 15–18th June 2016. In press.

Giannattasio, C., Pilia, E. and Pinna, A. 2016. *Urban tourism. A comparison with Anglo-American experiences for the regeneration of the historic centre of Cagliari.* In Lira, S., Mano, A., Amoêda, R. & Pinheiro C., TOURISM 2016 – Proceedings of the International Conference on Global Tourism and Sustainability, Green Lines Institute, pp. 189–199.

Giannattasio C., Grillo S. M., Murru S. 2017. Il sistema di torri costiere in Sardegna (XVI–XVII sec.). Forma, materia, tecniche murarie, Roma: L'Erma di Bretschneider.

Giannattasio, C., Grillo, S. M, Pilia, E & Pirisino, M. S. 2017. *Defence heritage in a state of ruin: the archaeometric study of 'della Fava' castle in Sardinia (Italy).* In International Journal of Heritage Architecture, Vol. 1, No. 2, WIT Press, pp. 237–246.

Ginsberg, R. 2004. The Aesthetic of Ruins, Amsterdam/New York: Rodopi B.V.

Giovannoni, G. 1945. Restauro dei monumenti, Roma: Cremonese.

Girouard, M. 1985. Cities and People: A social and architectural history. New Haven and London: Yale University Press.

Gizzi, S. 2006. *La condizione del rudere in Sardegna".* In Santa Maria di Curos in territorio di Monteleone. Studi e restauri di un edificio allo stato di rudere, edited by Frulio Gabriela, 3–5.

Glendinning, M. 2013. The conservation movement. A history of architectural preservation. Antiquity to modernity, London: Routledge.

Glendinning, M. and Mackechnie, A. 2004. Scottish Architecture, London: Tames and Hudson world of art.

Glendinning, M., Dakin, A & MacKechnie A., eds. 2011. Scotland's Castle Culture. Birlinn Press.

Göbel, H. K. 2015. The Re-Use of Urban Ruins. Atmospheric Inquiries of the City (Routledge Advances in Sociology), New York: Routledge, Taylor & Francis group.

Gómez Robles, L. 2010. *A Methodological Approach towards Conservation.* Conservation and Management of Archaeological Sites 12, no. 2: 146–169.

Gonza´lez-Ruibal, A. 2005. *The need for a decaying past: An archaeology of oblivion in Galicia.* Home Cultures 2, no. 2: 129–155.

Gordon D. 2010. 'Reanimating industrial landscapes': A session at TAG 2009 in Durham, UK. Papers from the Institute of Archaeology 20: 180–185.

Grillo, S. M. 2009a. *Le pietre usate nel costruito.* In Proposte per Stampace.Idee per in piano di conservazione del quartiere storico di Cagliari. edited by Giannattasio, C., Scarpellini. P., 79–83. Roma: Gangemi Editore.

Grillo, S.M. 2009b. *Notizie geologiche, petrografiche e storiche.* In Manuali del Recupero dei centri storici della Sardegna. Il manuale tematico della pietra, edited by Sanna, U. and Atzeni, C., 1–22. Roma: DEI.

Gruen A., Remondino F., Zhang L. 2004. *Photogrammetric reconstruction of the great Buddha of Bamiyan, Afghanistan.* The Photogrammetric Record, vol. 19, no.107: 177–199.

Guarnieri A., Remondino F., Vettore A. 2006, *Digital photogrammetry and TLS data fusion applied to Cultural Heritage 3D modeling.* International Archives of Photogrammetry, Remote Sensing and Spatial Information Sciences, 36, no. 5, on CD-Rom.

Guggenheim, M. 2009. *Building memory: Architecture, networks and users* Memory studies, vol.2, no.1: 39–53.

Guidi, G., Remondino, F., Russo, M., Menna, F., Rizzi, A., Ercoli, S. 2009. *A multiresolution methodology for the 3D modeling of large and complex archaeological areas.* Int. Journal of Architectural Computing, 7, no.1: 40–55.

H. Wolff, K. (ed.). 1959. George Simmel, 1858-1918. A collection essays, with translations and a Bibliography, Ohio: The Ohio State University Press Columbus

Hamlyn D. W. 1957. The psychology of perception: a philosophical examination of Gestalt theory and derivative theories of perception, London: Routledge & Paul.

Harald Fredheim, L. and Khalaf, M. 2016. The significance of values: heritage value typologies re-examined. International Journal of Heritage Studies, vol. 22, no. 6, 466–481, DOI: 10.1080/13527258.2016.1171247.

Hatherley, O. 2010. A guide to the new ruins of Great Britain, London: Verso.

Hell, J. and Shönle, A. eds. 2010. Ruins of modernity, Durham and London: Duke University Press.

Heritage Council of Western Australia. 2004. Heritage Impact statement, Guidelines.

High, S. and Lewis, D. W. 2007. Corporate Wasteland: The Landscape and Memory of Deindustrialization. Ithaca, NY: Cornell University Press.

Hill, J. 2006. Immaterial architecture, London: Routledge.

Howard, R.T. 1962. Ruined and Rebuilt. The story of the Coventry Cathedral 1939–1962, Hertfordshire: The Garden City Press.

Hudson, J. 2010. *Alternative cultural practices and (re)emergent spaces.* Paper presented at UGRC Conference 'Alternative Urbanisms', London, 10 November.

Hyppolite, P. 2015. La Ruine et le geste architectural. Presses Universitaires de Paris Ouest.

ICOMOS New Zealand. 2010. ICOMOS New Zealand Charter for the Conservation of Places of Cultural Heritage Value. Auckland: ICOMOS New Zealand. Accessed March 17, 2016. http://www.icomos.org.nz/docs/NZ_Charter.pdf

ICOMOS. 1994. *Nara Document on Authenticity.* Accessed March 17, 2016. http://www.icomos.org/charters/nara-e.pdf

ICOMOS. 2003. Measured Survey and Building Recording, Edinburgh.

ICOMOS. 2007. *The ICOMOS Charter for the Interpretation and Presentation of Cultural Heritage Sites: Proposed Final Draft.* Accessed March 17, 2016. http://www.enamecharter.org/downloads/ICOMOS_Interpretation_Charter_EN_10-04-07.pdf

Ingegno, A. 1993. Santa Chiara: restauri e scoperte, Cagliari.

Jäger, F. P.,ed. 2010. Old & New: Design Manual for Revitalizing Existing Buildings, Basel: Birkhäuser.

Jokilehto, J. 2009. A History of Architectural Conservation, Oxford: Butterworth Heinemann.

Jones, P. & Evans, J. 2008. Urban regeneration in the UK, London: Sage.

Kalman, H. 2014. Heritage Planning: Principles and Process, New York: Routledge.

Kaufman, N. 2009. Place, race, and story: Essays on the Past and future of historic Preservation, New York: Routledge.

Keene, S. 2005. Fragments of the World: Uses of Museum Collections. Oxford: Elsevier Butterworth-Heinemann.

Kent, R. 2003. *Heritage in ruins. The maintenance and preservation of ruined monuments.* In The Building Conservation Directory, 16–19.

Kerr, J. S. 2013. Conservation Plan: A guide to the preparation of conservation plans for places of European Cultural significance (7th edn.; Burwood, Victoria: Australia ICOMOS)

Kirova, T. 2009. *Assenze e presenze nella città storica. Il caso di Cagliari.* In Antiche ferite e nuovi significati. Cagliari e la città storica edited by Giannattasio, C., 185–198. Roma: Gangemi

Kirova, T., Masala F. and Pintus, M., eds. 1985. Cagliari, quartieri storici. Castello. Milano, Silvana ed.

Kirova, T., Masala F. and Pintus, M., eds. 1989. Cagliari, quartieri storici. Marina. Milano, Silvana ed.

Kirova, T., Masala F. and Pintus, M., eds. 1990. Cagliari, quartieri storici. Villanova. Milano, Silvana ed.

Kirova, T., Masala F. and Pintus, M., eds. 1995. Cagliari, quartieri storici. Stampace. Milano, Silvana ed.

Klanten R. & and Lukas Feireiss, L., eds. 2009. Build-on: converted architecture and transformed buildings, Berlin: Gestalten.

Lahusen, T. 2006. *Decay or endurance? The ruins of socialism.* Slavic Review 65, no. 4: 736–746.

Lamberini, D. ed. 2006. D. L'eredità di John Ruskin nella cultura italiana del Novecento, Firenze: Nardini.

Lambourne, N. 2001. War damage in Western Europe: the destruction of historic monuments during the Second World War, Edinburgh University Press.

Larkham, P. J. & Pendlebury, J. 2008. *Reconstruction planning and the small town in early post-war Britain.* Planning Perspectives, 23, no. 33, 291–321. Accessed: October 26 2015. DOI:10.1080/02665430802102807.

Larkham, P. J. 1996. Conservation and the City. London: Routledge.

Larkham, P. J. 2003. *The place of urban conservation in the UK reconstruction plans of 1942–1952.* In Planning Perspectives, 18, no. 3, 295–324, DOI:10.1080/02665430307975.

Larkham, P. J. 2013. *Continual change: a century of urban conservation in England.* Working Paper series no. 21 Centre for Environment and Society Research, Birmingham City University.

Latham, D. 2000. Creative reuse of buildings, London: Routledge (vv. 1–2).

Lavery, C. & Gough R., eds. 2015. *On Ruins and Ruination.* In Performance Research. A Journal of the Performing Arts v. 20, no. 3.

Lees, L., Slater, T. and Wyly, E. 2008. Gentrification, New York: Routledge.

Lefebvre, H. 1991. The production of the space, Oxford: Blackwell.

Lertcharnrit, T. 2010. *Heritage Values and Meanings in Contemporary Thailand.* In Heritage Values in Contemporary Society, edited by G. S. Smith, P. M. Messenger, and H. A. Soderland, 279–285. Walnut Creek, CA: Left Coast Press.

Levi, C. 1964. Tutto il miele è finito, Torino: Einaudi.

Levi Montalcini, E. 2002. *Introduzione.* In L'antico e il nuovo. Il rapporto tra città e architettura contemporanea edited by Massarente, A., Franco, C. and Tisciuoglio, Torino: Utet.

Lichfield, N. 1988. Economics in urban conservation, Cambridge: Cambridge University Press.

Lion Club, ed. 1986. Dentro Castello. Gli uomini, le storie, gli itinerari reconditi del più affascinante quartiere di Cagliari, Cagliari:

Lipe, W. 1984. *Value and Meaning in Cultural Resources.* In Approaches to the Archaeological Heritage: A Comparative Study of World Cultural Resource Management Systems, edited by H. Cleere, 1–11. Cambridge: Cambridge University Press.

Lo Curzio, M. 1992. *Architetture e ruderificazione* in Le rovine nell'immagine del territorio calabrese edited by Menizzu, Luciana, Roma: Gangemi.

Lumia, C. 2003. A proposito del restauro e della conservazione, Roma: Gangemi.

Lynch, K. 1960. The image of the City. Cambridge, Mass.: MIT Press.

Macauley, R. 1977. The pleasure of ruins, Thames & Hudson Ltd.

Mackee, J. 2009. Evaluation in Urban Conservation.

Madanipour, A. 2007. Designing the city of reason: foundations and frameworks. Routledge.

Madgin, R. 2010. *Reconceptualising the historic urban environment: conservation and regeneration in Castlefield, Manchester, 1960–2009.* Planning Perspectives, 25, no.1: 29–48.

Mah, A. 2010, *Memory, Uncertainty and Industrial Ruination: Walker Riverside, Newcastle upon Tyne.* International Journal of Urban and Regional Research, 34: 398–413. doi:10.1111/j.1468-2427.2010.00898.

Makarius, M. 2004. Ruins, Paris: Éditions Flammarion : Distributed in North America by Rizzoli International Publications.

Marconi, P. 1993. Il restauro e l'architetto. Teoria e pratica in due secoli di dibattito, Venezia, Marsilio.

Marconi, P. 2005. Il recupero della bellezza, Milano: Skira ed.

Marini, S. 2015. Architettura parassita. Strategie di riciclaggio per la città. Roma: Quodlibet Studio. Città e paesaggio. Reprint.

Marino, L. 1989. Conservazione e manutenzione di manufatti edilizi ridotti allo stato di rudere, Firenze: Opus Libri.

Marino, L. 2002. Restauro di manufatti architettonici allo stato di rudere, Firenze: Alinea.

Marzocca, F. 2014. *Il nuovo approccio scientifico verso la Transdisciplinarità.* In ÁTOPON Rivista di Psicoantropologia Simbolica, Special edition n. 10, Mithos Edizioni.

Masala F. 1995. *Le vicende storico-urbanistiche del quartiere.* In Cagliari, quartieri storici. Stampace edited by Kirova, T., Masala F. and Pintus, 23–82 M. Milano: Silvana.

Mason, R. 2002. *Assessing Values in Conservation Planning: Methodological Issues and Choices.* In Assessing the Values of Cultural Heritage, edited by M. de la Torre, 5–30. Los Angeles, CA: Getty Conservation Institute.

Massarente, A., Franco, C. and Tisciuoglio. 2002. L'antico e il nuovo. Il rapporto tra città e architettura contemporanea, Torino: Utet.

Matero, F. 2011. *Being Modern: The Currency of Conservation* in Architectural conservation in Europe and the Americas national experiences and practice edited by Stubbs, John H., and Makaš, Emily G. eds, xvi-xvii , N.J. Hoboken : John Wiley & Sons.

Matteini, T. 2009. Paesaggi del tempo. Documenti archeologici e rovine artificiali nel disegno di giardini e paesaggi, Firenze: Alinea.

Mcmillan, A., Gillanders, R. and Fairhurst, J. A. 1999. Building stones of Edinburgh. Edinburgh: Edinburgh Geological Society.

Melucco Vaccaro, A., Stanley-Price, N. and Kirby Talley, M., eds. 1996. Historical and philosophical issues in the conservation of cultural heritage, Los Angeles: Getty Conservation Institute.

Miele, C. ed. 2005. From W. Morris. Building conservation and the arts and crafts. Cult of authenticity. 1877–1939, London: Yale University Press.

Morris, R.K. 2000. The archaeology of buildings, Stroud: Tempus.

Mugayar K., B. 2009. *Il quadro pan-americano.* In Trattato di Restauro Architettonico. Primo aggiornamento: Grandi temi del restauro, vol. IX: edited by Carbonara, G. 115–146. Torino: UTET.

Musson, J. 1999. *Listen to the speaking ruins.* Country Life, Vol. 193, Issue 24: 92–93.

Musson, J. 2011. English Ruins, London: Merrell.

Nigero, C. 2008. *Centri storici allo stato di rudere. Strategie conservative a confronto.* Progetto Restauro, no. 47 (summer): 28–33.

Norberg-Schultz, C. 1971. Existence, space and architecture. London: Studio Vista.

Norberg-Schultz, C. 1980. Genius Loci: Towards a phenomenology of architecture. London: Academy Editions.

Orbaşli, A. 2000a. Is Tourism Governing Conservation in Historic Towns? Journal of Architectural Conservation, vol. 6, no. 3: 7–19.

Orbaşli, A. 2000b. Tourists in Historic Towns: Urban Conservation and Heritage Management, London & New York: Spon Press.

Orbaşli, A. 2008. Architectural Conservation: Principles and Practice. Oxford: Blackwell Science.

Ortu, G.G. 2004. Cagliari tra passato e futuro, Cagliari: Cuec.

Oteri, A.M. 2009. Rovine. Visioni, teorie, restauri del rudere in architettura, Roma, Argos.

Oteri, A.M. 2015. *Città e monumenti fra le due guerre. Un percorso fra critica, progetto d'architettura e restauro.* Archistor, 130–167.

OED. Oxford English dictionary, 2016. Oxford: Oxford University Press.

Paddison, R. 1993. *City marketing, image reconstruction and urban regeneration.* Urban Studies, vol. 30, no. 2: 339–350.

Palsson, G. 2013. *Situating nature: Ruins of modernity as náttú´ruperlur.* Tourist Studies, vol. 12, no. 2: 172–188.

Performance Research: A Journal of the Performing Arts. Special issue: On Ruins and Ruination. Vol. 20, Issue 3, 2015. Accessed June 23, 2015.

Perret, A. 1946. *La reconstruction du Havre.* In Techniques et Architecture, vol 6, no. 7–8.

Petti, B. 2012. I restauri e le ricostruzioni nel secondo dopoguerra. Il caso di Cagliari a confronto con il panorama nazionale ed europeo, Cagliari: La Riflessione.

Pickard R., ed. 2001a. Policy and Law in Heritage Conservation, London/New York: Spon.

Pickard R., ed. 2001b. Management of Historic Centres, London/New York: Spon.

Picone, R. 2012. *Il rudere architettonico nella storia del restauro.* In Confronti. L'architettura allo stato di rudere, Quaderni di restauro architettonico della Soprintendenza per i beni architettonici, 27–40. Napoli: Arte'm.

Pilia, E. and Pirisino, M.S. 2016. *Gaining knowledge of materials and chronologies of the ruins for the preservation of historical centers: the case study of Monteleone Rocca Doria in Sardinia (Italy).* IN HERITAGE 2016 – Proceedings of the 5th International Conference on Heritage and Sustainable Development, Green Lines Institute edited by Lira, S., Mano, A., Amoêda, R. & Pinheiro C., 1395–1404. Lisbon, Green Lines Institute.

Pilia, E. 2015a. *La catalogazione dei testimoni stratigrafici.* In Verso un atlante dei sistemi difensivi della Sardegna, edited by Fiorino, D. R. and Pintus, M., 164–165. Castella no. 100, Napoli: Giannini.

Pilia, E. 2015b. *Le sorti recenti nella documentazione dei restauri.* In Verso un atlante dei sistemi difensivi della Sardegna, edited by Fiorino, D. R. and Pintus, M., 346–347. Castella no. 100, Napoli: Giannini.

Pilia, E. 2016. *Wartime memories. The perception of nature in ruins within the historical centre of Cagliari (Sardinia, Italy).* In EAUH 2016 – 13th International Conference on Urban History, Helsinki, Helsinki, 24–27.08.2016.

Pilia, E., and Pirisino, M.S. 2016. *Towards strategies for the conservation and enhancement of the cultural landscape. The medieval fortified heritage in north east Sardinia.* In LA BAIA DI NAPOLI – Strategie integrate per la conservazione e la fruizione del paesaggio culturale, Naples 5./6.12.2016.

Pinto, J.A. 2012. Speaking ruins: Piranesi, architects and antiquity in eighteenth-century Rome, University of Michigan Press.

Porfyriou, H. 2010. Urban policies and monitoring tourist impact. The case study of Trevi-Pantheon itinerary in Rome. Rivista di scienze del turismo, 2/2010: 331–352.

Pretelli, M. 2011. *Germania Anno Zero tra ricostruzione postbellica e riunificazione della Nazione.* In I ruderi e la guerra. Memoria, ricostruzione, restauro, edited by **Casiello, S.**, 11–31. Firenze: Nardini.

Principe, I. 1981. Le città nella storia d'Italia. Cagliari, Roma-Bari: Laterza.

Pusca, A. 2010. *Industrial and human ruins of postcommunist Europe.* Space and Culture 13, no. 3: 239–255.

Putzolu, E. 1976. *Il problema delle origini del Castellum Castri di vallari,* in Archivio Storico Sardo, XXX.

Putzu, M.G. 2015. Tecniche costruttive murarie medievali. La Sardegna. Roma: L'Erma di Bretschneider.

Pye, E. 2001. Caring for the past: Issues in Conservation for Archaeology and Museums. London: James & James.

Quendolo, F., ed. 2014. Paesaggi di guerra. Memoria e Progetto, Udine: Veneto.

Qvistro¨m, M. 2012. *Network ruins and green structure development: An attempt to trace relational spaces of a railway ruin.* Landscape Research 37, no. 3: 257–275.

Racheli, A. M. 2003. Antico e moderno nei centri storici. Restauro urbano e architettura, Roma: Gangemi.

Randall, M. 2002. *Assessing Values in Conservation Planning: Methodological Issues and Choices.* In Assessing the Values of Cultural Heritage edited by The Getty Conservation Institute, 5–30, Los Angeles: The J. Paul Getty Trust.

Ranellucci, S. 2003. Il restauro urbano. Teoria e prassi, Torino: Utet.

Remondino, F., 2011. *Heritage recording and 3D modeling with photogrammetry and 3D scanning.* Remote Sensing, 3, 1104–1138.

Remondino, F., El-Hakim, S., 2006. *Image-based 3D modelling: a review.* Photogrammetric Record, 21(115): 269–291.

Richards, J. M. (ed.) 1942. The bombed buildings of Britain: a record of architectural casualties 1940–41, Surrey: The Architectural press.

Riegl, A. [1902] 1982. *The Modern Cult of Monuments: Its Character and Its Origin.* Translated and edited by K. Foster and D. Ghirardo. Oppositions 25 (autumn): 21–51.

Riegl, A. 1903. Der Moderne Denkmalkultus, Vienna.

Rizzi, G. 2007. *Preface.* In The conservation of ruins edited by Ashurst, xix-xxiii, John, Oxford: Taylor & Francis

Robertson, K. 2004. *The main street approach to downtown development: An examination of the four-point program.* Journal of the Architectural and Planning Research 21, Spring: 55–73.

Rodger, R. 2008. The Transformation of Edinburgh: Land, Property and Trust in the Nineteenth Century, Cambridge: University Press

Rodwell, Dennis. 2008. *Urban Regeneration and the Management of Change.* Journal of Architectural Conservation. Volume 14, no. 2: 83–106. Accessed January 16, 2014. http://dx.doi.org/10.1080/13556207 2008.10785025

Romeo, Emanuele ed. 2004. Il monumento e la sua conservazione, Torino: Celid.

Rosa, B. 2011. *Infrastructure and indeterminacy: The production of residual space.* Paper presented at CRESC Conference 'Framing the City', Manchester, 8 September.

Rossi, A. 1995. L'architettura della citta, Milano: Città studi.

Roth, M., Lyons, C.L. and Merewether, C. 1997. Irresistible Decay: Ruins Reclaimed. Los Angeles, CA: The Getty Research Institute for the History of Art and the Humanities.

Rudolff, B. 2006. *'Intangible' and 'Tangible' Heritage: A Topology of Culture in Contexts of Faith.* PhD diss., Johannes Gutenberg-University of Mainz.

Ruggieri Tricoli, M.C. and Germanà, M.L., eds. 2013. Valorizzare l'archeologia urbana, Pisa: ETS.

Ruskin, J. 1849. The seven lamps of architecture, London:Smith, Elder and Co

Ruskin, Jo. 1982. Le sette lampade dell'architettura, Milano: Jaca book.

Russo, M., Remondino, F., Guidi, G. 2011. *Principali tecniche e strumenti per il rilievo tridimensionale in ambito archeologico.* Archeologia e Calcolatori n. XXII: 169–198.

Russo, V. 2011. *Ruderi di Guerra nella dimensione urbana. Conservazione, integrazione, sostituzione in ambito italiano (1975–2010).* In I ruderi e la guerra. Memoria, ricostruzione, restauro, edited by Casiello, S., 127–151. Firenze: Nardini.

Sachs, N. 2011. *Be Berlin: vivere una nuova città.* L'industria delle costruzioni, 417, XLV, January–February.

Salmon, F. 2000. Building on ruins: the rediscovery of Rome and English architecture, Aldershot: Ashgate

Salvi. 1993. In Santa Chiara: restauri e scoperte edited by Ingegno, A. 38. Cagliari.

Scarrocchia, S. 2009. Max Dvorak. Conservazione e moderno in Austria (1905–1921), Franco Angeli.

Scarrocchia, S., ed. 1990. Il culto moderno dei monumenti: il suo carattere e i suoi inizi, Bologna: Nuova Alfa.

Scarrocchia, S., ed. 1995. Alois Riegl. Teoria e prassi della conservazione dei monumenti : antologia di scritti, discorsi, rapporti 1898–1905, Bologna: CLUEB, Accademia Clementina.

Schirru, M. 2017. Palazzi e dimore signorili nella Sardegna del XVIII secolo, Sassari: Carlo Delfino.

Schwalbach, G. 2009. Urban Analysis. Basel, Boston, Berlin: Birkhause.

Semi, G. 2015. Gentrification. Tutte le città come Disneyland?, Bologna: Il Mulino.

Serafini, L. 2005. *La progettazione per gli edifici allo stato di rudere tra realizzazioni e questioni teoriche.* In Conservare il passato. metodi ed esperienze di protezione e restauro nei siti archeologici edited by Varagnoli, C., 79–96. Rome: Gangemi.

Serra, S. 2015. *Piani progetti nell'evoluzione del paesaggio storico urbano del Castello di Cagliari.* In Paesaggio storico urbano. Progetto e qualità per il Castello di Cagliari edited by Abis, E. 58–71. Roma: Gangemi.

Sette, M. P. 1996. *Profilo storico* in Trattato di restauro architettonico edited by **Carbonara, G.** 109–299. Torino: U. T. E. T.

Settis, S. 1997. *Foreward.* In Irresistible Decay: Ruins Reclaimed, edited by Roth, M., Lyons, C.L. and Merewether, C., vii. Los Angeles, CA: The Getty Research Institute for the History of Art and the Humanities.

Settis, S. 2010. *Rovine. I simboli della nostra civiltà che rischiano di diventare macerie.* La Repubblica – cultura.

Siddi, C. 2015. *Programmazione spaziale vs Appropriazione sociale: l'uso come concetto centrale del progetto della città.* In Castello Toolkit. Cagliari, patrimonio storico vs usi contemporanei edited by Cadeddu, B., Cocco, G. B., Sau F. and Siddi, C, 8–25. Roma: Gangemi.

Simmel, G. 1911. Die Ruine, in Id., Philosophische Kulture, Gesammelte Essais, Kroner, Leipzeing

Simmel, G. 1958. *Two Essays.* The Hudson Review, Vol. 11, no. 3 (Autumn, 1958), 371–385.

Simmel, G., Frisby, D., & Featherstone, M. 1997. Simmel on Culture: Selected Writings. London; Thousand Oaks, Calif.: Sage Publications.

Simmel, Georg, David, Frisby, and Mike, Featherstone. 1997. Simmel on Culture: **Selected Writings.** London; Thousand Oaks, Calif.: Sage Publications.

Sitte, C. 1965. City planning according to artistic principles, translated by George, R. Collins and Christiane, Crasemann Collins. New York; London: Random House.

Slager, E. J. 2013. Touring Detroit: ruins, representation, and redevelopment. Ann Arbor, MI: ProQuest LLC.

Slater, T. R. 1984. *Preservation, Conservation and Planning in Historic Towns.* The Geographical Journal, Volume 150, no. 3, November, 322–334. Accessed: September 22, 2015. http://www.jstor.org/stable/634432.

Spence, B. 1962. Phoenix at Coventry. The building of a Cathedral. London: Geoffrey Bles LTD.

Stanford, C. 2000. *On Preserving Our Ruins.* Journal of Architectural Conservation. Volume 6, no. 3: 28–43. Accessed January 16, 2014. http://dx.doi.org/10.1080/13556207.2000.10785278.

Stead, N. 2003. *The value of ruins: Allegories of destruction in Benjamin and Speer.* Form/Work: An Interdisciplinary Journal of the Built Environment 6: 51–64.

Stephenson, J. 2008. *The Cultural Values Model: An integrated approach to values in landscapes.* Landscape and Urban Planning 84 127–139

Stoica, Ruxandra-Iulia. 2009. *Urban conservation and the international conservation charters: a theoretical overview.* In DO. CO. MO. MO Conference: Mirror of modernity, the Post-war Revolution in Urban Conservation, edited by Casciato Maristella and d'Orgeix Emelie, 8–12, Paris, Docomomo International.

Stoler, A. L. 2008. Imperial debris: Reflections on ruins and ruination. Cultural Anthropology 23: 191–219.

Strange, I. and Walley, E. 2007. *Cold War heritage and the conservation of military remains in Yorkshire.* International Journal of Heritage Studies 13(2): 154–169.

Stubbs, J. H. & Makaš, E. J. 2011. Architectural Conservation in Europe and the Americas. Hoboken, New Jersey: John Wiley & Sons, Inc: 423–484.

Stubbs, J. H. 2009. Time Honored: A Global View of Architectural Conservation. Hoboken, NJ: Wiley.

Stubbs, John H., and Makaš, Emily G. 2011. Architectural conservation in Europe and the Americas national experiences and practice, N. J. Hoboken: John Wiley & Sons.

Sulfaro, N. 2014. *Una memoria fatta d'ombra e di pietra. Conflitti, rovine, conservazione, processi sociali.* In Archistor, anno I, n.2, 144–171.

Tallon, A. 2013. Urban regeneration in the UK, London and New York: Routledge, Taylor.

Theodossopoulos, D. 2012. Conservation theory and fabric. From: Structural Design in Building Conservation, New York: Routledge.

Thiébaut, P. 2007. Old buildings looking for new use: 61 examples of regional architecture between tradition and modernity, Stuttgart/London: Axel Menges edition.

Thomas, J. 1987. Coventry Cathedral, London: Unwin Hyman.

Thompson, M. 1979. Rubbish Theory: The Creation and Destruction of Value. Oxford: Oxford University Press.

Thompson, M.W. 1981. Ruins: their preservation and display. London: British Museum Press.

Thompson, M.W. 2006. Ruins reused, changing attitudes to ruins since a late eighteenth century, King's Lynn: Heritage Marketing & Publications Ltd.

Throsby, D. 1999. *Cultural capital.* Journal of Cultural Economics, vol.23 n.3, 3–12.

Throsby, D. 2000. Economic and Cultural Value in the Work of Creative Artists. In Values and Heritage Conservation. Research report, edited by Avrami, E., Mason, R., de la Torre, M., 26–31. Los Angeles: The Getty Conservation Institute.

Throsby, D. 2001. Economics and culture, Cambridge: Cambridge University Press.

Throsby, D. 2002. *Cultural Capital and Sustainability Concepts in the Economics of Cultural Heritage.* In Assessing the Values of Cultural Heritage, edited by De la Torre, M., Los Angeles, CA: Getty Conservation Institute.

Throsby, D. 2005. On the sustainability of cultural capital (Vol. 510). Sydney: Macquarie University, Department of Economics.

Throsby, D. 2006. *The Value of Cultural Heritage: What Can Economics Tell Us?* In Capturing the Public Value of Heritage: The Proceedings of the London Conference, edited by K. Clark, 40–43. Swindon: English Heritage, January 25–26.

Tiesdell, S., Oc, T. & Heath, T. 1996. Revitalising Historic Urban Quarters, Oxford: Architectural Press.

Tortora, G. ed. 2006. Semantica delle rovine, Roma: Manifestolibri.

Treccani, G. P. 2008. Monumenti alla guerra: città, danni bellici e ricostruzione nel secondo dopoguerra, Milano: Franco Angeli.

Treccani, G. P. 2016. Monumenti e centri storici nella stagione della grande guerra, Franco Angeli.

Treccani, G. s. d. Vocabolario – La cultura Italiana (on line).

Treccani, G. P. 2008. Monumenti alla guerra: città, danni bellici e ricostruzione nel secondo dopoguerra, Milano: Franco Angeli.

Treccani, G. P. 2014. *Traces of the Great War. Architecture and restoration a century on | Tracce della Grande guerra. Architetture e restauri nella ricorrenza del centenario.* Archistor, Anno I, no.1 DOI: 10.14633/AHR005.

Treccani, G. P. 2016. Monumenti e centri storici nella stagione della grande guerra,

Franco Angeli. Trigg, D. 2009. *The place of trauma: Memory, hauntings, and the temporality of ruins,* Memory studies, vol.2, no. 1, 87–101.

Ugolini, A. 2010. Ricomporre la rovina, Firenze, Alinea.

Van der Hoorn, M. 2003. *Exorcizing remains: Architectural fragments as intermediaries between history and individual experience.* Journal of Material Culture 8(2): 189–231.

Varagnoli, C. 2008. *Antichi edifici, nuovi progetti. Realizzazioni e posizioni teoriche dagli anni Novanta ad oggi.* In Antico e nuovo. Architetture e architettura. Proceedings of the Conference, 31 March-3 April 2004 edited by Ferlenga A., Vassallo E. and Schellino F. (eds)., 845–860. Il Poligrafo.

Varagnoli, C., ed. 2005. Conservare il passato. metodi ed esperienze di protezione e restauro nei siti archeologici. Gangemi.

Vergara, C. J. 1999. American Ruins, The Monacelli Press.

Vittorini, E. 2000. Sardegna come un'infanzia, Milano: Bompiani.

Walter, N. 2013. *From Values to Narrative: A New Foundation for the Conservation of Historic Buildings.* International Journal of Heritage Studies 20 (6): 634–650.

Watters, D. M. and Glendinning M. 2006. Little Houses: The National Trust for Scotland's Improvement Scheme for Small Historic Homes, Edinburgh: RCAHMS and the National Trust for Scotland.

Whately, T. 1793. Observations on modern gardening, fifth edition, London: T. Payne.

Wilford, J. 2008. Out of rubble: Natural disaster and the materiality of the house. Environment and Planning D: Society and Space 2008 (26): 647–662.

Woodward, C. 2002. In Ruins. London: Vintage.

Zoppi, C. 2001. 'Comunita locale e scelte di piano: metodologie e casi di studio per individuare il grado di consenso nei confronti delle politiche del territorio', in Piano e consenso: nuove forme per il progetto del territorio, Deplano, G. (ed.),Trento: Temi.

Zucker, P. 1961. Ruins: An aesthetic hybrid. The Journal of Aesthetics and Art Criticism 20(2): 119–130.

ACKNOWLEDGEMENTS

I would like to kindly thank people who believed in me encouraging and supporting this research.

First of all, I am grateful to the supervisors of my PhD in Civil Engineering and Architecture (Department of Civil and Environmental Engineering and Architecture –DICAAR) at the University of Cagliari, professors Donatella Rita Fiorino, Caterina Giannattasio and Silvana Maria Grillo, for their passion for the research, positivity, and constant stimulus to do always my best. Each of them is a unique mentor, teaching me the important values of humility, respect, conscientiousness, determination, and enthusiasm.

I am deeply grateful to my second academic family in Scotland: the Scottish Centre for Conservation Studies (Edinburgh School of Architecture and Landscape Architecture - ESALA) at the University of Edinburgh. Special thanks to my mentor Ruxandra-Iulia Stoica for her trust in me, her encouragements, support, and guidance in my research, getting me involved in an exciting and interesting experience in all the UK and around. Thanks to professor Miles Glendinning for his advices and inspiring suggestions. Moreover, many thanks to Miguel Paredes for his innovative support and help to my research.

Furthermore, I would like to express my gratitude to other professors and technicians of the DICAAR who have joined this research: professor Giuseppina Vacca and her staff, Andrea Dessì and Monica Deidda, for their valuable academic contribution in the surveying phase; professors Vincenzo Bagnolo, Giovanni Battista Cocco, Andrea Pirinu, Marcello Schirru, and Cesarina Siddi for their professional and human support. I am thankful to the architect Ilene Steingut for proofreading my thesis with professionalism and meticulousness.

My most heartfelt gratitude goes to my family, cornerstone of my life, always supportive and present in every moment.

Finally, I gratefully acknowledge Sardinia Regional Government for the financial support of my PhD scholarship (P.O.R. Sardegna F.S.E. Operational Programme of the Autonomous Region of Sardinia, European Social Fund 2007–2013–Axis IV Human Resources, Objective l.3, Line of Activity l.3.1.), and all the members, supporters, and sponsors of the Literary Award "*La Calcina – John Ruskin – Writing on Architecture*", without whose support, this book would not have been possible.

THE ORGANISATION OF THE PRIZE
"LA CALCINA JOHN RUSKIN – WRITING ON ARCHITECTURE"
HAS BEEN POSSIBLE WITH THE SUPPORT OF:

The *Deutsche Bibliothek* lists this publication in the *Deutsche Nationalbibliografie;* detailed bibliographic data is available on the internet at *http://dnb.d-nb.de*

ISBN 978-3-86922-708-5

© 2019 by DOM publishers, Berlin
www.dom-publishers.com

This work is subject to copyright. All rights are reserved, whether the whole or part of the material is concerned, specifically the rights of translation, reprinting, recitation, broadcasting, reproduction on microfilms or in other ways, and storage or processing in data bases. Sources and owners of rights are given to the best of our knowledge; please inform us of any we may have omitted.

Proofreading
Laura Thépot

Design
Johanna Posiege

Printing
UAB BALTO print, Vilnius
www.baltoprint.com